Dedication

I dedicate this book to all women who would like to find and fully live with their ... mission.

Thank you!

Dear Reader,

Thank you from the depths of my heart for taking the time to journey through these pages.

Your support means the world to me, and I hope this book has brought inspiration, joy, or perhaps even a spark of something new to your life.

If you'd like to stay connected and explore more of what I create, I warmly invite you to visit michaelzettaking.com.

There, you'll find updates, insights, and more adventures to share.

With gratitude, Michael Zetta King

MICHAEL ZETTA KING

A *Queen* of a Charismatic Future

A

Queen

OF A CHARISMATIC FUTURE

Contents

INTRODUCTION

The Forgotten Sarcophagus

Night fell, and bright stars caressed Hanna's eyes, which closed in the unfinished melody of the day ... a long day. And not just a long one, but a most 'normal' one. And by a 'normal' one, she once again went through those experienced feelings of sadness, lack of confidence and all those things which she wasn't able to put words to. Because of the numbness she felt. It's just as well she wasn't able to. Because if she were, they would really be some sad words. At barely twenty-three years of age, she felt exactly like something that had always interested her: Archeology. Old. Even tombs, that had long been asleep, alongside her face, appeared more alive. And in not too long a time, she'd have in her hands a piece of paper, certifying her as a University graduate of Archeology. A piece of paper, which should hold some kind of value to her. It might even save her and tell her who she was. But, she was all the more aware that this probably wouldn't happen. The truth about it burned her, just like the desert sand burns your bare feet.

She asked herself if excavations really interested her all that much. Because deep down she knew, that she should, as a matter of fact, also dig down and excavate, within herself. In herself. She continued to try and find lost treasures from beneath the ground. Treasures, which enrich poor young girls and save them from themselves. As a matter of fact, she should have probably admitted to herself that she was looking for a different kind of lost treasure. Herself. That Hanna, who years before in despair, buried her abandonment in the ground. Her parents died young, far too young, in a car accident, which ripped the thread of love right out of a girl, who was barely six years old. Every now and then, Hanna remembered them, then buried the memory there in the chasm, where both her mother and father quietly rested, as did she. Her aunt and uncle, at every step of her young and deprived life, let her know how they loathed raising her. Oddly enough, this didn't seem to want to disappear into the darkness of obscurity. It was just as alive then, as it was today.

And now, she was there. Many friends, who attended the faculty only because their parents were able to afford it, secretly admired her as she was able to finance her studies all on her own. Many of them asked the question, how she could succeed in studying and working as a waitress at the same time. She probably fought for a better life and, at the same time, threw herself into her work to escape herself. And that better life should have been knocking on her door in the final year of her studies, but all she heard was the silence of her soul. She sat down behind the closed door and asked herself if she was capable of opening it to a better tomorrow, if a better tomorrow were to appear by mistake at her doorstep. And, an opportunity nevertheless did come her way during those days. She was invited to take part in an archaeological expedition, where she would gain a lot of practical experience. The future had opened a door for her, but as she stepped through it, she felt as if it had been slammed shut right in front of her face. Isn't that the way it goes, like in the movies? Shouldn't I be happy?

Instead of being in a time machine of her emotions, spinning faster and faster backward, it threatened, at any moment, to fall into the depths from which she wouldn't be able to escape, even with the strongest ropes of fate. Once again, she encountered an iceberg of relationships, just like she had when she was growing up. Scorn, and the lingering sounds of those humiliating words, cut into the heart of the young girl, like a sharp razor of hatred. At one time, it was her uncle, whom her aunt just didn't want to stop. She let him weigh upon Hanna, and waited for Hanna's tears of despair, thus enabling her to maintain her 'stone-like' heart. Now it was the head of the archaeological expedition, who seemed to live for the smallest of moments, in which he showed her, just how very much she didn't deserve to have faith in herself, or faith in anyone else. It seemed that every bit of her unease added fuel to his fire, which was able to burn for a damn long time. She was the only female in the expedition, and they let her know, without any doubt, that in truth, it was a very thankless role, and after the theatre curtain fell, it would leave her exhausted as well as even more unhappy than ever before ...

And that night, when she once again cried herself to sleep, it was different. It wasn't dissimilar to her archeological friends, who, as a matter of fact, they weren't. Friends, that is. For most of them, the expedition to Egypt, which, in itself, held something so very mystic, was something completely normal. Something they felt entitled to, which let you know that they were the supreme rulers of the golden land of power and influence. Some of them were so full of themselves, like turkeys strutting around the site, saying that they would find everything, except something nice to say. Their kind words had been, probably – just like their finds - buried deep a long time ago. But Hanna wasn't so sure that they wanted to find them. Even less so for her, the almost invisible shadow of the expedition.

"It's just another tomb ..." said one of them that day, when the underground doors opened their secrets to them.

Hanna, enchanted, entered the underground world, which invited her into its mystic embrace and asked if she wanted to discover its ancient treasures. Hanna was then admiring the sarcophagus, which supposedly reprimanded those that disturbed its eternal sleep.

Archeology was Hanna's true love, and her respect, which she found within her at a time when no one respected her. The fact that it was just a job to some of her colleagues and classmates, something that was handed to them, offering them a number of opportunities to travel and have a bit of fun between the sheets, was for Hanna, heartbreaking. And also, this time around, they broke her heart with such disrespectful comments about what those unimportant graves meant to them. But she could have sworn that every single one of those graves whispered their story to her and could only be heard by those who knew how to silence the screaming of their own vanity.

In those sarcophagi, people rested in eternal sleep; people who once lived and experienced their own endeavors, and were now there, anchored to the end path of their lives, many of them unimportant and overlooked. And just like them, young Hanna, who was observing them, quietly called out to them and asked: "Are we really so unimportant?"

Because the newly discovered tomb was so special. Hanna seemed to hear the whisper of some strange kind of echo that came from within, that ever so silently spoke the five letters that made up her name:

"HhhhAaaaNnnnNnnnAaaa ..."

The mummy in the sarcophagus revealed a mysterious woman, who seemed to be so intact, as if from the beginning of time. She was, as a matter of fact, ... yes, she was stunning. Hanna felt an irresistible desire to touch her. She wanted to hear her story. The mysterious woman was the only one in that dark world. Hanna knew all about that darkness because it also embraced her inner world. And oh, how she wanted to dig herself out of it, so that she could just find her way to the light and bathe her weary face in it.

She didn't have a lot of time with the sleeping queen (what if she really was a queen?). The head of the expedition came down and then sent her, as if she was some kind of annoying mouse, to where she 'belonged' - up on the surface in an improvised kitchen, to make some coffee for those, who were more 'important.'

She left the sleeping beauty and, in her heart, joined her parents, whom she was also forced to leave behind. The loss. The pain. "But why?" Hanna asked herself, leaving behind a friend, whom she would never have the opportunity of getting to know. The thought remained with her the entire day, even on her way home to the run-down hotel in the evening, after which she found herself delving into yet another night of unanswered questions.

Hanna closed her eyes. Just one single pearl of a tear ran down her cheek, after which she fell into a deep sleep. In her dreams, she finally found her way to the light, which took the lost girl into its lap and just like a caring mother, carried her off to the land, where once again her dying dreams were reborn, where she entered the Golden Temple, which had enchanted her. She was walking, in amongst some magnificent archways in a long dress, all until she saw a magnificent throne, right in front of her.
On it, proud as a lion, sat a Ruler with piercing green eyes, wearing a crown, proving her might and complimenting her immeasurable beauty. Despite the fact that everything was connected to her, letting you know that she knew what she wanted and that she was the Ruler, her eyes were so very warm and so kind. So inviting. And Hanna desperately needed a home. The Ruler seemed so familiar to her. As if she had known her a lot longer than she ever could have thought. If Hanna had ever thought about eternity, it now showed itself right in front of her very eyes.

"Hello. May I ask where I am?" asked Hanna shyly, finally interrupting the silence.

"Welcome to my home."

"Why am I here?" Hanna continued awkwardly.

"Because you need me. You've been asleep for a long time. And so, have I. It's time that both of us awaken. You're here so that we both fulfill each of our own ... missions.

Hanna wasn't able to say another word, but the Ruler continued: "Well, let me introduce myself. My name is Shanti ... "

In every woman, sleeps a 'Hanna.' And, in every woman, sleeps a 'Ruler.' Every woman is a ruler. The only question is, what does she rule over? Happiness or sadness? Does she rule herself, or do others rule her? Every woman has the sleepy truth within her. Some are able to awaken it, while others never do. But, the easiest way to awaken it is with honesty.

My name is Michael, and I'm a man. I wrote this book for women because men can awaken a Ruler with the honest truth. Quite often, women aren't able to see their own strengths, and what's even more common is that they don't even trust them. And why would they? Who wants to be a strong woman, capable of actually changing the world, when it's easier to maintain male-dominated systems, which subordinate and control? Who wants the love that a woman is able to offer when control is so much more appealing? But the time's come to turn everything upside down. A lot of men would probably think I've got a screw loose, for writing a book that'll awaken and transform women into rulers. And, many among them would argue that it'll bring nothing but 'trouble.' Oh yes, it will. Especially for those among them, who have built multi-colored (even golden cages for their women.

Why then, am I doing this? Why is it time that I openly reveal everything to women, particularly the things that they probably aren't able to see themselves? Because egoism, as it is today, has pushed us to the very edge of immoral life, self-destruction, disrespect for people, animals, and nature. Soon, we won't be able to leave future generations anything more than multiple battlefields, because I believe that women and men must balance the power on this planet between themselves. The earth is in imbalance, which can be seen every day by the number of calls for help. And so, this book might possibly save the world. For it to be saved, we first have to save those who don't even know that they're the key to a new, better 'fate' - the many women of this world. I bet that you're one of them. If you weren't, you wouldn't be reading these words right now. Perhaps you're surprised right now and aren't unable to believe that you could be so very important. That's your problem. You don't know. And so, it's time that you do.

And who am I? How is it possible that I can understand women and give them advice if I, myself, am not a woman? Maybe I really do live my own life and create things under the guise of a man's image, but within every one of us is a masculine side and a feminine side. Again ... balance. I know what both my sides need. I also know which one of them is being creative and which one of them is causing problems and trouble. But, I came into contact with both of them. And, when I did, I finally understood the Queen, alongside me. My wife. Time and time again, I watched her mend her bleeding heart, all up until the time when she placed a crown on her head. I saw a Queen, being born right in front of the eyes of her loving husband. My eyes. And so, I'm very grateful to her for showing me the way. So that now I can write even more FOR YOU.

This is a book, which will awaken you. It's time that you become aware of yourself. It's time that you move all that stands before you ... the things which have limited women for thousands of years. It's time that you realize that man is your friend, with whom you form a pillar ... and not a cornerstone, without which your life would collapse.

This book is a mission. It's your mission, your journey. It'll surprise you, again and again, dear Queen.

And some invisible force has put this book into your hands for a reason.

You can call that force whatever you want. You can even call it ... Shanti. Are you ready to discover who she is? Are you ready to discover who ... YOU are?

Michael

Mission no. 1:

The Mighty Bird

Already that the morning, the temperature of the air indicated that it was going to be damn hot. But, it was even hotter in the minds of the young archaeologists. It was only their third day in Egypt, and already they were on the brink of a new discovery. They came to the expedition as a support team to help the main group clean up the already discovered graves, but that day something extraordinary happened - by chance, another unknown tomb was discovered nearby, which lay not too far from the already discovered graves. But, in comparison with them, it seemed somewhat insignificant. The entrance into it was a simple asymmetric hole, concealed by a roughly carved-out rock.

The leader of the expedition, Mark, who made sure that no one forgot he was the leader, went inside and after a quick examination, said with some annoyance: "It's just another unimportant grave from someone of the lower classes."

He turned to one of his long-standing assistants and said: "Great. Now we have a job for the puppies. Call them."

Puppies was an expression Mark used for trainees and students, that the university sent to join him on his expeditions, to gain practical experience.

He lined them up just like an angry general would, and then said, arrogantly: "OK puppies, now prove that your university hasn't wasted its money by sending you here. Clean these walls and get rid of those stones. Most importantly, I don't want to see your pathetic green faces for the next few days, is that clear?"

The angry general spat fire, while the 'young soldiers' removed the ashes of humiliation from their hair.

"Spoilt brats," he thought, as he walked away. Truth be told, he didn't really appreciate them at all. Most of them simply came from wealthy and 'stuck-up' parents. He was convinced that they had no right being there in a place where history was discovered. He threw them all into the same basket, under the banner of 'undeserved.' Especially women. Who the hell allowed women to cross the threshold into the world of archeology?

"Archeology is a business for men!" he often said to himself, which he then had to urgently share with those who were of the same opinion, thus receiving thunderous applause, confirming him to be right. He argued that it's important to be objective and attentive, but women - well, with their sensitivity and idiotic emotions ... it all ends up being nothing more than failure, ruining the hard work and dedicated results of people, like himself.

This, or rather his way of thinking, strongly showed itself in his relationship to women in the expedition. And the only woman, this time around, was ... Hanna. At times, it seemed, she had to bear all of the burden that men put on women. And not just the burden. But also, the responsibility of those rocks of failure, which hung over her head and let her know that it would be better if she didn't make any mistake at all.

Over those past few days, Hanna felt what it was like not being equal. She had known that feeling before. And now, it appeared once again from the past and waited, reminding her that in truth, she would never be able to get rid of it. And, if she had ever really wanted to, she could now finally forget about it. And that feeling chuckled away like something that steals Christmas presents from children, while it took away Hanna's hope and joy for life. Her classmates quickly fell under the influence of the angry general and followed his anthem, which sang that archeology is truly a man's domain. The only bright light on the expedition was Peter, who wasn't there at the time ... her thoughts wandered to those warm eyes, the look from which Hanna so desperately needed at that moment. It seemed that silent words within her called his name, but the wind caught her call, and it never reached the ears of the friendly young guy. If only it would ...

"Hey, you with the tousled hair! The coffee's not going to make itself!" said Nick rather roughly, awakening her from her daydream, as he saw how Hanna was absently making note of some unknown symbols that were carved into the walls of the tomb.

"This isn't a place for women anyway," he added, which bought about some hearty laughter from some of the guys. All this did was remind them that they too would soon become just as harsh as their boss, who, in light of the fact, only reinforced the firepower.

Hanna lowered her head in sadness and headed out and up to the surface. Like a bird with a broken wing, she slowly walked away from whatever was left of her pride. As she was leaving, one of them called out: "I take two sugars in mine!" and in doing so made sure, that she would never fly again. If she ever had. Maybe a long time ago.

She hoped they wouldn't notice, but she was barely able to hold back her tears and begged them not to stream down her cheeks until she had left. The same relationship, which kept on slapping her fragile personality in the face, she had seen in the one her uncle had with his wife, her aunt, leading Hanna to sometimes feel pity for her. But in time, that pity faded. Her aunt was only able to survive because she was somehow energized by seeing Hanna tortured. It was probably easier for her that way. Maybe it seemed that her pain wasn't as bad as it actually was. But that was nothing but a lie, that hunted both Hanna, as well as her aunt.

Once, when things were a little better, Hanna promised herself that she would never allow herself to be in a situation like that again, where a man could so arrogantly look down on her and stand above her like a mountain, threatening to trigger a devastating avalanche. In her childhood, that was perhaps nothing more than a simple promise to herself, but down here, where the walls withheld secrets and supported men's wicked words, promises disappeared into the underground like a refreshing stream in a period of drought.
She cried as she made the coffee. But, this time around, she let her tears flow freely. It wasn't how she had imagined her life to be. She decided to join the expedition to experience the world, to enrich herself, to evolve, to discover ... she was searching for the hope that she wasn't able to find within the walls of the university and trusted that the walls there would be able to provide her with more. And when the offer came from the university, because she was one of the best students, offering her the possibility of some new hope, she felt that perhaps life was showing her a signpost on the road to happiness. And she was more than prepared to follow it.

And where was that happiness now? She was alone, in a tent that functioned as a kitchen, and like Cinderella, made coffee for people who made fun of her and made sure that she would never put on those tiny glass shoes of happiness and joy. And once again, she felt that feeling inside ... the one that overcame her, the moment she found out that her parents had died in a crumpled pile of metal ... something that barely even resembled a car which changed the fate of them and their poor, beloved daughter. She felt so lost, so alone. Her heart was crushed, just like that sheet metal, that had taken the life of her parents.

Meanwhile, the coffee was ready, as were the colorful mugs ... only that the fragrant indulgence was for those, who were ... worth more. She carefully added a little milk into each one and took care that her unhappy tears would not 'spoil' the coffee. When the last drops of milk were added to the heavenly, black elixir and the last mugs were filled, Hanna went to put the milk back into the refrigerator but noticed the milk she had just poured into the last cup was dancing on the surface, mixing in with the coffee, forming a white line in the shape of the letter S. Fixating on that milky outline far longer than she had on any archeological find, Hanna stared at it, motionless, until it spread out and disappeared into something unrecognizable.

She wanted to look away because she felt her heart wouldn't be able to withstand any more excitement, and then let out a soft scream. Her thoughts were immediately overcome by a forgotten memory. Suddenly, a tingling feeling came over her, and she had to sit down. Images began to appear in her mind. Images she had already seen somewhere before. But where? Last night's dream ... then her thoughts found their way to a merry-go-round, revealing to her its magic ride. A Golden Temple. A crown. A woman. Her stunning eyes. Her dress, so graceful, so special. What was her name again? S ... Shanti! And then, Shanti came to life. She stepped out of the sarcophagus into the young girl's milk of hopelessness.

Even though Hanna knew it was only a dream, an unusual but warm feeling came over her. The same kind she felt that morning when she hugged her wonderful mother for the last time. That morning, when everything changed. She remained seated and cried. Destiny, again and again, reminded her how very much she missed her. She missed the feeling that a warm embrace gives you when everything seems possible. She wiped her nose and cheeks, and with shaking hands, picked up the tray of coffee and headed out towards her classmates.

Something invisible was following her. As she walked towards the excavation site, a strange kind of pressure began to rise in her heart.

The closer she got, the stronger it became, while at the same time, the image of the mummy began to flood her thoughts. And with every step, it became clearer and clearer. From beneath the grey bandages, she began to recognize the outline and shape of her face. And then she caught sight of her eyes. Her green eyes. She could have recognized those emerald eyes anywhere. She had only seen them once, and she knew exactly where. In her dreams. They were Shanti's.

"What's going on?" Hanna asked herself. "Is this really possible? Is that mummy ... Shanti?" she was barely able to register the fact in her exhausted mind, which wanted to spring back to life, just like the mummy from the sarcophagus wanted to.

The more her head resisted the thought, the clearer the feeling became in her heart. "But it's not possible ..." said Hanna, trying to convince herself, but at the same time knowing, in truth, that she wouldn't be able to. Did she even want to believe that it wasn't possible? Or did she urgently need ... someone? A female friend? An ally? Anyone?

The closer she got to the tomb, the faster her heart was beating, on account of the unknown force. She had to see her again. She hurried up. With a tray full of coffee, she stepped into the tomb, and in a wave of confusion and enthusiasm, she forgot that food and drinks were forbidden at the excavation site. She accidentally bumped a piece of rock that was jutting out from the wall and spilled coffee over the bottom part of the wall. When Nick noticed her awkwardness, he roared and erupted in a series of insults, blaming Hanna for her incompetence, for destroying important work and confirming what Mark had already said ... that it was so embarrassing to have women in archeology.

"From now on, you're banned from entering this space!" he said gruffly. And continued harshly: "As far as I'm concerned, you can pack your things and go on home! That is, if anyone at all wants you there, you incompetent fool!"

The other guys who were witness to the attack on Hanna didn't say a word, nor did it occur to any of them, to stand up for her. Their place in the expedition of 'very important people' was more sacred than life itself. And far more sacred than the life of Hanna, or anyone else like to her. And so, they quietly congratulated Nick, who drove her out of the tomb, just like some kind of unwanted dog.

But all she wanted was to see her, Shanti ... and for the very last time she looked back and for a moment saw the open sarcophagus, and in it, the outline of Shanti's face, which with every step on her way up and out of the tomb, drowned in a world that Hanna no longer had access to. The next thing she saw was the blinding light of the sun.

That evening, Hanna cried uncontrollably. Her schoolmates had hurt her. They killed the hope she had inside, of ever becoming a proper archeologist.

"What if they're right?" she asked herself. "What if I'm really not good enough?"

Perhaps her cruel uncle was right when he said that she would never amount to anything. Maybe she should just be satisfied with making coffee, which would constantly remind her of her pointless existence. But the thoughts of her destroyed fate got mixed up with something else that was sad ... with Shanti. She would never see her again. Despite the fact that the mummy in the tomb was just one amongst many finds for some of the others, it was special for Hanna. She had no understanding why, perhaps because of her dreams, perhaps because of the feeling in her heart ... after a while, her crying had taken its toll on her eyes, and she slowly fell asleep. Invisible arms waited, once again, to embrace the girl with no hope for a bright future.

She felt a gentle breeze embrace her, when the queen of the night, the moon, shone a path towards the Golden Temple. The tall, luminous door slowly opened of its own accord, and an amazing, extremely bright interior was revealed to her. Every single corner of the temple was stunning, but her eyes stopped when they saw the mighty, golden throne on which she sat ...

"Shanti!"

"Hello, Hanna," she smiled kindly. "How are you?"

"I'm well?" Hanna replied with some confusion and realized that her answer was more like a question than a statement.

Shanti looked into her eyes, then said: "Hanna, you don't have to pretend in front of me. You can be who you really are. I can see your heart and the key to your soul. So, once again, I'll ask you. How are you?"
Hanna burst out into tears. Tears, from the depths of her heart, streamed down her face. She didn't need to say a word, because as her tears fell, the fairytale of Cinderella in deep sorrow, was once again recreated.

"You know, Hanna," continued the Queen, "I know your tears. Far too many have also slid down my cheeks. They were fueled by an intense feeling of fear in the face of the world, helplessness in the face of life, and the many unanswered questions I had. Like a princess in the courtyard, I had everything, but in reality, I lived in a golden cage. I had to live that way because my father wanted me to; my friends were chosen by his advisors

and I wasn't able to venture out further than the courtyard gardens. The courtyard was surrounded by walls that suffocated me and took from me what was true. And so, I was faced with a choice. To take the crown and become a mighty queen, or to relinquish it and continue to live the safe life of a princess, the only difference from the life of a slave being the beautiful clothes and better food. I decided and then realized that my decision was the right one. You know, Hanna, everything begins with you ... but first, you have to know who it is you are, to know where to begin. Don't worry. I'll help you find your beginning ... to become a mighty bird, which freely soars without fear of having her wings broken ..."

Mighty birds. Freely soaring about the sky and allowing themselves, with every feather, the entire time, to experience the unlimited possibilities, which have been given to them. They can turn to the right, or they can turn to the left. They can catch a hot air vortex, which takes them higher and higher, and which can show them a new horizon, a new reality. They can, like a spear, hurtle directly downwards, exactly to where they want to go. If they want, they can flap their wings, or if not, they can simply sail the skies. They can admire the untouched mist of the clouds, which are inaccessible to most, and they can touch the blades of grass on the meadows, along which anyone can walk. They can land on the very top of a mountain, and they can land on a simple tree in the valley. They can silently observe, or they can fill the sky with their shrieks. Yes, these are mighty birds - creatures, that were born to be free. Creatures that were born to fly. Creatures that were born to rule their own world.

Did these words stir up a bit of admiration in you? Did you feel the wind embrace the faces of these birds? Did your heart get carried away when you sailed the heavens with them, and did you feel anything other than absolute limitlessness? If so, then the sleepy Ruler has begun to awaken within you, because she too has felt that a life like this belongs to her. It's time to have a talk.

Every woman, in her heart, wants to be enriched and appreciated. But above all, happy. But the truth is that many aren't. Why? Because that's what they decided. Yes, maybe that sounds a little too simplistic, but it's true. The difference between a slave and a ruler is in their decisions. When a baby is born, it's neither of these - a slave nor a ruler. But, a few years, or decades later, they wear the 'clothes' that reveal the decisions that were made. These days, we no longer live in times when only 'blue blood' allows a woman to become a ruler.

These days, every woman can become one. Every woman can master her own life and ensure that it has meaning and purpose. How? That she finds and carries out her ... mission.

Rulers, as we knew them before, have become just a memory from the past. Nobody can truly rule over someone else. The only person you can truly rule over is yourself. And so, a new era is in the making. An era of individuals, who'll rule over their own lives, by virtue of knowing their mission. An era of Queens is on its way. And you, my dear, are one of them. Congratulations!

The Gift Of Decision

The primary strength of every woman is that she can decide for herself, who she wants to be. This is incredible strength. Her entire truth is, therefore, in her hands. The Creator, Nature, the Universe ... whoever or whatever she believes created her, gave her that gift when she was born.

Some use it faithfully and cleverly. With it, they create fairytales and castles. Others are unaware that they have it, and so it lays dusty and deeply buried under layers of disappointment and unfulfilled dreams. Those women need the winds of change to blow away the dust and once again show them what they are truly capable of.

The big 'secret' is that you can be anything you decide to be. You can take on any kind of role you want. Yes, I know, it's a bold statement. If you're a little skeptical, then that's exactly what you need - a little more boldness. If you've got dreams you don't think you can accomplish, then it's time to start listening. Your vision and dreams are simply energy, that come from your soul. If your soul has shown you a dream, then it has also provided you with a map, which will lead you to it. To every goal, there is a path. Many paths. Which one you choose depends on you. If you want to be happy and fulfilled, then let that path be yours. Only yours.

But you have to know where to find it. So many women feel trapped because they look in the wrong places. Allow me to direct you there, where your most honest and purest truth is, about who you are and what you're capable of - for you.

A woman's power is exceptional, but even the most powerful animal becomes docile if it gives it over to others. Most women have given their strength to the people around them. How? They've taken on roles that were assigned to them by others. And so, it's time that I remind you of the gift of decision: "You can decide for yourself, the kind of woman you would like to become!" You can decide for yourself, the throne on which you'll sit. Will that throne be in a castle or in a jail ... it depends on you. You know which one you would like more. But, let me tell you a secret - every kingdom needs a Queen. Even yours. And your throne in the castle, of course, if you're not already sitting on it, will be waiting - for you. So, raise your head and make your way to it. Because, the moment you take your place on it, you'll also find a crown on top of your head. A crown, which will confirm that you've made the right decision. A crown, which will always, when you look in the mirror, remind you that you rule your own life. A crown is a valuable thing. Do you deserve it? Do you believe you're worth it? Gold and precious stones are otherwise owned only by those who appreciate their beauty ... especially those who believe they deserve them.

An Inferiority Complex

But the beauty and majesty of a crown are the two things many women don't believe they deserve. A lot of women, deep down inside, have a feeling, and because of it, think the way they do – an inferiority complex, given to them by the society in which they live. Sadly, most of them aren't even aware of it. It's hidden and does absolutely nothing ... until a woman like that needs to decide on something. When she has to make a decision and stand behind it, the creature, which is capable of almost anything, changes her into a meek and frightened mouse, which unassumingly lowers its head and suppresses its true feelings. For whom? For others.

Women were born with their own power. And so, they were entrusted with one of the most important jobs in nature - childbirth. Have you ever asked yourself why it wasn't given to men? Let me tell you a secret: Because men wouldn't be able to do it. The demands childbirth puts on a woman, exceed the capabilities of most men. And I'm not just talking about biological boundaries, but more so emotional and energy-based ones. For such a feat, it's necessary to have strength; the strength of a woman. The same strength that allows a ruler to be able to rule. Why then does she hand it over to others? Why does she get caught up in her dreams and the expectations of people around her, who demand from her that she follow and believe in them?

I have met hundreds of wonderful women attending my seminars and workshops, who have been locked up in golden cages. Behind the images of diligent housewives doing tens of things per day, behind the images of loving mothers, who are always available to their children, and behind the images of loyal partners, who support their husbands, are all the more the cries of lost souls, who feel that their stories, in which they're trapped, are suffocating them. Stories from which they are unable to save themselves. When some of them looked out from their cages, they didn't see a thing, as they were so blinded by the golden bars of their cages, which were holding them there, as prisoners. Yes, this was the truth for a lot of those women, who wanted to be 'Rulers,' but ended up becoming 'laundrywomen.' But more such prisoners walk the streets, not knowing, that they, in fact, are prisoners.

Others have determined to a number of them what they should be and what they have to do. And so, the profile of women was formed, which shapes what society expects from them. A lot of women were burdened with a multitude of tasks, only because they were women. A lot of women were determined, what they were capable of, only because they were women. A lot of women are discriminated against, only because they're women. A lot of doors are closed to women just because they're women. And now's the time to open them wide and throw away the key.

The time has come for women to decide for themselves, what, and how. It's time for you to decide. If you want to, of course. Some women deliberately give up their power, which means they can avoid the responsibilities they should otherwise take on. If you've decided to go on this journey, I believe that you're not one of them.

Every woman, who wants to awaken her true inner strength, has to step forward on her own path and answer a few key questions. Perhaps it's time that these wonderful answers also resonate in your heart so strongly that you'll hear them, as well as the whole world around you.

Who am I?

Only you know the answer. As a little girl, you were aware of it at every moment; you felt it in every one of your cells. But, over time, most girls lose the thread, which connects them to who they actually are. They grow up and gain valuable life experiences, while at the same time allow that others determine what they should be. And for most girls, it's true: The more they develop into adult women, the more they lose contact with their inner ruler. When a person, at a certain moment, is distanced far enough from herself, she loses the essence of her soul, meaning that her higher self is no longer able to guide her in the right direction. And then, for most people, the search for direction in their own lives begins, through other people.

My dear, your parents, relatives, partner ... they love you very much, but their direction, unfortunately, is not the right one for you. Their direction can only lead you to their island of happiness. You need your own. And so, it's time, that you once again listen to your inner voice. Call your inner friend. The one who has accompanied you all the way from childbirth, and ask her: "Who am I?" Look at yourself in the mirror, and you'll see who you are. Somewhere under the masks that you wear in order to please those around you, hides your true 'spark' ... which shines only for you. So, remove the masks you wear and save them for the day when masks are worn: At Carnival. For all the other days, let the world see your true face.

Throughout history, humanity has steered the world in very different ways. Someone, a very long time ago, said that women aren't as important as men. Many among them accepted that absurdity. They put on veils that covered their true beauty, and positioned themselves in the background, hoping that one day they would be allowed to live in the way they had always wanted to. But the truth, which many don't want you to find out, is that you don't need permission from anyone. No one owns you. You're as free as the most wonderful forest birds. You can fly wherever you want. But, beforehand, you have to know that you have wings, which will open the moment you honestly answer the most important question in life. Then, the bird in you will awaken and show you that the sky is the limit, and open, just for you to experience ...

1. **Take a sheet of paper and write down: "I am ...",**
   then write down your truth. Maybe you'll have some reservations at first and will have to think about what you're going to write. Don't think. Thinking will take you back to that part of your memory, where others told you about yourself, which you don't need right now. You need the energy which comes from your heart, not your head. So, don't try to understand what is written, but just simply feel. And write ...

   Once, at one of my workshops for self-confident women, I was working with one of the ladies that attended ... a younger woman, who didn't know who she was. When I put a sheet of paper and a pen in front of her, her hands began to shake so badly that in the beginning, she wasn't even able to pick the pen up. She was so afraid of the truth, that could be written down on an empty sheet of paper. Then, she began to write.

2. **Write down all your feelings and thoughts.**
   While writing, your truth will begin to appear on the paper.

It's important that you realize that you haven't expressed some parts of yourself for a long time, so they'll appear to be a little strange to you. Don't discard them as nonsense because they'll awaken the ruler in you. Just as they began to awaken the ruler in the woman attending my workshop. From not being able to even pick up her pen, she went on to write many pages. She wrote down everything her heart told her to, even some forgotten feelings, which then led to her cheeks being covered in tears, streaming down her face. Because the spring from which they came, was a hot geyser, in which all possible feelings were boiling.

3. **Remove the Band-Aids.**
   When you face your own truth, you'll be confronted with strong feelings. Because from some of the things you've written, you'll feel strong emotions of happiness, joy, satisfaction, and hope, as you'll once again remember your greatness and truth. When reading this truth, you may possibly want to laugh. So, laugh. Some lines will reawaken sensations of sadness and entrapment in your heart, as you'll remember where you trampled on your truth, and pushed it away. Then, you may want to cry and scream. You may even be angry. So, if you feel like it, then cry. Or scream.

   Believe me, the list of sincere words will awaken feelings of sincerity in you. Your task is simply that you accept them as they are. Completely, and without censorship. Maybe you won't be so comfortable, and maybe you'll even feel pain. Your mind will want to turn you away because the human body is geared to avoid pain. But don't allow it to happen. The feeling of pain is only an illusion, only a Band-Aid on a wound, covering the reality of the situation. And we can only see the real state when we remove what's covering it.

When the woman read in the end what she had written, she was speechless. There was no time for words, because in her head and her heart, hustle and bustle ruled, caused by memories of forgotten greatness. Tears flowed down her face, which reminded her of what she had once given up. And now, her greatness was once again visible. The light of truth, which she wrote down on that piece of paper, that day, shone upon her new rays of hope and prompted the desire inside of her to once again take things into her own hands. And the ruler in her began to awaken.

4. **Over the coming two weeks, read that sheet of paper every day, over and over again.**
   And read it out loud. Why? Because it's important that you come into stable contact with yourself. The words you've written on your piece of paper will fill the truth in you, and will, with every new drop, grow and grow. Why is it important that your truth is strong and stable? Because nothing will then be able to knock it down. Anyone can walk over a sapling, which has barely begun to put its roots down, but a tree that has its roots deep down in the ground and its tallest branches high up in the sky is strong, stable, and unyielding. So too, should be your truth.

The woman who attended the seminar reminded me of the strength of those roots and, two weeks later, she wrote me an email, in which she enthusiastically said that she had put her sheet of paper with her truths onto the wall in her office and that she reads it every day. She simply didn't allow herself to forget once again.

5. **Your sheet of paper should be read by a person you trust, and one who respects you.**
   In this way, you'll share your truth with others, and, in a moment's notice, it'll become even more true, as it'll no longer exist just in your heart, but also in your surroundings. It's just as important that you have support in the beginning, and that you can lean on it when the winds of change blow. A good, honest, and respectful friend, your mother, friend, or father can be of invaluable support. Don't forget, even a young tree needs a strong stake, alongside it to grow, until its roots are strong enough that it can grow independently.

The stake of support for the woman from my workshop was her colleague, who asked her one day, what was written on that piece of paper on her wall. When that woman read the words on her colleague's sheet of paper, she realized that they finally showed her who, in truth, the woman was, who had been sitting on the other side of the office for the past five years. Between them, an even stronger friendship was woven, and the walls of their offices soon began to be adorned by new sheets of truth, this time belonging to her colleague.

That sheet of paper, dear Queen, is possibly one of the most important pieces of paper in your life. It's important that you know what's written on it and that you really feel it in the only authentic place of judgment for you - in your heart. And because of that, you'll be able, from now onwards, to always understand your decisions and ways of looking at things. And because of that, you'll no longer need to behave in accordance with the opinions of other people. Never again.

May the winds of truth blow away the cobwebs from your heart. Who in truth are you? Who are you? ... Who are you ...? Who ...?

"Look inside,
and you'll see who you are."

Hanna opened her eyes. She felt how strongly she was clutching onto her blanket. It was really cold in her hotel room ... the window was open, and the curtains were flapping about gently. A cold breeze was drifting into the room, and a draft could be felt. She was confused ... "Is it possible I forgot to close the window?"

She looked at the clock ... it was 3:40. Wrapped in her blanket, she got up. As she walked towards the window, she heard the wind blowing outside ... and she could have sworn, that she heard the wind whispering ...

Mission no. 2:

True Colors

Hanna was lying in bed and looking up at the ceiling, which seemed to be somehow, and rather unusually, 'alive.' She wasn't able to fall asleep, nor was she able to look away from the ceiling. Although it was completely cracked all over and was 'decorated' with a dirty yellow blotch in the corner, which looked like someone in the hotel room above hers had forgotten to turn the water off, she didn't see anything.

Instead, on it, she saw images from her past. One of her father and how he surprised her on her fourth birthday with a brand new bike. And of him, on the same day, pushing her down the street from their house and with a smile on his face, calling her 'Teddy bear," and telling her with pride that she was his greatest treasure. Of a dark day, when her tears got mixed up in the rain, as she stood before the dark hole of dread, into which they put her parents' bodies, at which she wasn't able to say a single word, because she was all choked up inside. Of her wonderful teacher, who in the second grade, emotionally adopted her, when she most needed her mother and who, during the break between classes, taught her how to plait a ponytail. Of the angry old Chinese man, who let her, at fifteen years of age, earn enough money by washing dishes in his small restaurant and was unable to show, beneath all his anger, that he genuinely had a beautiful heart. Of the first time, she was teased by her classmates in high school, who made fun of her because she wore the same jeans the whole time and said she would never get a boyfriend because girls like her don't deserve even the tiniest bits of love. Of Peter, a special guy, who moved to their town when she was in the third year of high school, and for a moment shed light on the darkest of dark things, when he joined her class ... because he was the only one who, because of the passing of his own father, understood the pain and loneliness of losing a parent, and knew how to quickly comfort her between classes when she needed a shoulder, for her and her heartbroken from life head, to rest on. Of her extraordinary professor at university, who gave her hope, that she too could one day be truly exceptional at something. Of Mark, the leader of the expedition, who every day, over and over, stole this hope like a vulture, and who proudly elevated himself high, without letting anyone else come close.

The sun woke her from her thoughts, shining a thin line between the curtains, in search of her face, as if it wanted to tell her something. Perhaps, she wasn't able to understand its force. However, she knew that it was time to get up. With a heavy heart, she left the safety of her bed, which had magically led her to her Shanti, and headed for the bathroom, to prepare for yet another day in the arena of gladiators, in which her schoolmates, with their thumbs turned downwards, would once again show her, where her place was.

She looked at herself in the mirror, and through her tousled hair, looked into her eyes. Even though they were still sad and 'decorated' with dried-up tears, that morning, they were different. She stopped. The longer she observed them, the more they became, somehow ... stronger. She remembered her dreams and Shanti ... "Look inside yourself, and you'll see who you really are." For a moment, she seemed to see something in her eyes ... only that ... she didn't know ... but other people would call this spark, simply ... hope.

That day, Hanna spent it far removed from the other members of the expedition. She ran into them three or four times, most often when she brought them coffee, otherwise she did her best to avoid them, as she didn't want to be on the receiving end of another bout of humiliation, which would shout quite a different opinion at her, as the one Shanti had. She didn't want to hear, once again, how terribly incapable she was and how women are an unnecessary problem or even a mistake of nature. Her already too often wounded heart would not survive yet another stabbing with something sharp, held in the hands of those who God himself gave the right to do something which was not theirs ... not today. A tent, a few meters away, was an excellent hiding place, where no one would insult her, and a place that provided her with some time for reflection.

She remembered her dreams, but in them, everything was so much simpler. In them, there was no Mark nor her rude classmates. There were none of their demons, who persistently ran their claws down her face in the hope of scratching her eyes out and blinding her for life. In her thoughts, there was only that magnificent Ruler ... so beautiful ... so understanding ... Shanti. Oh, how she wanted to be able to see her again. She had seen her mysterious face only for a moment ... it might have been while she was calmly and peacefully sleeping. But the scepter of courage was lost in the moment when she remembered the humiliation down in the tomb, which painfully reminded her that visiting it was a forbidden palace, and that girls like her were not allowed to enter.

In the evening, she lay down in bed. Confused. Like so many times before. She didn't know what was going on; her thoughts were spinning around like a merry-go-round that just didn't want to stop. Shanti's words about a strong woman sounded so nice, but there, in the real world, just one look from her now reprehensible classmates, and in a split second, they were trampled over, like gentle grass, being crushed under the pressure of unyielding steps. "If only dear Shanti knew that it wasn't so easy," even though Hanna, deep down inside, sometimes wanted it more than life itself. And that thought led her to close her eyelids, inviting her to a new night, in which she would perhaps ...

"I know what it's like, Hanna. I understand you better than you think," echoed in her ears. "I know how you feel."

Hanna looked around and quickly discovered that she had once again found herself in the Golden Temple. She sat down next to Shanti and, with her hand, fleetingly touched her long dress made of golden thread and thousands of small pearls. Hanna looked at her. She said nothing. Her look, which desperately sought answers, was enough.

"Once, I also had to deal with the world and show it how strong I was," continued Shanti. "I had to show it that I deserved to be a part of it. Who wrote the rules that determined who deserves something and who doesn't? Hasn't this always been the undoing of love for most people? When my father died, I became heiress to the throne. And then my uncle appeared, who was, during the time of my father's reign, one of his advisors. He didn't like me. He was of the opinion that he deserved the throne, not me. He screamed in his demands, and his voice played the notes of hatred. He wanted to take away my crown. He scared me and threatened me. And, I had to stand up for myself. And then, I realized that I deserved ... myself. And I had to show him who I was ..."

The earth, a beautiful planet, which offers thousands and thousands of possibilities. And its treasure trove is open to only a few - to those who take action. To those who move. To those who show others who they are. The earth demands from its inhabitants that they also express their thoughts and words outwardly. The laws of nature are otherwise very clear. Dear Queen: Show yourself, and you shall be seen. If you don't show yourself, you will be overlooked.

Millions of women around the world are bound by chains, imprisoned in jails where the sun rarely shines, and are caught up in life's stories in which they have no part. Who put the chains on them? Who threw them in jail? Most of them did this ... to themselves. I know you're reading this with slight disbelief, possibly even with your mouth wide open, so let me explain what's actually going on.

A woman who has decided to live a life she no longer likes has voluntarily given up her freedom. From a once little girl, who with every step knew who she was and what she wanted, she changed into a slave, who now holds her head low, while her dreams scream out for her to take action. Her main challenge is not a lack of economic opportunities or a lack of respect for equality, but it is her preparedness to accept less than what she's capable of. She voluntarily buries the power she has into the sand and throws it away in exchange for passiveness.

Every day, rulers lose their crowns everywhere ... when they go to work to a job they hate, when they're together with a partner for reasons other than love, when they measure themselves up to men's criteria which they work so hard to achieve, or that in the end they discard their femininity and take on the part of them that is masculine. Can such a life enrich you with happiness? No. A woman who doesn't listen to her heart, can't be happy. And as such, she can't be truly active in her own power.

Modern slavery doesn't take place in detention centers or in jails, but every day on the streets and in family homes, where women, instead of expressing themselves and their needs, bite their lips and remain silent. Praying in the hope that one day, it'll be different. But the truth here can be very unpleasant - without change, things will stay the same. This is the fundamental law of nature and mankind. Humanity always functions along the lines of least resistance.

I'll never forget a woman in her fifties, who came to me for an individual consultation, with the intention of me helping her regain her confidence. After an introductory conversation, I decided that we should first look at her partner relationship. Already after having answered my first question, I began to realize where this woman was challenged, and shortly after, I discovered that I was right - she was a slave. She was subordinate to her husband in absolutely all areas of her life. She did the things that he liked, wore the clothes that he wanted, even ate the food he liked. When I asked her why she was doing that, she answered because she loves him. Of course, my next question was whether he demanded such behavior from her, or not. She replied that he had never directly demanded anything from her, but that many a time, he clearly mentioned what he liked.

And she somehow decided to start dancing to the way he played. And so, she danced the following twenty-eight years in that way. For almost three decades, she lived like a slave, not knowing that she had invisible chains around her wrists, which reminded her of her own feeling of incompleteness, which after many long years, finally fought its way to the surface. When I explained to her the true circumstances of her life, she happily thanked me. We agreed to meet again, as an hour and a half was simply not enough time to resolve thirty years of such behavior. Two days before our next meeting, she called me and canceled. The reason - she felt that her life was actually not so bad and that if it were on the cards that she had to change, then she would change by herself, naturally. In other words, once again, she bit her lip and allowed others to control her chains.

You know, if the railway tracks of your life have been built with you having your head bowed all the time, then the dynamics of your energy will continue to flow as it has until now, without change. Life won't change the circumstances so that you'll be able to change the causes, from which those circumstances arose. Things work the other way around. First, you have to change your behavior. Then things start to change around you.

Remember now your gift of decision. The best thing in your life is that you can change it whenever you really want to. Nothing is permanent. Something is the way it is because someone decided so. And now is the time that you decide, how you want that something to be. The world has often convinced women that they're not good for some things, or that for some things they aren't suitable, only because they're women. I've got no idea where this way of thinking began, but the fact is, that in the world as it is today, there's a completely absurd selection, that divides people into two groups: men and women. And, surprisingly, many people on earth still accept and even encourage such a division. Most likely, it's not necessary for me to write this here, but the main advocates of this division are men. But we're now in a time, which is no longer called the Stone-Age, so it would be good to update this old fashioned way of thinking, as many ancient beliefs, which support it are highly illusionary, if not even stupid, and many women continue to have their spines broken and are slowed down on their way because of it.

Therefore, Queen, have you ever heard that:

- Women should stand behind the stove and cook for their families? Interesting, because as far as it's known, men also eat. The irony is that most of the professional chefs in the world are men;
- Women are responsible for their children's homework and for their upbringing? Even though both mother and father are equals in the role of parents;
- Women are bad drivers? But despite this conviction, most accidents are caused by men;
- Women are gentler creatures and physically more sensitive. But a simulator replicating the contractions a woman feels during childbirth was placed on men, and the results show the opposite to be true ...

The list could go on, and on ... just as a person could get caught up in an infinite number of their own convictions. And so, my dear, perhaps it's time that you rejuvenate some of your strengths, which may have been weakened a little in light of these convictions and which will once again help you to place your crown on your head.

1. *POWER: Self-respect*

Your greatest allies are not other people, but you yourself. And your greatest enemies are not other people, but you yourself. The anvil, on which you forge your power, is otherwise your self-respect. It depends on the strength and stability of the anvil, how strong you can forge, and how strong a scepter you can create.
Self-respect is a fundamental energy, around which you build your life. Everything comes from this - the people you are surrounded by, the career you build, your health, finances ... everything. All of this simply responds to your request of love for yourself. You can't demand health, but you can get it when you respect your thoughts, feelings, and body. You can't get a nice partner relationship until you have a good relationship yourself, with yourself. When you demand a good relationship from yourself, you automatically expect it from others. A lot of women are challenged by this because people in their surroundings don't respect them. And then they demand respect. My dear, you cannot demand anything. Least of all respect. The attitude people have towards you is chosen depending on your attitude towards yourself. As a matter of fact, the energy of respect can only come to you from others, if you set up the foundations to receive it. And you lay those foundations. It's called self-respect.

Everything in your environment is simply an expression of your inner demands. A lot of women continue on in relationships, in which their partner, superiors, coworkers ... behave badly towards them. Many are verbally, psychologically, emotionally, sexually, or even physically abused. But know what follows: A woman who strongly respects herself, would never allow, that anyone in any way abuses her. Instead of that, her life is full of gifts in the form of beautiful relationships, material rewards, and good health.

How strong is your self-respect?

All the decisions you make in life, you make according to the level of self-respect you have. If you decide to drink only fresh, clean water, this shows a different level of self-respect, as opposed to if you consume sodas with added sweeteners and colorings. If you do a job which makes you happy, it shows a different level of self-respect, as opposed to working in an environment in which you are unhappy. Absolutely everything in your life is a reflection of your self-esteem. Even in other people, you can see from a distance their level of self-respect by observing the kinds of people they associate with and the kinds of things they've chosen in their lives.

My wife, Christy, was at one stage in her life at the very bottom, with respect to her level of self-esteem. That was at the beginning of our relationship. Some of the ordeals she went through were a serious car accident as well as the death of her mother, who was taken from her, and together, they pushed her into an abyss of self-destruction. That's why all the things around her conspired against her. There was no other way for things to go because she herself had created them. Then, she began to face up to her grief, got through it, and slowly began to get back on her feet. The first results could be seen very quickly. They came in the form of a new job, the loss of some excess weight, and even improvements in our partner relationship. Now, years later, her life is completely different, above all, more beautiful. It's filled with extraordinary people, and equally exceptional are her decisions, which she makes every day. And all because of the respect for herself, which she forged on her own anvil.

Homework

Begin to consciously observe what your life is made up of. Look at everything: The kind of food you choose, the people you associate with, how you spend your free time, the kind of movies you watch ... everything. Then, look at how everything affects you. Go through everything, and simply take a look to see if they affect you positively or negatively. At the same time, check your feelings in relation to them: Are they friendly or unfriendly? Through this, you can find out how much you truly value yourself, as you yourself choose the circumstances in your life on a conscious and subconscious level. Why is it such an extraordinary indicator of self-esteem? Because everything influences your body, your thoughts, and your emotions. And that is, essentially, what makes you, you. Which means that you're the person you are because of the way these things influence you.

An example of a movie:
Horror movies fill people with fear, while comedies fill you with joy. A woman, who consciously chooses a comedy, has a lot more self-respect that a woman who chooses a horror movie, as the first woman chooses feelings which will make her happier, calmer and more satisfied, while the other chooses feelings which will make her more frightened and emotionally damaged.

An example of food:
Fatty and fried, animal-based food in the human body adds to the level of bad fats, leading the body to become all the more fatty, deteriorating its functionality. On the other hand, fresh vegetables ensure the body gets lots of vitamins and fiber and leads to better functioning. A woman who chooses fatty foods has a much lower level of self-respect than one who chooses lighter foods.

In the world, you have one best friend who loves you unconditionally. Her love is so strong that she's almost prepared to forgive you for anything. She's with you when you reap the fruits of your successes as well as when you fall from your defeats. So, love her back. Help her so that she understands her true value and appreciates herself in every moment of her life. And that girlfriend is you.

2. *POWER: Decide what you want (especially what you don't want).*

The best thing in the world is that everything is here, just for you. Just like what it would be like to be in a huge store, where the shelves are full of everything you can imagine, and you get to choose whatever it is you want. But a lot of women, who enter this 'global store,' come without two things: a shopping list and a shopping cart. One of the qualities of a ruler is that she very clearly knows what she wants and takes care that she also gets it. If you knew in every single moment what it is you wanted, then every day would be like Christmas.

Write down a list of things that you WANT to have in your life.

On that list, write down absolutely everything you want to be, become and have. Include absolutely all areas of your life. It's very hard to get something if you don't know what you want. Be honest with yourself. Don't look at what it pays to do, what others advise you, or if you're strong enough. Just focus on your heart. While writing, release all the things you've learned about the world and 'naively' listen to your heart. It's also important that you don't stop yourself writing for any kinds of feelings of guilt, obligation, or doubt. Write from your heart, and don't be surprised if you find things on the list which you may have forgotten about. And, don't limit yourself - put everything down on the piece of paper.

Write down a list of things you DON'T WANT in your life.

Sometimes it's easier to write a list of things we don't want, rather than a list of things we do want. Some women tend to be a little pessimistic. Usually, they're rather unhappy in life and live their truth, but only in a very small way. For such women, it's a bit of a challenge, in the beginning, to see all the beautiful colors of life, as they've been caught up in the greyness for years and years. Therefore, it's easier to determine and define what they don't want. Knowing what you don't want is just as important as knowing what you do want. As a matter of fact, most people more clearly know what it is they don't want, rather than what they do. Things you don't want, but nevertheless have, cause you pain and other unpleasant feelings, which are rather strong and let you know that they're there, even if you don't see them.

Once, a young girl came to me, who had been sexually abused as a teenager. Even though the location where I held workshops and consultations was particularly warm and safe, she was shaking on the inside. Her inner world was very dark. Sexual abuse and ridicule from her peers, cultivated dark thoughts within her as well as a strong resistance to trusting the world. Even though she was only in her twenties, she wasn't able to see anything bright or optimistic in her life. She disclosed to me that she'd been contemplating suicide for some time. The pain was too much. She'd lost hope in the world.

Usually, when people lose hope, I help them to once again find the little bright lights of their dreams, which illuminate the twilight, but this wasn't the case with her. With her, we began with this list - with the things she doesn't like. Inside, she had too many things which triggered pain, and too many burning memories which had burnt her young soul. It was important that she get them out of her system.

The consultation lasted almost three hours. And because of that, I canceled the client I was supposed to have later that day. For three hours, we tore up everything she hated, everything she didn't want, and everything she was afraid of. Her list was endless. In the end, there was nothing left, and she was exhausted. But after a long time, a smile lit up her face. It didn't burn her as much. She wasn't afraid as much. Piece by piece, she began to remove the toxic energy of resentment, anger, and pain. She had a long way to go, but at least, she was able to walk. And she clearly knew what she didn't want.

In writing this list, it's crucial that you're honest with yourself. It could happen that a person appears on your list, who you otherwise love, but don't want to continue having a relationship with. Maybe you'll write that you no longer wish to live with your parents or that you no longer want to be a mother, twenty-four hours a day. But understand two things: Whatever you want to write, know that you have the right to do so. Every person has the right to express their own truth. And, don't feel guilty or have a bad conscience. Having a bad conscience is nothing more than a feeling that arises when you look at a particular thing differently than others, and then when you try to compare them. As you've already discovered: Your truth is not comparable to anything, and it's always right.

3. *POWER: Discover the world of your thoughts and feelings*

If you don't disclose your thoughts and needs, people around you won't know what you need, and therefore, won't be able to help you to achieve them. Don't allow the thoughts and skepticism in your mind to consume an idea, even before you're able to express it. Your task is to tell people what you want and what you need. And, of course, what you don't want. This is key because only on the basis of the information people get are they able to build relations. And if the information is incomplete or even incorrect, it's very difficult to build a quality relationship. The main reason why most women don't express their needs clearly when they already know them is two-fold: Because they've been intimidated or because they've been manipulated.

Intimidated women:

A lot of women have a tightly-closed chakra of the throat (this is the energy center in the area of the neck and the lower part of the head which takes care of expression and the receipt of information). They're not 'allowed' to express their own truth.

This senseless prohibition comes from very long periods of time when, for expressing the truth, thousands and thousands were punished at the stake, by imprisonment or even by death. And so, many suppressed it. And who could have blamed them? Authorities and systems sometimes didn't like smart and independent people, particularly if they were beautiful women.

Fear of expression is firmly rooted in the minds of many modern women. Despite this, it's important to know that today's world is different. There are no more stakes upon which people are burned. You can express your truth. Authorities won't lock you up (well, okay, in 'developed' countries they won't), the only thing is that you'll get under someone's skin, but that's more his or her problem. Usually, these people will only be in a bad mood or angry at you, which is a small price to pay in comparison with not expressing your own truth.

Of course, some people, on rare occasions, can express their disagreement with you and your needs in a way that is damaging, or even dangerous. Some people, when others express their own truth to them, begin to psychologically, emotionally, or even physical abuse or intimidate their partners, their friends, coworkers, employees ... This is in no way acceptable. If this happens to you, stop such action immediately, and if necessary, put an end to the relationship. Even if it hurts and stings. Do this for your own personal freedom. In an extreme case of intimidation, seek help from organizations that can support you in this, or official bodies, such as the police. Intimidation is abuse, and abuse is not acceptable, in any way, shape, or form. It's very important that you know what's going on. If you discover that it's actually taking place, stop it immediately. Why? Because you deserve people around you, who'll encourage you on your path, and won't stop you. No woman in the world should have to suffer from any kind of abuse, especially if some of the people around her are emotionally unstable, or simply mean.

An exceptional example of a woman, who saved herself from the claws of an intimidator and came out of it as a proud ruler, is Tina Turner. As a young singer, she got married, and shortly after the wedding, her husband began to abuse her in all kinds of ways. The physical and sexual violence lasted many years, before the final blow, which triggered something in her - she had had enough. Enough blows, enough blood, and enough humiliation. She deserved to live peacefully and freely, in the same way that every woman deserves to. She gathered all the strength she had and left. Of course, he wanted to stop her with even more intimidation, but she didn't give in. She was prepared to leave absolutely everything behind. And she did. The only thing she took from their marriage was her name and the permission to continue to use her name, Tina Turner. You know how things turned out after that - Tina is one of the icons of modern woman, a world-renowned singer, and actress, proof, of how a woman can go from being a slave to becoming a ruler.

How to recognize intimidation and abuse? Some women don't even know what intimidation and abuse actually are. As a matter of fact, they probably don't even want to admit it. Many women, who could be queens, in truth are slaves and turn a blind eye to the abuse. Some are even of the opinion that they deserve it, others think that it's not so bad, while others still think that it's normal.

Once, I was having a drink with a female friend. During our conversation, she told me about a female friend of hers, who had a new guy in her life. When my friend asked her what he's like, she said: "My new guy's great. Do you know, he doesn't even beat me?" Excuse me? What's wrong with that answer? Everything. It's extremely important that a woman is aware of the reality of the relationships she's in. Abuse is the execution of any kind of emotional, verbal, psychological, sexual, or even physical violence. No one has the right to do this, irrespective of whether they agree with your truth, or not. The law is there to protect you from abuse. So, always take measures, if it happens. Just like Tina did.

With the women I've worked, there have been many cases of intimidation. Most of them were expressed through prohibitions, demands, stipulations, a denial of rights, direct threats, ...

Therefore, Queen, have you ever heard that:

- being prohibited by their partner not to socialize with their friends, families, to not undertake any activities they want to, or to travel on their own, etc.;
- demands of being constantly reachable by telephone or the execution of other forms of control, such as tracking, checking their activities, even checking the call history on their cell phones, etc.;
- stipulating what and even how much they can eat;

- denying them fundamental rights to freedom, food, and other existential things, that arise; as a consequence of disagreeing with the person providing it;
- mobbing at the workplace, etc.

Manipulators:

Some women don't express their needs and thoughts clearly enough, because it gives them the feeling of controlling the person they're in a relationship with. Manipulation in this way mostly takes place in partner relationships and in employment-related relationships, where the manipulator has the role of being a supervisor.

Once I spoke with a female friend who was angry at her boyfriend because he didn't buy her a present for her birthday. A lot of women would sit down with their partners in such situations and tell them that they're sad because they forgot to buy them a present. But not my friend. She decided to be angry at him and to give him the 'cold shoulder.' Instead of talking to him, she was cold towards him and so distanced herself from him. When I asked her what good that kind of behavior would bring to their relationship, she replied that she had to teach him a lesson. Of course, I interested to know what kind of lesson. "He has to learn what's important to me."

Then we talked a little bit more, and I told her that people in relationships are constantly learning. And that, in some way, we're learning more and more about our partners, the whole time. Her response was that she wasn't interested and that if he truly loved her, he would have known. Yes, it's true that a lot of partners don't listen enough and pay attention to their partners but being offended is not the key to a better relationship. Relationships are a lot easier to build if both partners clearly express their thoughts and needs. And so, playing the 'diva' and that everyone around her 'should know' what her needs are, is not exactly the role that helps women strengthen their relationships, and even less so to help them become a ruler. Usually what happens, at best, is the opposite - partners, subordinates, friends ... begin avoiding such women, because the way they are, in that they have to be attentive to her the whole time, or that they have to be careful what they say to her the entire time, and that it's too much of an effort. If you recognize yourself in this role, stop passively expressing your wishes and emotions and help others around you find out who you are and actively help them understand that part of you, which for whatever reason, they haven't until now.

4. *POWER: Informing*

Now that you know what you want, or rather what you don't, you have to inform the world around you. A lot of women run into trouble here because the message they send out to the world about their needs is simply not strong enough. All too many women shyly announce their wishes and seek permission from others for it to be realized. Stop asking for permission. You're nobody's owner, why should you have to ask anyone for permission? Thousands of women seek approval from their partners if they want to do something on their own. What's then the difference between a slave and them? Slaves also have to (or had to) ask for permission. Stop doing that.

I first thought about the power of informing one evening after I had a small fight with my wife. We argued about the uncut grass around the house, which was already so high that almost any kind of ball would get lost in it, which we usually threw for our little dog to go and fetch. Although the entire argument was completely unimportant, it otherwise created some kind of tension between us, just like every kind of argument does. A little before that, my wife and her girlfriends arranged that they were going to go for a girls' weekend away, the following weekend. When, during the argument, she said that I would have the entire upcoming weekend to cut the grass because I would be home alone, I replied that she can't go because we had other things to do. Then she looked me in the eyes and said: "I wasn't asking you for permission, I was telling you." Although my male ego wanted to fight back and win in the 'battle of the grass,' that statement came to mind. It was so strong. So clear. It was the statement of a ruler. And, at that moment, I knew that her statement was one of the most important, which I want to instill in our yet-to-be-born children.

Never allow anyone else to determine your place. Determine it yourself. If you want to do something, do it. A queen never asks for permission, she just states. And that's why she's a ruler. To state means to pass on a message, which is based on already accepted decisions, and that demands you to stand behind them. But now, because you know what you want, it'll be a lot easier. If you inform people of your intentions, they won't interfere as much in what you're doing. The energy of informing is a lot more stable and a lot stronger than the energy of asking for permission. Besides that, people will have a lot more respect for you, as they'll see that you have a solid standpoint and goals.

Queen, you can do this. You deserve absolutely everything that comes to your mind. Now, go and get your crown.

"The anvil, on which you forge your strength, is your self-respect."

Hanna opened her eyes in a state of confusion and looked around. She was looking for Shanti. But only the plaster, which was falling down from the walls and ceiling told her, that she was no longer in the Golden Temple, but in her hotel room. For a moment, stars danced all around her and, almost helplessly, she remained there, lying in her bed. She had a feeling that she had to, somehow ... come back down to earth.

She had obviously been dreaming again.

Was it true?

Mission no. 3:

A Ponytail of Changes

Hanna awoke with a feeling that today was going to be different. Instead of her morning headache and those unhappy dried tears on her face, this morning, her body was flooded with something, which she hadn't felt in the past seventeen years, something, like a flower of despair, that had been withered already for a long time - like some kind of ... self-confidence? Burning sensations of power mixed in with her blood and made her ask herself anew, who she was. She wasn't used to such sensations. It seemed that the frightened little girl, who looked at the clock all confused every morning, was still asleep. There was no anxiety indicating a new day that she had to spend with her rude schoolmates, and there were no cramps in her legs, preventing them from doing what they were told, and getting up. No. That day, she almost jumped out of bed, as if her legs were playing with the idea of some kind of invisible trampoline, inviting her to the game of her life. An unknown energy even encouraged her to do a couple of pushups, showing her that there was some strength hiding within, which resolutely wanted to be awakened.

"Is it really possible that a person can feel so different, simply because she remembers who she really is? Or, did I maybe just recall ... something?"

With that question in mind, she headed off to the bathroom. She wanted to quickly get herself ready, just like she had every morning for the past couple of years. A few quick brushes of her tousled hair, a bit of water to freshen her face, and the job was done. Her makeup remained carefully packed and unused in her toiletry bag, and grumpily asked her why she had taken it along with her if it wasn't allowed to express its colors.

Then, an inner voice loudly and clearly stopped her: "Slow down, Hanna. Not today. You deserve more."

Her eyes remained focused on the mirror, and it seemed as if they would begin to talk all by themselves. She knew exactly what the mysterious voice wanted to tell her. Her thoughts were flooded by a photograph from a glamorous fashion magazine, which she had flipped through years before and which was adorned by the image of an attractive woman with exceptionally long hair, just like hers, which was tied together in a ponytail from the top of her head and then fell down past her neck. And because it was tied in three places, it had the look of a long plait. She was like a goddess, who ruled her own temple, and everything about her spoke of love for herself.

Hanna, in the evenings, when nobody knew, had arranged her hair in that kind of way, already a thousand times before. But whenever she wanted to go out like that and be among people, something stopped her and convinced her that her long hair, which wasn't tied back and that somehow encircled her face, was a lot safer. After all, she was able to cry at school behind her hair, without anyone noticing. It was a good front for someone who so desperately wanted to hide her pain. For many a year, it had offered her a safe haven, behind which she could hide whenever she wanted to escape the world. But not today. Today would be different. Self-confidently, she took her hairbrush, brushed her hair back, then skillfully tied it together at the top of her head, exposing her slender neck, which altogether hadn't happened in a long time. Then she added three clips to her ponytail and tied it together so that it fell in a straight line. No more protection. No more hiding. The time had come to show her 'true colors'. Or at least the first shades.

She stood at the door of the large tent for a few seconds, where her coworkers from the expedition drank coffee every morning before heading out to work. The coffee not only gave them the impetus for work but also unwound their sharp tongues. The echo of laughter echoed from behind the door, from which some male competitiveness could be perceived. Nervously, she straightened her ponytail, breathed deeply, and entered.

Her schoolmates were confused for a moment which silenced their endless banter: "Who's that?" whispered one of them. Then, their eyes almost fell out of their sockets: "Hanna? Is that you? I was already overjoyed at the thought that such a beautiful local girl had come to say hello ..."

But already in the next moment, the energy changed, and the image of the beauty vanished, which had caressed the eyes of those who knew only to value beauty based on external appearances.

"What's this? You're late!" hissed Nick, and everything went back to the way it had been. "We had to make our own coffee! Why do we even have you? Next time, stop playing hairdresser and get here on time!"

But, in spite of his rude words, Hanna felt that morning, that strength was on her side. She walked over to Nick and said: "Can you please give me the phone number of your mother?" "Why?" Nick grumbled confused, which didn't stop Hanna, who added ice-coldly: "That I congratulate her for succeeding in teaching you how to make a coffee before your twenty-third birthday. Because as far as teaching you good manners goes, she obviously failed miserably."

Nick stood silent. He wasn't used to anyone even thinking of opposing him. It seemed that the unexpected shock had erased all thoughts from his head, and so words weren't able to find their way to his mean mouth. He looked like a fish out of water. He didn't expect such a response. Not him, nor the others. A deep silence prevailed, like the sleep of those in the tombs they had discovered.

But one of them had quietly noticed the rising of a mighty beauty, who until that moment was only known by the name, Hanna. In the back part of the tent sat Peter. "I knew it. I knew you would one day arise," said his mysterious smile.

For a moment, Hanna herself was surprised. She hadn't expected that. Not from herself. She had no idea she had it in her. Was Shanti right? Could she really change like that? Could she ever be happy? Was there really a chance for those who had lost it such a long time ago? She felt some unusual energy shooting through her ordinarily hunched-over spine like a snake lifting its head demanding respect and that boundaries weren't be crossed. She had a feeling that her body was on automatic pilot as if she was dancing to an awakened rhythm, the tact of which was silenced the loss of love. But now, the rhythm was all the more faster, and all the more louder. She looked at Nick, all confused, winked at him like a mischievous flirt, then turned and like a proud black cat, and walked out of the tent.

"What just happened?" the guys silently asked themselves as they watched Hanna walk out with her ponytail swaying behind her back like a sharp sword, cutting through their astonished gazes.

Hanna walked out of the tent and took a deep breath of warm desert air. Her lungs welcomed her with the breath of life. But her legs were shaking. She had never confronted anyone before. She had always run away and hidden like a vampire from the light. "What was that?" she asked herself with a smile, which adorned her now, changed face. She thought she knew herself. Who was that girl in the tent? Did she really have this inside herself? Do Phoenixes really rise up from the ashes? For a moment, she held her breath, then exhaled. Her thoughts began to relax and caress her new reality. Obviously, an unknown part of her existed, which she had just started to discover ... and started to like. Just like the sarcophagus with Shanti - so very hidden, but so very ... beautiful.

The week passed in the blink of an eye. Hanna quickly got accustomed to her new 'energy' and was enjoying herself, just like a child enjoys playing in a sandbox. The quiet mouse within her all the more began to hide in its hole, its place taken by a self-confident feline, which was moving, all the more decisively. Her relationship with her classmates had mellowed, and no one wanted to be the next target of her scoffing, as had happened to Nick. Her goddess-like, carefully tied back hair had become a part of her every day. With it, she felt strong. Her ponytail was like a reminder to her, hanging back there. Whenever the end of it touched her back, she felt some kind of self-confident force flow through her. Even Nick reverted to not antagonizing her anymore, as she had decided that no iceberg was going to sink her ship. Otherwise, they hadn't formed a strong friendship, but at least there was no more friction between them. Which was more than good enough.

Hanna was finally able to experience beautiful Egypt that day in a way she had only imagined when at university, she found out that she had been chosen to go on the two-month expedition. The guys had, above all, accepted her, and somehow she had become a part of the team, breathing with them in an equal rhythm of life. And finally, she was able to be with her, once again - with her sleeping Ruler. No longer did she spend most of her time in the improvised tent kitchen, but there, underground. With her. With Shanti.

One day, when she was carefully cleaning the walls of the tomb with her archeological shovel, her gaze fell on a faded stain, which had come about a few days earlier, when she spilled the coffee.

"At the time, she felt frightened and discarded, humiliated and wounded, but today she was calm and accepted. How quickly things change in life ..." thought the girl, who was once again aware of the smile on her beautiful lips, which then remained with her to the hotel and kept her company like a faithful friend and promised never to leave her again. The feeling in her heart, when she was getting ready for bed, reminded her of her greatest victory in life. A win over herself. "Maybe this is how courageous and

daring people feel?" she asked herself and smiled. Although on the outside, she possibly looked rather ordinary, that evening, Hanna knew that she had begun to mature. The little girl in her said goodbye, and a woman arrived, who was aware of herself, who promised her a new world, and a new future. "Thank you, Shanti," were her last thoughts, before the stars once again danced ...

Although it glittered quite strongly, the golden reflection didn't bother her eyes at all. "The Golden Temple. Shanti ..." were her first thoughts. She looked around and saw her and noticed how she was sitting on her already familiar throne. She ran to her and, in a wave of joy, hugged her. Never before had she hugged her. A second later, she pulled back and said: "Oh, I'm sorry, I didn't mean to ... it just happened automatically ..."

"Hanna, embraces are to be shared," said Shanti with a divine smile, pulling her back in. Hanna caught the intoxicating smell of jasmine, and on her skin, she felt some soft fabric, which reminded her of silk. At that moment, she felt as if she was in heaven.

Releasing herself from their embrace, she crossed her legs, then sat down on top of them and, with a certain amount of pride on her face, stated: "I did it. I did it. I stood up for myself. Do you know what? It felt amazing. And my classmates have also changed. Now, we're digging together. Finally, I feel like a part of the team. And everyone likes my new ponytail. And it's all because of you!" Hanna's smile said it all. And the sparks in her eyes glowed even stronger than ever before.

Shanti took her by the hand and said: "My dear, that's how it goes. Life just reacts to you. And know that it's primarily because of ... you, yourself."

External circumstances only confirm what you've already accepted internally. Therefore, when you change your inner perceptions, the outer world also changes. Why does the life of most women, who decide to change it, change so slowly? Because they change it in the wrong places. Instead of changing their inner perception and themselves, they try to change their external circumstances and others. And so, they focus on something, which in reality, they can't control. Therefore, they can't achieve the result, they initially wanted. If we direct our attention to circumstances instead of the source, we're usually tired and disappointed after trying for a long time. This isn't the kind of result women want. Especially so, because results in life are so very important. We all want to be rewarded for our work. If we invest energy, time, and money into change, it's right that our investment is somehow returned. So, dear Queen, it's important, if your actions are to bring success and everything you want, you have to truly understand the relationship you're working on, as well as your circumstances.

A lot of women seem confused and unsuccessful because they don't understand where they have to begin to create change if they actually want to change something. And so, most of them focus on what they can clearly perceive. Usually the things and people who make up their lives: Their children, partner, job, money ... in other words, circumstances.

Yes, absolutely everything which builds your life and which isn't you, are your circumstances. Maybe you'll hear this now for the first time, that your child is your environment, that your job, which you go to, is your circumstance, that all the people around you are just your environment. Some things and people are close to your heart, and you love them, while some you don't see and take for granted, but they're all just your environment. All things, happenings, and people, who make up your life are just a consequence. Of what? Of your decisions. It's important to remember that a scepter in the hands of a ruler is only a consequence of her decisions. Nothing else. A scepter is only a confirmation of decisions. And different decisions bring about different confirmations. That's why some women have a scepter in their hands, while others have a stick. That's why some have gloves on their hands, while others have handcuffs around their wrists. So, what now determines what you'll have on your hands? Will you put gloves or cuffs on?

Do you remember the gift of decision? This was shown to me very clearly once by a woman who came to a workshop, which I had organized for women who wanted to work on their self-confidence. Her main question was how to change her husband - who was obsessively enthusiastic about football. She thought that their entire relationship was suffering because of it. Every day after work, he would go to the football field, where he volunteered his assistance to football teams in their training, and in the same way, he spent his entire weekends at matches, at training sessions or in front of the television, where he watched past matches. "Football is ruining our marriage. We never go out, and he never takes as much time for me as he does for that stupid sport. If I had a button to wipe it from the face of this Earth, I would press it," she said, blaming her husband's hobby for her unhappy marriage. I advised her that it would be good if I could also speak to her husband. Despite the answer that he wouldn't be interested, she at least agreed to mention counseling to him. And a few days later, they really came.

And do you know what the main reason was why her husband spent so much time with his football buddies? He was running away from her. There was nothing in her life that she actively participated in, no hobbies, no activities, no friends. Consequentially, she was chronically dissatisfied with her environment, and because of that, she 'hung' onto her husband every second, as he represented the only living thing in her life. Everything else, including herself, was half dead. The problem wasn't with her husband, but with her. During counseling, he looked into her eyes and said: "Darling, I love you. But you're not my whole life, but an important part of it. I hope you can understand that." His wife was, of course, shocked, and I myself quietly applauded his courageous answer.

That lady needed her own life. She came to me for counseling, three more times after that. I helped her find her passion for life and to set some new goals. A few months later, she wrote me an email, in which she thanked me for all my help. Among other things, she wrote: "I found out that I have a fantastic husband, who really knows his football." I still have this email as a reminder of how quickly things around us fall into place when we begin focusing on ourselves.

The main reason why some women are so concerned about their circumstances and want to change them is that by doing so, they don't have to deal with themselves. And so, they always look for those who are guilty and responsible in their surroundings, so as not to point the finger at themselves. It's a lot easier to accuse a partner in a bad marriage, a boss for a low salary, the country for a low standard of living, etc. And women, who do this, all the more sink into the quicksand, in which they are stuck. To change their lives, they need energy. The greater the changes, the more energy is necessary. By pointing their fingers at others, saying that they're guilty for their circumstances, and the reason for their dissatisfaction, and then pushing it away from themselves, they lose instead of gain. And so, they become weaker instead of stronger. And so, their possibilities for positive change decrease, instead that they would increase.

My dear, focusing on your circumstances is like trying to change your shadow. You can't. Your shadow is simply a consequence of the fact that you are there. You can draw on it, scream at it, threaten it, but you'll never change it. If you want to change your shadow, you have to change yourself. Putting on an additional 100 pounds or cutting your hair short will change it. Understand? Your shadow is only a consequence of you, just like everything else.

A lot of women get 'caught up' in circumstances where they feel bad. Some have partners or colleagues around them who don't respect them, or even humiliate them. Some are trapped in jobs where they're unhappy, while some are without money, and even others are physically ill, etc. Perhaps, while reading these lines, the painful feeling in your chest is a reminder to you that some of these circumstances are also ones that you experience. But don't worry. You can change them. You can change absolutely everything! But you have to understand where change really begins. For your life to be truly comprised of the most beautiful colors that flow into the shades that you want for yourself, I'm going to pass on some knowledge to you that'll help you make that happen.

1. *KNOWLEDGE: You're the center of the Universe.*

Sounds good, doesn't it? It sounds good because it's true. You are the center of YOUR OWN Universe. The entire energy, which creates your life, comes from you. Everything in your life is a consequence of your internal processes. Has anybody ever said to you: "What do you think, that you're the center of the Universe and that everything revolves around you?" Actually, it's true. As a matter of fact, everything does revolve around you. And that phrase is actually one of the most powerful phrases that an individual can use. People think that only one center exists in the Universe, around which everyone lives. But it's not like that. Every person is the center of the Universe for themselves. Which means, there are as many centers of the Universe on Earth, as there are people. If you understand this, then you understand the concept of circumstances and their creation. In truth, everything comes from you.

2. *KNOWLEDGE: Always take action, starting with you.*

When there's something you don't like, you want to do something and change things. Always take action, starting with you. Because you're the center of your own Universe. Everything in your life comes from you, which, as a matter of fact, makes things a lot easier for you. Why? Because now you know that it's not important to deal with a thousand things in your surroundings, but with just one -

with yourself. Why are so many people tired? Because they try to change a whole lot of circumstances in their lives - their partners, children, careers, etc. And, of course, over time, they run out of energy. If you devote your energy to yourself and not to others, very rarely will you be tired. Consequentially, your circumstances will be as you want them to be, as they'll come from you. A woman, who is self-confident and strong inside, automatically has circumstances around her, which confirm this.

3. ***KNOWLEDGE: Think with your own head.***

Other people are just your circumstances. Which means that you're also just a circumstance for others. And, in line with this, they'll also behave that way to you. Therefore, it's important that you think with your own head. If you behave according to the opinions and instructions of others, you'll be dealing with circumstances, with shadows. Other people form their own opinions based on their own truth, their own center of the Universe, which isn't the same as your truth. As a matter of fact, they can't even give you the right information for you, because they've got their own point of view, which, in most cases, is different from yours. Therefore, the only source of credible guidance for your life, is, as a matter of fact, you.

4. *KNOWLEDGE: You're never really 'caught up' in certain circumstances.*

Sometimes it seems that you're caught up in certain circumstances, against your will. You think you would never have chosen them yourself. I'm thinking of circumstances in which abuse, manipulation, etc. take place. But despite the emotional strain which such circumstances demand of you, be aware that it was you who chose them at some stage. People choose their circumstances consciously, but more often subconsciously. If you don't like a particular circumstance, it doesn't mean that you didn't choose it yourself, but only that you'll have to dig a little deeper within, to find out why you did, in fact, choose it. Whatever happens in your life, you've allowed and accepted it at some level to occur. A woman, who has a partner that beats her, has, at some level, decided herself to persevere in such a circumstance and allow that kind of behavior to go on. Let it sound as terrible as it is, because it's true. This otherwise doesn't excuse the actions of her partner, but it's important that the woman knows that she can put an end to it.

Some reasons for the choice of circumstances are superficial, others originate from the depths of our subconscious, or even from karmic decisions. A person can, in the wish for the approval of a certain type of behavior, draw on subconscious patterns of behavior, fear, etc., which were perhaps created in their childhood and have been consciously forgotten a long time ago, but this doesn't mean that they no longer exist.

One day, a young woman, around twenty-five years of age, approached me. She was interested in why she always seemed to end up with 'idiots' (if I can quote her) that cheated on her. When we delved into her subconscious, we discovered that she had, herself, chosen such partners. Her father had otherwise cheated on her mother. Which she discovered when she was just a little girl. But her mother kept saying that there are no ideal relationships and that sometimes it's just necessary to have a little patience. As a young girl, she accepted her mother's truth, which was then expressed in her choice of partners as an adult, who behaved towards her in the same manner as her father had behaved towards her mother - they cheated on her. Although she consciously didn't want that, she somehow called it into her life, subconsciously. So, it's important that you're honest with yourself, that you harmonize your conscious and subconscious, and that they become all the more similar, which will reduce the number of 'unexplained' circumstances in your life.

Karmic 'circumstances'

Karmic circumstances are a special kind of circumstance, which don't necessarily originate from the current embodiment, but from past lives. Karma, otherwise, balances energy and experience very well. Man is a multi-faceted being, whose different levels of energy determine the circumstances in his life. Some levels are quite basic and everyday, and so it's easier for us to be aware of them, while others can be strongly etheric and astral, so they can be a little harder to understand. Karmic circumstances thus derive from the latter. Sometimes, as a soul, you decide to go through a painful lesson, and there's nothing wrong with that because you've chosen to do so at the level of the soul. What's wrong is if you repeat it, over and over again.

Once a young mother came to me, who had lost her two children and her husband all before the age of thirty-six. She was without hope and didn't know what to do. She was drowning in deep sorrow and was searching for a culprit for the three painful blows she had to endure. She was afraid of living because she didn't know what awaited her the following day. Who would be next? Her parents? Her brother? When we began mourning therapy, we didn't know what the purpose of the three departures in her life was, but I had a feeling that the circumstances might be karmic. And they really were. At the level of the soul, with all three of those loved persons, she had a karmic agreement about a 'premature' departure, because she, as a soul, chose one of those lessons, in which she wanted to understand it in her current embodiment, and also to understand the feelings of loneliness and abandonment. And in this, her three boys just helped her. Yes, these types of karmic circumstances come as a package with all earthly feelings, but if you want to understand them, you have to look to higher levels of energy. I know that sometimes some experiences are very difficult and at first glance rather pointless, but every one of them has its own beginning.

5. *KNOWLEDGE: Ask yourself about your life all the time.*

If you always ask questions, you'll always get answers. A woman who consciously or subconsciously accepts circumstances she doesn't like, doesn't know what she wants. And so, it's important that you ask yourself about yourself the whole time. That you ask questions and look for answers. Because you'll be able to choose your life for you and make smart decisions.

Once, at one of the workshops I organized for self-confident children, a young Queen came along. She was eleven years old and was the youngest in the group. Sparks of life shone from her eyes, which hinted to the fact that a massive fire burned inside of her. And it really did. When we began the workshop, she began to ask questions. For the following five hours, she asked dozens and dozens of questions. Everything interested her. She had a clearly defined opinion about everything we spoke about. Hats off to her parents, as her broad-minded way of thinking simply surpassed that of average eleven-year-olds. I believe that the young lady will grow up into a self-confident woman, who'll know what she wants. Provided, of course, that she continues to ask questions. You, too, should ask them. When you do, you allow life to deliver you an answer. Who wouldn't want answers, right?

6. *KNOWLEDGE: Learn from existing circumstances.*

Circumstances are a result of your thinking and your actions in the past. If you look closely, you'll be able to learn a lot about yourself from them, as they'll show you the state of your inner thoughts and emotions from another perspective. And so, you'll be able to work through the lesson life presents you even faster.

Once, to one of my workshops for self-confident women, a mother was enrolled, who half an hour before the beginning of it sent me a text message saying that she had been unexpectedly held up because of her children and asked me if it was possible to come half an hour later. I said it wasn't a problem, and that such things happen. The lady then really came, calmly settled in, and joined the group. When we came to the part where we analyzed their relationships, she told me that she had eleven children, from one to sixteen years of age. We were all stunned. There was nothing about her which indicated that fact: She was well dressed and looked great, relaxed, calm, happy, and above all, not nervous at all. When I asked her how she succeeds in being like that, she answered that she has eleven mirrors around her, that show her every day, who she herself is. Eleven teachers, who teach her the whole time, how to be a better mother, a better friend, a better her. "And in sixteen years, you can learn a lot about yourself," she playfully added, then continued listening with interest. Her attitude to life strongly and positively surprised me, but I admired her even more by virtue of the fact that the day of the workshop, Sunday, was her only free Sunday of that year.

So, now this knowledge about circumstances has been passed on to you. Now you've got an excellent opportunity to show your strength. Now, you know. A woman's ignorance is her only real weakness. Only an ignorant woman succumbs to her circumstances, which then makes her a prisoner. And the opposite: A Queen finds the way to her throne by virtue of her behavior, which comes from within.

To create a life that will support you in every part of your mission and purpose, follow the steps below to create exactly the kinds of circumstances you want.

1. **First, recognize the circumstances you want to change.**
   Look at your entire life: the people in it, the things you do, the relationships you have, etc., and decide what you no longer want. Help yourself here with a list of things which you don't want, from the 2nd chapter.

2. **Then, look deep down inside and find out why you've accepted these circumstances in your life.**
   It's important that you find out why you're still holding onto them. The simplest way to find out is to ask yourself what they provide. Some provide you with security, others love, while still others provide you with encouragement, etc.

3. **Then, think about where else you can get the things you need.**
   There's not just one possibility. There are hundreds of them. Usually, a person, who's surrounded by circumstances he doesn't like, feels a little trapped, which is just an illusion. Other options always exist. Play with your thoughts and find them.

4. **Then, listen to your heart's desires.**
   You create a new reality, so you're the most important. Listen to your heart and do what it tells you to do. Don't focus on the circumstances and the people around you. They're not so important. If you focus on yourself, the appropriate circumstances will automatically form, in line with your heart's desires.

It's time for you to soar higher, above the life you have built for yourself. Life works through mirrors, and in every single part of you, they show you who you are. Circumstances are your reflections, which shine everywhere around you. When you look at them, you always see yourself.

"The scepter in the hands of a ruler is only a consequence of her specific decisions."

Hanna woke up. She looked around for Shanti ... "Ah-ha, my room ..." she thought when her gaze stopped at the cracked plaster, "I'm sure I didn't see that in the Golden Temple."

And it was time for a new smile.

Mission no. 4:

A Bucket of Strength

That morning was simply wonderful. It was bathed in new, fresh colors. Hanna finally had a feeling that things were moving in the right direction. She went to the window, opened it, and although the view was of an old apartment block with balconies, onto which the inhabitants dumped everything they no longer needed, in her heart, she felt that life was becoming beautiful. Above all - different. Quickly, she put on some dark blue shorts and a white top. In the bathroom, the 'goddess-like' ponytail created its new star, and before leaving the bathroom, the girl with green eyes and long, ebony-like black hair, looked in the mirror and gave herself a mischievous smile.

Twenty minutes later, she opened the tent flap, which led into the kitchen, took out a pot, poured some water into it, turned on the cooker, and allowed it to pamper her, just like she deserved. A few moments later, the scent of chamomile filled the tent. And it wasn't just chamomile tea. Because she always drank chamomile tea when she was in a good mood. It was a real little magical potion of happiness. It was some kind of memory of her parents. When she was just a little girl, they had a garden behind the house, and on the edge of it, chamomile grew. Together with her mother, they waited until it bloomed and were then able to pick the small flowers, which they put into a woven basket. They dried them and then prepared delicious tea, which her mother always said was special and magical. And today, she believed her.

But her inner goddess was still scared of someone. His five-day-old beard and sharp facial features surrounded his piercing eyes, still scared her, over and over again. Mark. If she dared to stand up to her classmates, she would never be able to do so with him. It seemed that with just one look, could he destroy everything inside her that was worth destroying, in a split second. She was genuinely scared of him. And, as always, whenever they ran into each other, she subconsciously began to stare down at the tips of her shoes. Even her classmates, who played the game of not being afraid of him, didn't feel terribly comfortable in his presence. And so, the possibility to be once again able to dig down in the tomb, was even more joyful for Hanna, as she rarely went down into the world of moles where there was no light. At first glance, he saw the strange tombs of unimportant mummies as just obstacles, which slowed him down in the search for his holy grail.

That evening, as Hanna was taking the last bucket of sand from the site, she stumbled awkwardly, halfway up the steps leading from the tomb. The bucket fell to the ground, and sand spilled over a few of the steps, which captured the attention of the fiery general. And got it. Destiny played with time, so that right at that moment, his highness, together with his toxic attitude, passed by.

"With you incompetent fools, there's no hope for a person!" he screamed at from afar, without noticing that the lip of the bucket had cut into a part of Hanna's leg, inflicting a deep wound. Hanna, with her heart racing, quickly covered her injured leg with one hand, while she began to gather up the sand that had fallen out from the bucket with the other, almost pleading for it to jump back in and hide her more than apparent fear.

Mark came down and hissed at her bad-temperedly: "Do it slowly, Your Highness, because I've got time ... just for you! The expedition can wait! The world can wait. It's not a problem. Take your time!"

Then his hissing grew into a deafening shouting: "Have you gone mad? Or are you truly incapable of even the stupidest of work? What are you even doing here? We've got so much work, and the excavation time is limited, and all you're doing is causing us to lose more valuable time, which we'll never get back!! Every second here costs money, and it doesn't grow on trees. Which you probably didn't even know, you pile of misery!"

He kicked the bucket, which was lying on the floor, and added: "Spoilt brat!" Then he continued his battle march.

Hanna was barely able to contain her tears. With her palms, she feverously gathered the fine sand with her hands, begging it to get back into the bucket. In between, she wiped the sweat from her face with her back of her hand, which got mixed up with her tears. She quickly got the sand back into the bucket and disappeared into the hotel in the hope that she would disappear forever.

Warm water rinsed the small grains of sand which had found their way into the narrow cut on her leg. A burning pain flowed through her body. Not so much from the wound, but from Mark's words.

"How could he be so cruel? Doesn't he see how hard I'm trying?"

She quickly washed herself, then with so many unanswered questions, hid her tired body underneath the blanket. Despite the demoralizing attack at the hands of the fiery general, the sixty-odd, full buckets of sand she carried out of the tomb that day had taken their toll, and she immediately fell asleep. An unknown vortex began to take her farther and farther away. Somewhere far, far away. Exactly there, where she wanted to go. There, where it didn't hurt ...

"Hello, Hanna, welcome. May I sit down?" said Shanti, greeting her and waking her from her sleep.

"Of course," Hanna replied, cheerfully, then already in the next moment remembering that she should have been the one asking that question. But, she asked her something else. "Shanti, sometimes some circumstances are more difficult than others. How should I deal with them?"

Shanti mysteriously smiled: "You know, Hanna, searching for inner strength is one of the most important journeys a person can take in their lives. I'll give you all you need. Just trust yourself to it. Trust that it'll always lead you somewhere ..."

Women around the world have been given enormous power - power, enabling them to change, and to create. Their role is so important that without them, the world would in no way work in the way it does. Even though many women are possibly still not aware of this power, the truth behind it all is fundamentally different. Have you ever heard of things like: "Behind every successful man is an even more successful woman" or "In a home, a man supports one corner, but a woman supports three?" Believe me, these phrases didn't just appear from thin air; people use them because they're true. Because women, in truth, own this power.

Witch Hunt

The world is full of amazing women who are entrepreneurs, mothers, writers, adventurers, inventors, etc. Women who've discovered inexhaustible sources of power within themselves. Ladies who are aware of their potential and make sure that they include it in everything they do. They're creating a strong life for themselves and for others in which they're happy and better off. Yes, they're Queens, who are aware that they've got enough power to carry out their missions. Brave women, already for centuries, have been carrying out their missions and so, consequentially, changing the world around them. And so, on many occasions, they tried to stop them. Strong women are otherwise harder to subordinate than those who aren't aware of their power. Strong women are less obedient because they're not dependent on the leadership of others. They have their own, and they don't need it from any external sources. That's why they tried to suppress them so many times in the past. Many different religious and political systems have been trying for thousands of years to suppress women's power. They even invented the term 'witch,' that they used to label those women who were a little out of the ordinary and stood out. Then they began to attach this label to an even greater number of women. And interestingly, all those 'witches' had something in common: They were smart, independent, and thought with their own minds. In other words, they were aware of their power.

I know strong 'witches' really well. I actually live with one of them. My wife is a typical example of a woman who would have been persecuted and who a lot of men would have even been afraid of. Not because she would have been evil. Quite the opposite, because her heart is as open as one can be. Because every one of her words, and even her look, emotes energy which says: "I know who I am, and I know what I want." In other words: "You can't subordinate me." And so, she always has a clear point of view regarding things that are going on around her. Not only that, but her energy is also very stable energy, with which she creates life.

Some of my friends said to me, when we were just starting out together, that my girlfriend, at the time, and now my wife, is someone they otherwise appreciate, but that it might otherwise be a little overwhelming living with her. I have to admit, in the beginning, when we started dating, I thought the same. The whole time she was demanding something, and it seemed to me, that I had to continually watch what I was doing, that I had to continually pay attention to her emotions, and it seemed to me that alongside her, I wasn't able to breathe normally, because she was continually bringing my soul down.

I have to admit it was, at times, quite difficult. Then, I began to notice a particular pattern. She was almost always right. Although it seemed, in certain difficult situations, that her 'preaching' was draining me of energy and stopping me, later on, I always seemed to come to realize that in truth, she was saving me and encouraging me to become even better. On the outside, she may have, from time to time, really looked like she was a difficult-to-deal-with emotional vampire, but in truth, behind her emotional mask hid a princess, who was slowly coming out.

In the first years of our relationship, as a couple, we went through a couple of more significant tests, in which we were somehow forced to change. The experiences molded us into different people; for me, from a little boy into a man, and for her from an emotionally confused girl into a strong ruler - a 'witch.' These days, I totally respect her, so much so that I married her. And the term 'witch' is one among those expressions, I affectionately call her. A witch in our house doesn't mean a mean, hunched over old woman with a wart on her nose that cooks her brews in the light of the moon, but a strong woman, a ruler, who knows what she wants and where she's going.

As you've probably already realized, a lot of men don't marry strong women and are even afraid of them. Why? Because a strong woman influences her surroundings in only two ways: they respect and encourage her, or that they fear her and try to put her down. Unfortunately, men in the past misunderstood the power women had and even were afraid of it. And, face-to-face with them, they wanted to protect themselves by putting them down. Men took away the power women had, when they convinced them that they were less worthy, and burdened them by saying they were 'less' important and that they had a less respected role in society, as well as telling them that it would be better if they stayed in the background. And, equally responsible for the removal of that power were also women, because they believed and accepted the opinion of men and, in doing so, gave it up.

Training Elephants

Do you know how they train an elephant so that it obeys and humbly performs in circus acts? As you know, an elephant is incredibly strong. Actually, it's the most powerful land animal of them all. With their trunk, they can uproot a small tree or even overturn a car.

How can one then capture such a mighty animal, put it in a cage, and convince it to cooperate in stupid circus performances? Because it has been convinced that it's got no power. They begin to train them already when they're young. They put chains around their legs and attach them to a sturdy post. In the beginning, the elephant tries to break the chain but doesn't succeed. Then, after a while, it gives up trying. It's learned that the chain is too strong. What happens when the elephant grows up? Nothing. It's still chained up, and whenever it feels it on its leg, it subconsciously stops, because it's learned that it can't break it. It remembers that it tried to break it a thousand times before but wasn't able to. However, it's not aware that it's now an adult. If it wanted to, it could break it in the same way that it could uproot a tree. But it's unaware of that because it was convinced that it doesn't have the strength.

Can you see yourself in this story? Have you ever felt that you had a chain around your leg, that constantly reminds you that you don't have any strength? Maybe it's time to break it. Now's the time to do it. There are no more witch hunts, and the world around you has changed. The world, especially the male part of it, has begun to appreciate the power women have. We men are aware that we need strong women alongside us because, without them, we're not enough. Most systems that govern this world are powered by male energy, and because of that, the world is unbalanced. The world will fall back into place by use of a secret ingredient - female energy. The world is prepared for it. An era of female presidents has come, who have led world powers, female directors who have managed multinationals, mothers who have skillfully navigated children, and their careers. An age has come, in which you, as a woman, are safely able to express your power and are freely able to enjoy it. What you do with it is your decision, but the mere knowledge that you can do with it as you wish is very, very liberating.

Queen, the power has been given to you to use. What's the difference between having power and not using it and not having it at all? Nothing. Therefore, it's crucial that you're aware of it in all its greatness.

1. *AWARENESS: You're 'beautiful Helena".*

A story about 'beautiful Helena'

Beautiful Helena was the wife of Menelaus, the Spartan King, who was so beautiful that the Trojan prince, Paris, also fell in love with her. One day, with her consent, he 'kidnapped' her from Sparta and took her back to his homeland, Troy, which triggered such rage and humiliation in King Menelaus, that he gathered his strongest fleet and sailed off to war with Troy, which lasted ten years and in which thousands of people died. All because of the mysterious power held by the beautiful Helena ...

You also have that mysterious power. Every woman has it. You have it by nature. But only those who are proudly aware of their femininity evoke it. That power comes from an inner knowing, which is confirmed by their uniqueness and divinity. Some connect that mysterious power with sexuality, others with mysticism. Whichever way you look at it, it's there. Therefore, it's time that you're aware of it and that you radiate in it; in the power that some women are very aware of and because of which some men, alongside such women, make some very unusual decisions. It seems as if women have enchanted them with something. And they really do. With a mysterious inner power, which only those women who are aware of themselves have. Once, I was talking with a friend of mine about his girlfriend. He said to me: "There are a thousand things about her that get on my nerves, but with just one touch, she can make it happen that I fall in love with her again every day."

2. *AWARENESS: You possess unique power.*

Every creature is born with its own unique strength, which it needs to survive. And so, every animal has its own unique strength - the sharp sight of a falcon, the exceptional flexibility of a cat, the sharpened scent of a dog, the strong jaws of an alligator, etc. - which they also use. And if they don't, they don't survive. And so, animals don't copy one another. Have you ever seen a monkey build a dam or a beaver that would jump from branch to branch? No. Because they're both aware of their unique strengths, which they've developed from what they have within.

People, from that perspective, are no different from animals. Every woman has her strengths, which only she can develop. So, never compare your strengths with the strengths of others. If you want the strength of others, then at the same time, you're giving up on your own strength, which can, as the only thing in life, make you happy and lift you in the long run. Be aware that you're unique and that there are no circumstances in life you cannot resolve. Your task is simply to focus on your strength and then use it.

I remember a woman who once came to me for advice regarding relationships at work. It seemed to her that all her coworkers were doing was taking advantage of her. Whenever a dispute arose, they talked about it with her, which somehow dragged her into the conversations and conflicts, which didn't have anything to do with her whatsoever. And so, she wanted to learn how to set boundaries. When she described one of those situations to me, I realized that she was, in truth, a natural mediator. As such, she had a natural ability to calm people down very quickly as well as help them, once again, to reset the loving energy between them. Her co-workers subconsciously knew this, and so they always included her in their disputes. When this lady became aware of her 'unique power,' she began to look at it differently, and above all, she began to use it more often and more wisely.

3. *AWARENESS: True force is triggered by energy, not form.*

The story about David and Goliath

Once there was a battle between the Philistines and the Israelites. One of the Philistine soldiers, Goliath, was particularly big and strong. One day, he challenged the Israelites to a fight. He said that they can choose anyone from their ranks, to fight against him. And if Goliath won, the Israelites would become slaves to the Philistines, and if he didn't, it would be the other way around. A small shepherd, David, who had just come to say hello to his brothers, volunteered to fight Goliath. Even though everyone laughed at him, when he said he would fight, he nevertheless went to battle. Goliath was on one side, armed with a shield, a sword, and a spear, while David, on the other, was armed only with a slingshot and river stones. When the battle began, David slung a stone with his slingshot into Goliath's forehead, killing him. David was able to win, because he was aware, what in truth, releases energy.

Because there's quite often a conviction that women are physically weaker than men, a lot of women live in fear and avoid confrontation. Thousands and thousands of robberies and rapes go on around the world in which most women give in and allow things to happen to them, because of the mindset that they are physically weaker, and are of the opinion that they can't stand up to men. Which is simply not true. Women are not weaker. They just think they are. Weak are only those who aren't aware of how strong they are. The following statement can literally save the lives of a lot of women: "True force is triggered by energy, not form." It's time that you understand where the real principles of strength reside. Just because something is bigger or that it has more muscles doesn't necessarily mean that it's stronger. The strongest is the one who's aware of his or her own energy and knows how to use it properly.

Quite some time ago, I met a young female athlete who was training aikido and was genuinely enthusiastic about that form of martial arts. At the time, I didn't know a lot about the sport, so I was interested in the way they trained. Above all, if they also fight against men. "Of course," she said. "There are only two girls in our club. Most of the time, I train with the boys." That girl was a lot smaller than the average woman, so I was interested in how she could train with the boys in an equal manner, them being many tens of kilograms heavier than her. She told me that in aikido, height, or body shape is not important, but the understanding of the principles leverage and energy. And so, with her fifty or so kilograms, she was able to throw down men weighing around thirty kilograms more. In the end, she told me: "Do you know, sometimes it's good to be smaller. People quickly underestimate you, and so, they don't take you so seriously. When they see they've underestimated you, they're usually already on the floor." In the end, she added the well-known saying: "Poison can be found in small bottles."

When I was writing this book, I called her and asked her for some advice about how women can learn to protect themselves as quickly as possible against attackers. She said: "There's not enough time for Aikido lessons, but for a woman who is being physically attacked, a well-directed strike with the knee into his temple - between his legs - will surely help remind the attacker of her strength. I've never seen a man remain on his feet after a good kneeing." My memory, of course, led me back to my youth on the basketball court when I also got such a kneeing. Yes, the male testosterone factory is otherwise a synonym for strength, but is also, at the same time, his weakest point.

4. *AWARENESS: Strengthen ambition.*

There is no such thing as an ambitious woman who doesn't have strength. Strength otherwise comes in a package, together with ambition. The law of nature says that the bigger the intent you have, the more power is given to you to realize. The bigger the desire in you for something, the more inner energy you will create. For a person, it's already enough that they simply think of their true dreams, and within them, some force is triggered, which didn't exist beforehand. This explains 'unusual' cases, when averaged sized women, with their own hands, lift a part of a car, because someone they love was caught underneath. When you have a strong enough reason, an equal amount of strong enough energy is released for you to realize it.

A lot of women lack that inner strength, primarily because they don't need it. Many among them live along the lines of least resistance. A lack of ambition ensures that a minimal amount of energy is required to maintain their current quality of life.

I've noticed that there's a direct correlation between the level of a person's 'life energy' and the level of success they have in life. Sometimes a woman comes to me who has such little energy that she even speaks slowly and in a somewhat 'tired manner.' Then, I usually find out that she doesn't even have any goals, wishes, or ambitions.

It's really hard to work with such people, as I sometimes get the feeling that I want success for them, more than they do themselves. Therefore, if you want more inner power, increase your demands and standards, as they'll also lead you to new power.

5. *AWARENESS: Power attracts power.*

When you start working from your inner power, you begin to see it all around in your surroundings. The structure of your relationships with people changes: You find yourself surrounded by people who are self-confident and who are equally strong internally. Your business environment also changes: Because of raised standards and increased self-confidence, opportunities that were sometimes not possible open up, and your financial flow is strengthened. Choices and decisions become stronger and more favorable, which leads to greater flow and a greater abundance of all sorts. Your life becomes ... strong! The common thread with all women who come to my seminars and who genuinely desire to change their reality is that their lives begin to improve in all areas: Health, relationships, career, etc. Of course, energy only responds to energy. I've never seen a strong woman with a weak mission. I've never seen a strong woman with a weak partner. Have you ever seen different birds fly together in nature? No. The same birds fly together. Power attracts power.

So, inner power begins to strengthen YOU. And your true power will most firmly put you on your ruler's throne, so do everything, to continue to express and enhance it. The workings of your inner power create the circumstances which are automatically aligned to your true heart's desires, represented by one more among all the exceptional features of inner strength: If you work with it, you simply can't miss the right path in life.

Now, dear Queen, your decisions will also change. Why? Because people basically decide on things for two reasons: Out of selfishness, or out of helplessness. Because your helplessness is now on the garbage dump of history, your decisions will only come from selfishness, or rather, power. Which means that you'll no longer create and allow circumstances to humiliate you, abuse you or whatever else might negatively affect you. Yes, maybe it's sometimes true that you need to make an effort to work from your inner power, but nevertheless, for such efforts, you will be rewarded in a big way.

Moral Compass

Like every kind of power, inner power also brings with it and demands responsibility. It represents energy. And energy influences the environment. When you have power, use it appropriately, as it can create, just as it can destroy. Some people spread the light with their power, while others darken it. What you spread is your choice. Will you work well and help yourself and the world, or will you create new barriers and setbacks?

Often, I observe how people try with all their might to get strength. At the beginning of my career, a young woman came to me once, who at the time had been working for a private company for around four years. The director, that particular month, announced that over the following two months they would be expanding their business into a new country and would, therefore, need a new sales manager. That young woman, at the time, worked as one of four sales representatives for the domestic market. Of course, all four were 'grappling' for the new work position. The promised promotion offered higher pay, more responsibility, and more power.

When the young woman told me about her new goal, at first, I thought she was just ambitious. But the truth was different. She was in conflict with a colleague, whom she literally hated. And she wanted the promotion, only so she could, later on, make sure that her colleague would lose her job. I have to admit that I was a little shocked when I discovered her real motives. That woman was more than competent, and would have achieved a lot, had it not been for her moral compass, leading her in the wrong direction. When I advised her that she should rather direct her energy into creating instead of destroying, she replied that what she ends up doing with this colleague had nothing to do with me. And she was right. It really didn't. So, I stopped working with her. I felt my moral compass direct me away.

You know, power requires responsibility. And that's why not many people have real power. Can you imagine anyone becoming the President? Anyone accessing a bank vault? Anyone piloting a plane? Anyone performing heart surgery? Anyone taking care of your child? No. Before you get power in your hands, life usually puts you through some training. Training, which strengthens those qualities in you, which ensures that you use that power 'correctly.' If your moral compass isn't 'on-track,' real power can do you harm or can even destroy. You can see thousands of these kinds of examples throughout the world. Wars, violence, manipulation, abuse, etc. belong to a whole series of consequences, owing to the wrong use of power. As you can see, they're consequences that can really affect you. Therefore, decide what your inner power will be: A shovel, that'll help you dig a hole, into which you'll plant a tree, or a saw, which will cut it down.

So, dear Queen, now you know the meaning of inner strength. With it, you can build a kingdom and accomplish your mission. It's time that you add one more color to your life; the color of inner strength.

"True force is triggered by energy, not by form."

Hanna opened her eyes. Even though the muscles throughout her entire body were telling her that they hadn't rested enough, she felt peace in her heart. Peace, which she felt throughout her entire body, which told her that she was safe and strong. Her dreams had given her new hope.

"Thank you, Shanti."

Then she remembered Mark and his words, but they were so far away. They seemed so ... unimportant.

Mission no. 5:

A Blade of the Heart

Hanna wanted to get up out of bed, but already in the next moment, she felt a burning sensation in her right calf. The wound, which made the previous day even more complicated, demanded that she do something, threatening that it wouldn't accept things if she didn't take care of it. The cut, around eight centimeters long, was widening more and more, and opening like a crack, hungry to swallow up a new victim.

"It's just a scratch," said Hanna, quickly consoling herself, although, on the inside, she felt it would need a little more attention. And now wasn't the time for that. There was no time for feeling sorry for herself. Not now, when she and the team had just begun to get on really well, and that she had tried, every day, to prove that she deserved respect, something that was still in its infancy. Mark was perhaps really rude and cruel, but she had to accept the fact that they were only going to be digging for one more month. And she couldn't afford to make another mistake. Even though he was the one she was terrified of, each and every day, he obviously knew what he was talking about, as he was, after all, one of the best archeologists in the world. That was her only option.

She encouraged herself: "I can't leave the team now. The guys need me. And, after all, ... Shanti needs me!"

She washed away the blood from the wound on her leg and quickly bandaged it using the first-aid kit she always took with her, whenever she traveled. Just in case. And that was today. Then, she headed off towards camp. She knew she would have to face Mark. With the person who obviously hated her and could send her home and ensure that her career in archeology for him would be just a fading memory, but for her, a very vivid memory, which would always remind her, that she had failed. And she didn't want to put off the crucial confrontation any longer. It would have to happen - today.

Mark was sitting at the table in front of his tent and was looking over some papers.

"Good morning, Mark. Can I have a word with you?" Hanna began, approaching carefully.

Mark didn't say anything and continued to look over his papers. For him, the sound of Hanna's voice was like a couple of annoying flies that didn't want to leave the food alone that was placed on the table.

"Mark, please ..." said Hanna, once again.

At that moment, Mark nevertheless looked at her, and without a word, motioned towards the stool on the other side of the table and abruptly replied: "I'm listening. Be quick and don't waste even more of my time. You're lucky I'm in a good mood."

"What are you like when you're not in a good mood?" thought Hanna, then quickly remembered that she already knew the answer.

She immediately took the offered stool, and nervously sat down. She took a deep breath, which reminded her heart that she was alive, thought of Shanti, then began to speak. In the following ten minutes, she told the fiery general about her effort and dedication, which she had invested into her work on the expedition, as well as how her feelings had been hurt because of his attitude towards her. She also told him about the fear, which she feels towards him every time she looks at his not-so-friendly face, and of the constant feeling, that she's not good enough, and asked him if such a relationship between the two of them could change - of course, because of their common love, which was, without a doubt, archeology.

Peter, who had accidentally walked past, watched everything that was going on from a distance. When he saw Hanna and Mark at the same table, he was shocked. He knew, otherwise, how Hanna was so terrified of him, even he himself, from time to time, felt uncomfortable around him. Who wouldn't? The fiery general, time and time again, proved that he could, at any moment, erupt into fire, which could burn the hearts and hopes of a young talent. He waited for them to finish, then ran up to Hanna, as she was leaving.

"Hanna, is everything okay? I saw you were talking to Mark."

Hanna confidently looked at him and calmly said: "Yes, I told him about a few things, which a few times over in the past days wouldn't let me breathe. Let's just say that I got sick and tired of the feeling, which kept telling me that I shouldn't take in the air which belonged to me as well as to him."

Peter was shocked. "What exactly did you tell him?"

Hanna looked at him, deep into his eyes, deep into the depths of his soul, then replied: "You know, sometimes in life, it's not about what you say, but how."

Immediately after, she felt her lips form a slight smile. "Just as if I listened to Shanti," she thought, then winked at Peter and left.

Some invisible force, proud of her student, brought her hands together in applause. "Sometime, somewhere she will become a Queen," she thought and disappeared into the invisible world of love.

But Hanna's smile didn't last long, and immediately after she had disappeared from Peter's field of vision, her lips came together in an attempt not to give in to the sharp pain. Her leg. It was becoming worse and worse. She limped off to the kitchen tent and wanted to sit down when Nick came in.

"Look, look what the cat dragged in. You've just arrived. I hope you slept well and got some rest. Today, we're going to move the stone slabs along the northern wall of the tomb, because yesterday Josh noticed that underneath them is some kind of line. As if there was another room. Maybe it's nothing, or maybe we've discovered something new. If we want to finish this today, we'll all have to work late into the night. So, join us as soon as possible. You've slept enough, haven't you? Mark promised us if we finish investigating and documenting the site by the end of the month, then he'll enter into his report that we were an official part of the team, and not just assistants. So, we need all hands on deck. Even yours."

There was no lack of sarcasm, but despite this, Hanna replied: "Of course, I'll be right there," and grabbed her leg, which bit back at her, opposing her answer.

She felt guilty. The guys had been working hard, and were trying to finish the work in time, while she was contemplating taking the day off! Wounded or not. She only had herself to blame. If she had been a little more careful with that damn bucket. And now, she just couldn't abandon the team. They needed her.

She slowly headed off towards the tomb. When she thought that no one was watching, she heard Peter say: "Hanna, are you okay? It looks like you're having trouble walking."

"Oh, it's nothing, I accidentally knocked it," she replied quickly and began working.

An hour later, she was crouched down, cleaning some sand away from the edges of some stone slabs when one of the guys came up to her. He accidentally knocked her leg with his foot and revealed the truth of her wound, which from minute to minute threatened that if she didn't take the time it deserved, then she also would be buried right there, between those walls. The sound of Hanna's piercing scream filled the tomb, and was even heard by the dead, which then was followed by tears of pain.

"Stop exaggerating!" Sam said to her, but in the next moment, when Hanna lifted the leg of her pants, he saw that her tears were more than justified. He saw a long, swollen and reddened cut, throbbing in rhythm with the pain.

Peter ran over and shared the same look that Sam's had on his face, which, after the accident, revealed that which Hanna had so desperately tried to hide.

"Hanna, what the hell ...?! You have to go and see a doctor!"

"It's nothing, it's just a cut," replied Hanna, trying quickly to cover the wound by pulling down the leg of her pants. She then attempted to put on a brave face by adding: "Stop wasting time, we've got a lot of work to do. History won't write itself."

"No!" Peter said decisively and added salt of anger to Hanna's already painful wound with his words: "You will not be working anymore today. Right now, you're going to the doctor!"

All the others supported Peter by nodding, and Hanna was left with no choice but to lean on his shoulder and hobble out. The show was over. And this time, no one clapped.

"You're very lucky, young lady," said the doctor. "The wound was very dirty, but it obviously hasn't led to any infection. Oh, by the way, you won't be needing any stitches. But, given the conditions in which you're working, I'd say that you came at the last minute. But, you won't be able to avoid a tetanus injection!" the doctor said, trying to add a little humor to the situation, as he had noticed Hanna grimacing while he was cleaning her wound.

He disinfected the wound, put cold cream on it, gave her an injection then prescribed at least one day of rest in bed.

"Young lady," the doctor added, "I advise you not to lift any heavy loads for at least a week so as not to strain the calf muscle and, consequently, stretch the skin. And if I were in your shoes, I'd take that advice."

"I've let the team down," said Hanna sadly, as she and Peter left the doctor's surgery, putting an end to her plans to help the team.

Despite Peter having calmed her down, saying that everything would be okay and that the most important thing was that her leg gets better, the guilt she felt, didn't allow her to hear him. The only sound that echoed within her was the sound of guilt, accusing her of betraying her team and all who believed in her. Finally, when she got the opportunity to prove herself, she gave up because of a scratch.

When they arrived at the hotel, she said goodbye to Peter, headed to her room, and with the last ounce of strength, dragged herself to bed. The antiseptic injection, which the doctor had given her for precautionary reasons, was obviously beginning to work, as her eyelids were becoming heavier and heavier ...

She grabbed her leg but didn't feel any more pain. And the wound no longer bothered her whatsoever. How was that possible? She looked around and saw a very familiar golden-colored window with rainbow glass. "The Golden Temple," she smiled.

"Shanti?"

"Hello, my dear, how are you today?" the ruler greeted her with genuine interest.

"Not so good. For such a long time I had tried to prove that I was good enough, and now, when I finally got my chance, I let the team down, and Mark ..., and because of me the expedition won't be able to finish the job, and the guys won't get the recommendation that they otherwise would have. I feel so guilty."

"Hanna, everything's fine," Shanti said, comforting her like a mother does her child, then continued: "I know how you feel. The year I took over the throne, my kingdom was caught up in a severe drought. The irrigation reservoir quickly dried up, and the crops began to die as if Mother Nature wasn't able to provide for our hungry mouths anymore. There was less and less food, and people demanded that I, their Queen, take care that there is enough. But I didn't know how. It wasn't in my power. At the time, something stronger than me was in charge. But the sharp guilt cut at my heart. Guilt that I had left my own people in the lurch, which every day, over and over asked me, if I was at all worthy of my crown ..."

Mission Complete

Once, some woman approached me. A week before, she had sent me an email in which she wrote how for the past half a year, she hadn't been feeling well and was extremely tired. She decided to turn to me after her doctors pronounced her to be physically healthy. Most physical sensations come from deeper worlds (mental, emotional, etc.), so I decided to meet up with her and find the cause.

When she came, I noticed that she had outstanding energy. She was smiling, was positive, and communicative ..., she had completely different energy than that which tired people have. First, I thought that she was a hypochondriac and was only seeking attention. Then, very soon after, I began to notice a pattern in her behavior. She apologized for everything. Although she wasn't late, when she came, she apologized for the congestion on the road, then she asked me for a glass of water and apologized at the same time because she was thirsty. When we began the consultation, she began to talk about her life and again apologized for talking too much, and so on.

In the first ten minutes, there were quite a lot of those apologies. Too many. I asked her why she always apologized if she did nothing wrong. She replied that it was the way she was raised. As a personal coach, I, of course, know that people really only apologize when they think they have done something wrong. Only when they have a feeling of guilt, that they want to get rid of, with an apology.

Therefore, this lady constantly felt she was, in some way, guilty. And I was right. Ever since she got married and had children, she began to live for her husband and for her children. For her, everything was subordinate to her family. She had given up her own free time, hobbies, and a lot of her dreams. In those relationships, she had somehow gotten lost. She never asserted her own wishes, never demanded, and, consequentially, didn't create anything. When I advised her to take a few hours for herself every day and do the things she felt in her heart, she said that in the past, she had tried attending dance and yoga classes. For a few months, then she slowly gave up. Whenever she went to those activities in the evening, she didn't feel so good. Instead of being happy that she was doing something for her soul, and that she would meet others who were also attending the same activities, she felt a great deal of guilt in her chest. Guilt, because she was wasting time; guilt because she should have been spending time with her children; guilt because she should have been doing something 'more' useful. In the end, she felt guilty, even for just looking at the yoga mat. So, she quit.

But someone didn't. Her inner child. Although she had come to terms with the guilt that was limiting her, the little girl inside of her wasn't able to. She wanted to have fun, some time for herself, for something dynamic, and in line with that, she also began to create and demand some decent energy, which the woman didn't want to express or admit. And so, she expressed this by feeling bad and through tiredness. I advised the woman to once again fill her life with activities, while at the same time to also invite her husband to the counselling sessions, who was very understanding, and above all, highly intelligent. He immediately understood his role - encourage his wife in her new activities and to never let her attach a feeling of guilt to what she was doing. He was her pillar of support, and over the following few months, she sought out his support in relation to her guilt. He kept telling her, over and over again, that she deserved time for herself and that he and the children would be able to manage somehow. He even didn't allow her to stay at home.

Half a year later, the woman came to one of my guided meditation sessions. When she entered the room, she radiated ... and not once did she apologize. When I looked at her, I smiled to myself and said: "Mission accomplished."

Examples like this are widespread. Have you ever heard of anything like this? Maybe it's similar to your story?

Guilt is one of the main reasons why so many women don't become rulers, and one of the strongest tools, with which they can be very quickly turned into slaves.

Guilt in women is otherwise different from that in men. Why? In a large part of history, women held a different position in society than men. Man, as a matter of fact, determined that he was more important. On the basis of that, society was thus formed, which consequently sent different signals to women concerning acceptance, than men. As a matter of fact, most systems and things were set up in such a way so that they glorified men even more, but not women. Usually, a man was more important because he performed more valued work, which had a more significant contribution. And because of all this, it was quite easy for a woman to be burdened with a sense of guilt, as it stemmed from the fact that as a woman, having the same needs for food and shelter as a man, nevertheless, wasn't able to contribute in the same way men were. Then, the creation of guilt was added to by the desire for male descendants. Many ancient cultures, and sadly still a lot of 'modern' ones, still believe that men are of more value as successors because they can provide better quality care for their parents. That's why many parents still prefer to have a son as their first child than a daughter. If a daughter is born as the first child in a family in which that kind of mentality rules, the family members, subconsciously, and sometimes even consciously, implant a sense of guilt on her because she wasn't born a boy. Stupid, I know, but unfortunately very true. These, and other such cases throughout the centuries, have heightened the sense of guilt in a lot of women. Just because they exist.

That's the main reason why guilt in women is so 'different' than it is in men. These patterns in our upbringing are otherwise so strongly embedded into the collective consciousness of society that even a lot of women themselves believe them. This will change only when society stops dividing things up into 'men's' and 'women's' things because guilt is almost considered now a more 'female' thing.

But although a lot of women don't do anything wrong, they all too often feel guilty. And not only that, some of them even additionally apologize for it. A woman today can be equal to a man, but beforehand she has to do away with her feelings of guilt. As long as she has this within her, it'll occupy the place which should be held by her dreams. Thousands of smart, good-hearted, and beautiful women walk the streets, whose souls are just waiting for them to remember who they are and what they decide to find, as well as fulfill their mission. And so, instead of dreams, they fill their lives with circumstances, people and thinking, which from moment to moment also latch onto that underground, unpleasant feeling - a feeling of guilt.

A lot of women can identify with the following claims, as some of them use them almost daily.

I feel guilty because:

- I went out to lunch with a friend, and my husband had to cook lunch for himself,
- I went on a trip without my children, and deprived them of a new experience,
- I gained a lot of weight after giving birth, and I know my husband doesn't like it,
- I ate some chocolate cake and knew that I shouldn't have, as I already have a few pounds too many,
- on Saturday I slept in until ten, although my partner got up earlier and went to mow the grass,
- I bought a new t-shirt for myself, instead of buying something new for my children,
- I'm not a good enough wife, and so my husband left me for another woman,
- I took the evening off, even though my partner is always at work.

And even: I feel guilty because I got sick and now I have to rest.

There are hundreds of these internal monologues, and almost every woman has at least some of them. But why? Why do most women who have a family, feel bad, if they go and spoil themselves? Why do most women think that their children and partners have to be the center of their lives? Because they were taught some stupid rules, that they should abide by. Rules which were imposed upon them by their parents, partner, or someone else. Maybe you also live by some of these rules, so it's time that you look to see if they're justified, then get rid of them. And when you do, the curtain of guilt will also fall. And remember - the 'hook' of guilt, which catches you, is, as a matter of fact, always thrown by you, yourself.

1. *A NONSENSE RULE: Sacrificing for othersis noble*

A lot of women spend their days sacrificing themselves for others - for their partner, for their children, for their family, for their job ... if they're not available all the time, or if they don't respond to all the wishes and demands of others, they feel guilty. Somehow, they've accepted that they're available the whole time for many a thing. Why? Because someone has taught them that this is what mothers, wives, and daughters do. Because if they don't accept these roles, they'll be bad mothers, wives, daughters ...

You know the phrases, like:

- You go and have fun, dear. I'll stay at home.
- You sleep a little longer, I'll get up and change the baby.
- You buy it for yourself, I'll buy something for myself next time.
- You stay at home, I'll do it.

It is nice to help people and do them favors from time to time. It's right that we help people. But that's not sacrificing. That's help. Sacrificing arises when you accept that you'll do something that others don't want to do while you see yourself as someone (or even as the only person) who has to do it, even though in truth, you maybe don't want to.

So that you understand a little better, let me explain what sacrificing actually means - sacrificing means giving up something for someone else. And what do people usually sacrifice? We sacrifice things that are less important than others, right? If you had your child in one arm and a backpack in the other and you wanted to board a plane, and then they tell you that there's not enough room for both, what would you give up - your child or the backpack? Of course, the thing that's least important in line with your criteria and values. Most likely, the backpack. When most women sacrifice themselves, as a victim, they choose on a subconscious (or even conscious) level, the thing they think is less important - themselves and their time.

And now the question: Are you less important than others? Or is your energy less important than the energy of other people? Or is your time less important than the time of other people? Honestly think about your answers, as they can determine if you'll wear a crown on your head, or not.

Sacrificing for others isn't noble, it's unwise. Helping others is noble. But those who really deserve your help will also appreciate it. A lot of women otherwise think that people around them will love them more if they sacrifice themselves by doing various tasks and chores. And, on the contrary - that they won't love them if they don't sacrifice themselves. Perhaps this will open up your eyes: It's only worth sacrificing for those who would never expect or demand that you sacrifice yourself for them. So, stop doing it, praise yourself, and appreciate yourself some more.

How To Stop Sacrificing Yourself?

1. Begin to appreciate yourself more. Respect yourself to the extent that you recognize when you want to help others and when you want to please them. A woman who appreciates herself, never allows anyone to exploit her: Not others and not herself.

   Once, a student came to counseling, whose primary way of building relationships was by sacrificing herself. She believed that people only accepted and appreciated her when she offered to take on some of their burdens. Later, I found out that she learned this from her mother. Therefore, she usually volunteered to take on a lot of obligations and tasks for other people, as she thought that was the way you build relationships. She did this, year after year, but over time she became the 'on-call caretaker' for everyone. This was mainly the case with her peers.

   Then, something happened, which clearly told her that she was obviously doing something wrong. In her third year of college, a three-day excursion was being planned. And by chance, it happened that they found a travel agency with a suitable package, but which was ending that day. From an organizational point of view, it meant that they would have to collect, that day, the money from thirty-five people, all-in-all something more than difficult to execute, otherwise they wouldn't be able to take advantage of the special price. So, this girl volunteered to pay, out of her own pocket, the money for almost half the students studying that year. And that day she was, of course, the main savior and was very popular.

What happened later? The girl went to the bank and paid for the trip for herself and for her friends. But, because the offer was at a special price, it had different conditions from regular offers. And one of those conditions was that she wasn't able to take out insurance against the risk of cancellation. When she asked her classmates the following day to each bring her the money which she had paid in advance on their behalf, she found out that they'd reconsidered, and the trip was called off. Only sixteen people brought her the money; the others said that they were only talking about the trip the previous day, and weren't sure if they would actually go, or not. That was the result of her self-sacrifice. She was left without a significant amount of money, which she had worked hard for over the weekends, in her father's company, and instead of being refunded by her schoolmates, she got disrespect. When I asked her if she wanted to use that money because she wanted to help, or because she thought that they would like her better, she replied the latter - she thought she would be able to 'buy' their love.

2. Know that you're no better or no worse than those around you. Everyone has the same human value. A homeless person on the street and the owner of a large corporation, both women, have exactly the same human value. No one is better or worse. Therefore: Your time and energy are of the exact same value as those around you. I still notice that some women 'fearfully respect' those who, in their opinion, are more successful, richer, and more influential. Once I attended a gathering, where I saw how a woman, working as a cleaning lady, offered her seat to another, who was the owner of a successful beauty clinic. Just because she felt less worthy as she believed that

the woman from the clinic deserved the place behind the table more than she did. An undeniable example of self-sacrifice, which came from an extreme lack of self-confidence.

3. People should do the things they are able to do themselves. Don't carry the burden of other people. Every person in this world should carry their own burdens. If you carry your own burdens, as well as those of others, you'll become exhausted.

4. Stop doing things 'to buy' love. The right people will love you even when you don't 'sacrifice' yourself. If you have to fight for love and the affection of people around you by doing things for them, then they're not the right people for you. I know a guy who liked a girl, but before they started dating, he wrote a list of things, she would have to learn, if she wanted to become his partner. On that list were: Baking cakes, cooking goulash, and having a home-made lunch and dinner every day, etc. That girl was a lot younger than him, so, of course, she naively accepted his demands and obligations. Then, one day, she got a job, and so, she wasn't at home a lot. Consequently, she didn't have as much time for housekeeping. When that guy didn't get a freshly cooked lunch a few times, he ended the relationship with her and found another.

5. Stop being a sacrificial lamb. Then you'll also stop feeling guilty for being one. And your life will become more pleasant, and above all, freer.

2. *A NONSENSE RULE: It's my job.*

A lot of women take care of a lot of things - going to work, caring for children, cooking, washing, cleaning, etc. Over time, these things become somewhat automatic and are, above all, taken for granted. If you do things where it seems that others don't notice anymore or don't even thank you for anymore, then they've taken it for granted. Thousands of women, every day, cook lunch, without being asked to. And, there's nothing wrong with that. What's wrong is this: First, very few of these women receive an honest thanks for lunch; and, secondly, if others don't like it, then they feel guilty.

And now a question for you: Do you take the people around you for granted? Or is it taken for granted that you do something? Or do you feel guilty if you do nothing when something is expected of you?

It's important that you know that you don't have to do something just because you're a woman, a wife, a mother, or a daughter. In the same way, you don't have to feel any kind of guilt, if you don't want to do anything. Things don't belong to people simply because they're next to them. A home-cooked lunch doesn't belong to your children simply because you're their mother. You prepare lunch for them because you love them. Don't forget that ..., not you and not them. Your partner isn't entitled to sex, simply because he's married to you. If you have sex, then have it because you love each other, and you both want to, not because you're afraid that if you don't, you'll be a bad partner.

I first began thinking about taking things for granted when I moved out of home. For as long as I lived at home, a home-cooked lunch was always waiting for both my brother and me, all our clothes were washed and ironed all by themselves (and found their way into our wardrobes), the house was clean the entire time, the bills were always paid, the gas tank of the car was always full, the fridge was also always full, and if I ever needed anything, in the space of a few days I got it in the palm of my hand ... yes, my parents were incredible. I've got the best mother in the world and the best father in the world. But, I often took them for granted.

When my girlfriend and I, who is today my wife, decided to move out on our own, we also decided to concentrate on our careers at the same time, so we spent a lot of time away from home. When we came home, a freshly cooked dinner was not waiting for us on the table, our clothes, instead of being washed and ironed in the wardrobe, were stuffed in the dirty clothes basket to be washed, my car had lost that magical ability to fill itself with gas, and we had to pay our bills ourselves. Even the fridge went on some absurd strike and told us that, just like the car, that it also wasn't able to fill itself. At the time, I often remembered all those unbelievable dining tables, wardrobes, cars, and fridges at my parent's place. Thank you, mom and dad, for all those 'taken for granted' things. I appreciate them today. I appreciate everything that other people do for me. When my wife does something on her computer in one hour that would take me the whole day, I'm grateful to her. When I go and visit my parents, lunch is often waiting for me, but now I thank my mom for it. When my grandmother bakes her incredible poppy-seed cake, I eat it with pleasure, but also with gratitude.

How do you do away with being taken for granted?

1. Think about everything you do or provide for others, that they are not sincerely grateful for.

2. Then, talk with them and remind them about taking things for granted. If they change their attitude and become thankful, continue to do those things.

3. If they don't, then stop providing that kind of support (a lot of women at this stage ask: "What if they won't love me anymore?" Answer: "You don't need people who are there, alongside you, only when you provide them something, but not when you don't." As a matter of fact, you'll find out people's true colors in this way.").

4. The result in both cases will be energy, which won't awaken feelings of guilt in you, if you won't succeed in doing something, or won't want to do something.

A woman who's aware of her own mission never takes things for granted. Not herself, nor others. A Queen knows what she does and what she provides. So, get rid of 'being taken for granted' from your life so that you'll never feel guilty because of it.

3. *A NONSENSE RULE: It doesn't belong to me.*

Let me tell you a story. Even though it's short, it might be familiar to you. I've heard it many times before, from many different women, so I decided to include it here.

The story begins one fine day in a handbag store. A lady is taking a look around. All of a sudden, her eyes see a beautiful handbag, which would go exceptionally well with her new shoes. Her first thought is that she just has to have it, which is then followed by a second thought, that she shouldn't. But her enthusiasm prevails, and a few minutes later, on her way home, she has her new 'baby' in her hand. She's thrilled to have it but at the same time a little frightened, what her husband will say. Before entering the house, she carefully hides it and takes care that her new acquisition finds its way to the back of the wardrobe as soon as she possibly can. A few days later, she and her husband head off to dinner with friends. She does herself up, then adds the last detail to her elegance - her new handbag. Her husband looks at her, but her beauty doesn't attract enough attention ... his gaze otherwise finds its way to her handbag. He asks her: "Have you got a new handbag?" The lady waves her hand in dismissal, and quickly replies: "Oh, this bag; I just pulled it out from the back of the wardrobe ..."

Many ladies, who deserve a nice life, feel guilty in the face of new and, above all, beautiful things. In some way, they think that they don't belong to them. That they don't deserve them. Quite often, their partners also ensure that this way of thinking is truly anchored in their minds, and in doing so, do themselves and their ladies a disservice.

A woman, who has been exposed to that kind of psychological pressure for a long time, begins to believe that she honestly doesn't deserve such things. They begin to use sentences for themselves, such as: "Why would I have that" or: "That's not for women like me." The thinking that "it doesn't belong to me" ranks among the main reasons why so many women in their lives don't live out their dreams. Because they think they aren't worth it, important enough or good enough for something. Because, whenever the world wants to give them something, someone appears and tells them they don't deserve it. When a woman stops accepting the gifts that life gives you, she stops accepting life itself. What's the quickest way you can check if you also have this guilt complex? Look at what's going in the way you accept beautiful things. If you have difficulties accepting gifts, prizes, etc., if you feel uncomfortable in such situations, then you've also succumbed to it. It's time that you get rid of it.

How to do away with a guilt complex?

1. Go into a store and buy something, just for you. The conditions of the purchase are:
    - it mustn't be practical, because its purpose is just to make you feel good,
    - it can't be for anyone else, except you,
    - if possible, the thing should be more expensive than things you ordinarily buy (for example: If until now you have only bought things from a middle-class range, the thing should come from a higher-class range); the purpose of that is to shift the scale of self-worth one step higher in your head. Needless to say, carry out this purchase

within the framework of your financial capabilities and never threaten your own existence with it.

2. Then go somewhere, where you'll be alone, and admire it, accept it and relax with it.

3. Then, look for good feelings to associate with it, and focus just on them.

4. Show it only to people who honestly love you and who'll be genuinely happy for you. (jealous people, in the beginning, can arouse a sense of guilt in you).

Then enjoy it, until you are relaxed with it and realize that you deserve it and that it belongs to you.

These rules can strongly cuff you in their chains, so get rid of them as soon as you can. It's important that you understand that most guilt-related feelings come from these senseless rules, which as a matter of fact, means that these feelings in themselves are senseless, as the basis of them is already absurd. In fact, they're founded on a fabrication. Let me explain in other words - Feeling guilty based on senseless rules is the same as being wrongly imprisoned in jail, where you're serving a senseless punishment. How would you feel behind bars? Most likely, you'd do everything in your power to prove your innocence, right? You'd call all the lawyers, legal experts, criminalists, etc. because deep inside, you'd know that you're innocent and that you deserve freedom. No, these feelings of guilt are the bars in your heart. To remove them, you don't need to call any lawyers, you just need to admit what you already know inside yourself - that you deserve a life without feelings of guilt.

Other People

A woman's heart has an extreme capacity for love. Sometimes, even a little 'too much.' Often, it's an illusion of love that time and time again pushes it into a sea of guilt. Sometimes, there are people in her life she loves very much and would do anything for. She'd even give up the peace in her soul - in the name of love. But these people often not who she thinks they are. Sometimes the people around her, time and time again instill in her a strong sense of guilt. Why? Because, for some reason, they want to slow her down or even destroy her.

Guilt as a manner of psychological abuse

A lot of women are dedicated to their partners and would do anything for them. But, a lot of their partners take advantage of this. They instill a sense of guilt in them. Women and men have otherwise quite often different outlooks on the same thing. So, in such circumstances, a compromise is necessary, which is only possible when both sides are strong and self-confident. If one of them is not, then they're usually subordinate to the other, stronger one. The weaker side of many cultures is still represented by women. At the same time, a lot of men have discovered two things: First, that their partner loves them, and second, that they can take advantage of that. They've otherwise found that instilling a sense of guilt in women is an excellent way of preventing them from doing something the opposite of what they (men) think is right, or that with guilt they can even convince them to act the way they want them to act. But, in both cases, women lose. In both cases, they distance themselves from who they are and also from their strength.

A lot of men instill a sense of guilt in their partners every day. This behavior, in most of them, comes from deep subconscious patterns of a lack of self-confidence, and convictions that they're not good enough. If a man who lacks self-confidence accuses his partner of some unpleasant circumstances or some event in his life, he has, in other words, blamed her, even shifting his own responsibility onto her, which means that all focus is directed towards her, and therefore none on him.

For example:

A lot of men, when their children don't clean up after themselves at home, blame their partners. They base their accusations with words that their mother should have taught them the rules of the house. Is that true? Don't fathers and mothers have the same responsibilities to teach a child order and discipline? They do. And because a lot of men still think that women are responsible for things around the house, they justify their way of thinking by laying the blame onto them.

Subconsciously laying blame

Men, for whatever reason, subconsciously lay the blame onto their partner, because of their own feelings of unhappiness and incompleteness. Because they need someone who would be guilty for the circumstances in their lives, someone who would be responsible for them. People who don't accept responsibility for their circumstances, look for culprits elsewhere. Usually, they choose a weaker person, from an energy point of view, and upon whom they can exert some influence with relative ease, as with them, it's easier to implant feelings of guilt.

I also know about the subconscious laying of blame. My wife was once one of those women with handbags. At the beginning of our relationship, I often asked her why she bought things for herself. As if I wanted to instill a feeling of guilt into her for every purchase, that was, in my opinion, unnecessary. These days, I don't do it anymore. She's a mature woman. She can buy whatever she wants. Which I only realized when I myself grew up. Only then did I stop projecting my own patterns of dissatisfaction onto her. It's interesting that when I accepted responsibility for my own life, all of a sudden, new handbags didn't bother me anymore.

If there are people like that in your life, do the following: First focus on yourself and on your inner feelings. Relax and make sure that you really know what you feel. When you're at peace with your innermost feelings, mentally evaluate the circumstances you've found yourself in. Evaluate the concrete circumstances of it as well as the person who wants to instill in you a feeling of guilt. Do this as objectively as possible. Think, if the attempt at instilling guilt is justified or not. In most cases, you'll discover that there's no need to feel guilty, and in truth, the source of your emotional confusion is, a matter of fact, the person who wants to instill it into you.

The conscious laying of blame

Men who consciously lay blame onto their partners, do it because they want to manipulate them. Guilt is a feeling to which other feelings of fear, doubt, mistrust, and lack of confidence attach very well. If we deliberately lay blame on someone, we intentionally take away their power. A lot of men don't want to have a strong woman alongside, but a humble slave, who would do exactly what they want. These are people with serious emotional problems, not to mention a lot of problems with their egos. They need a weaker person alongside them to feel strong because, in truth, deep down within, they're frightened little boys, who aren't capable of doing anything with their lives. Their ego is so fragile that even the tiniest tremor would break it, so they try to take care, in advance, that anything like that wouldn't happen.

If you've got people around you, who want you to be weak, put an end to the relationship as soon as possible. If you're in that kind of relationship, it's essential that you understand that, in truth, you're stronger. This knowledge will give you strength, so you'll be able to leave that person with greater ease. Why is it best to leave if you're in these kinds of circumstances? Because the chance, given those circumstances, of you, changing that kind of person, are, in fact, very small. For that kind of change, you need to have a lot of strength, which you don't have because this is what that person is taking from you. If you want to get it back, you first have to end the relationship. If you feel that you would then help the person return later, but only when you once again have your strength and when the person won't be able to influence you anymore like they did in the past.

Guilt is a strong psychological manipulator, which can truly burden your life and change you, extremely quickly, from a ruler into a slave. And so, it's vital that whenever you feel it, you begin to work on its resolution and elimination.

An example of the resolution of guilt:

Once, a young lady came to counseling who wanted to become independent and move out on her own. However, she had a challenge - a feeling of guilt, which had been instilled into her by her parents when they mentioned that she should stay at home and take care of them. Because her wishes were not in-line with theirs, she thought she was a bad daughter. Here, are some of my questions, which we used to work through a good part of her guilt:

1. ***First, be aware of the unpleasant feelings that are eating away at you.***
   The feeling that I'm not a good enough daughter eats away at me because I want to move out of home. I feel egoistical and ungrateful. My parents have enabled me many a thing, and now I'm leaving them and leaving them alone.

2. ***Why do you think that your feelings are justified?***
   Because I've noticed that my parents don't have anyone to take care of them when they get old. It seems to me that somehow they expect that I'll do that, which they mention in conversation with them. I've got the feeling that I'm obliged to take care of them.

3. ***Who, in your opinion, is responsible for the life of your parents?***
   Well, basically themselves, but nevertheless I think that I'm obliged to help, now, that they're older.

4. ***Great. Help. Therefore, you would like to help them, right?***
   Yes.

5. ***When can you best help others: At the time when you're happy, and you have what you need, or at the time when you're unhappy and limited?***
   Of course, at the time when I'm happy and have what I need.

6. ***Why, exactly then?***
   Because then I ... I don't know ... because I feel good. Because I would be strong.

7. ***And what do you currently need to be happy?***
   I need a life, that's mine. I want to live in my own home and do things on my terms.

8. ***Therefore, you agree that you have to, if you want to help your parents best, move out on your own?***
   Yes. I agree.

That girl had conflict within herself because her definition of happiness was different from that of her parents. They thought that happiness was living together with your children, while she thought that happiness was becoming independent. Because she looked at the circumstances through the eyes of her parents, of course, she felt guilty when it came to her wishes. The moment she began to focus on her own feelings and her own point of view, the guilt in her began to evaporate. When her parents were thinking that she would stay at home, they looked at the situation as a form of help, in that her presence would offer them support. But that was not the case for her. She looked at this as some form of subordination. And so, she wasn't capable of being seen to be happy in the given circumstances. Therefore, it was necessary to find a solution in which she would understand how to fulfill her own dreams, while at the same time offering them help.

That example of guilt, which parents or grandparents lay onto their children is widespread. It's important to understand that no one owes anyone anything. And so, parents, in reality, cannot really demand anything from their children. They have their lives, and their children have theirs. The responsibility of every individual is that they should, in their own lives, take care of themselves. If parents take care of themselves, so that they're independent, their children will take care of themselves and arrange their lives as they wish. Then they'll all be happy. And no one will create feelings of guilt, but a wonderful atmosphere can be created, in which they all help each other, without any insinuated feelings of guilt whatsoever. For that to be possible, everyone has to take responsibility for themselves.

Two paths to internal liberation

Sometimes you're the source of your own guilt because it comes from within you. Sometimes you do something, which you're not proud of, and that you later regret.

If you feel guilty for something, you've got two options:

- The first is that you fix the mistake and move on. Fixing the mistake is a very good pardon, which gets rid of the guilt (or the better part of it) in most people. So, if you can actually change and fix it, do so. Get moving and do what's in your power. Advice: Give it your all. As such, you'll know that you did everything in your power, which will greatly contribute to your liberation.

- The second option is that you forgive yourself. Sometimes you can't fix things, and so the only option you have is to forgive yourself. Which, at the same time, is also the most liberating. It's important to know that you're human. And humans sometimes make mistakes. Making mistakes is human. So, don't be so tough on yourself as you can't always do everything perfectly. You have to learn somehow. And most people learn the quickest from their mistakes. So, forgive yourself for everything you can, finish up what you have to do, then go forward, freer.

So, my dear, guilt can now be just a part of history. The world offers you millions of gifts, and all of them belong to you. But the Universe has a hard time delivering them to you if you're of the opinion that you don't deserve them. So, open your heart and your arms, because you can become and have everything you can imagine. Without any feelings of guilt whatsoever.

"The hook of guilt which you get caught up on, is, as a matter of fact, always thrown by you, yourself."

Hanna, all of a sudden, woke up. There was a light knocking at the door. She got up, but the moment she put her foot on the floor, she was once again overcome by a stinging pain. Because of the treatment, the wound was even more painful and even more decisive in not letting her escape from the embrace of her bed. But nevertheless, she slowly limped to the door and opened it.

On the other side of the door stood a sight for sore eyes - Peter. "Indiana Jones, how's it going?" he said, trying to cheer her up a little when he noticed her puffy face and added: "How's your leg?"

His comment put a tiny smile on her face. "Indiana Jones? Peter, seriously?" she answered with a smile and added: "My leg's better, but it still hurts. I've got to rest a bit. I guess."

Peter smiled: "It's great that it's better. Yesterday, when I took a look at your awful wound, I was simply horrified. You really frightened me.

"What do you mean, yesterday?" asked Hanna surprisingly. "Don't you mean today?"

Peter looked at her, all surprised and said: "No, yesterday, before I took you to the doctor's."

Hanna didn't give in: "That was this morning."

Peter had to gently tell her: "No, Hanna, that was definitely yesterday."

"Are you trying to tell me that I've been sleeping for ..." she looked at the clock: "for twenty hours??"

She also checked the time on her cell phone, which would possibly show her to be mistaken, but it too confirmed Peter's words. That had never happened to her before. That she had slept the entire day?

"I obviously needed the rest. Otherwise, I came around last night and knocked, but because you didn't answer, I assumed you were sleeping, so I didn't want to bother you," replied Peter.

Hanna opened her eyes and breathed deeply. She was still a little shaken. Obviously, time goes by a little differently in the Golden Temple.

"How's the excavation going?" she asked when she was able to gather her thoughts.

"Quite slowly," replied Peter, "there aren't enough of us in the tomb. First thing in the morning, Nick and Mark left for the national archives in Cairo in the hunt for some information. Sam had to help another team at the site where Mark works, meaning that there was only Josh and me in our tomb. Everything will take a little longer. I hope we'll be able to finish because already in two weeks we have to go back home. The guys are asking about you, how you are ... and when you're coming back ..."

Hanna soaked up his words like a sponge, and her body was overcome by a strong wave of guilt, but, before she was even able to become aware of it, the image of Shanti, sitting on her throne and watching her appeared like a flash of lightning, cutting it off. Oh yeah, the dream.

Guilt ... for a moment, she got caught up in her thoughts, and it seemed as if she had been taken away somewhere. Then she woke up from her 'daydream,' looked at Peter and said: "Tell the guys that I'm there in spirit, but that I'm still not capable of coming today. My leg still hurts a lot, and

I need to rest. I tried to work with my injured leg for two days and found out that I had dug myself into a hole. Tell them that I'm coming tomorrow; today, I'll keep resting."

Peter looked at her surprisingly. He didn't expect such a clear and direct answer. Least of all from her, a quiet mouse, whose words were always modestly hidden from the world. What's going on with her? First, Nick, then the same conversation with Mark, and now this ... she's changing. So strong. So ... beautiful.

Slightly confused, he nodded and stuttered something like, " You just rest ..." and left, surprised.

Hanna was also surprised. Words flew from her mouth like a butterfly having just magnificently transformed from being a caterpillar. A butterfly, aware that nothing could limit it anymore, and that allowed itself to express the colors of its new wings.

It seemed to her that she wasn't the one that had expressed those words. As if they had come from her mouth, but at the same time not. As if they originated from some unknown, hidden part ... part of a butterfly. She closed the door to her hotel room and leaned against it as if she had taken a significant step in her life.

That inner feeling was something unfamiliar to her. She had always been available to others, always helping, and frequently even at the expense of her own happiness or well-being. She always felt responsible for others and never said no to them. And rarely could she say that others ever returned the favor. But today, something was different. Today, she felt different. The feelings within her were made up of themselves, just like a jigsaw puzzle of meaningless pieces, which, when put together, formed a beautiful picture.

She knew what she wanted. Peace. Time for herself. The guys and Mark would have to do without her. After all, the whole time, they said that they would be better off without her. Maybe they would soon experience the 'fittingness' of what they said. Maybe she would also soon discover her own real value ... maybe.

Mission no. 6:

An Open Lock

Hanna, just as she had promised herself and Peter, spent the day in bed. Despite the fact, from the outside looking in, it seemed as though she was doing nothing, on the inside, it was more like in the middle of an anthill. Her thoughts shot left and right, just like fireworks shoot up in the sky on New Year's Eve. What was going on with her? Who was she? She had a feeling that she didn't even know herself anymore. Everything about her had begun to change – her speech, the way she looked, even the way she walked. A month before, she wouldn't have dared to even think of standing up to anyone, least of all to a person like her boss, but now words boiled from her that she didn't even know. Bubbling like lava from the depths of a volcano, which had long before claimed to have extinguished.

Was it really possible that until now she hadn't known who she was? She understood that people change, but as far as she was concerned, she thought that all the changes had already been made. She had almost graduated, and somehow knew what she liked, had her own opinion on things, even though, more or less, she didn't dare express it. Now, far away from everything, in the heart of Egypt, her life had been turned on its head like a court jester in its own chaotic show. Sticking up for herself, a new hairstyle, unknown words said to those who underestimated the strength of her innocent appearance ... what was going on?

Even though the transformation was rather strange to her, she had to be honest with herself and admit that she felt better. A lot better. It seemed that every one of her newly discovered words opened a new clip on her corset, which had been stifling her the last few years. Now, it had finally begun to release her from the rather rough hold it had on her and allowed her to fully breathe.

For a moment, her thoughts escaped back to the tomb in which the guys were feverously working, but then they persistently went back to the sleeping ruler, the mummy, which lay quietly in the middle of the room and gave her the feeling that it was not even in the slightest interested in what was going on around it. It lay there, completely at peace. As if it wanted to convince the visitors, who were stealing glances at her, that she was just deep in meditation.

All around it was chaos; the guys were digging, cleaning, carrying buckets full of sand and talking one over the other, and everywhere there were tags, ropes, bags, etc., but for her, it seemed as if she was there, just for ... herself.

Her thoughts took her to unknown worlds, which then took hold of her in such a way that she didn't even notice that night had already come to the city. Lost in her dreams, she stared out through the window. Another day in her life had come to an end. But that day was different.

Today, she had put herself first. "Well, as a matter of fact, my leg," she smiled to herself and asked if perhaps that didn't mean that she now had her own throne, just like Shanti.

She wasn't used to such feelings. She had always been there, available for others. The woman, who lived in Boston in the neighboring apartment, always brought her spoiled cat over to Hanna's place, saying she had things to take care of. It was always Hanna who was the last to leave the lecture room, cleaning up the little bits of paper that others had left behind. Usually, it was she who went in search of books for their research projects, while her workgroup members emptied their glasses of sparkling self-indulgence. And in the restaurant where she worked weekends, it was her who most often substituted for her co-workers, who wanted the night off to go on their hot dates, thinking that Hanna didn't have them anyway.

Even a part of her savings, which were put aside for a planned trip to Rome upon completion of her studies, were instead devoted to an animal shelter. Others always took first place.

She liked helping out, but now she realized that in all her efforts to be a good schoolmate, niece, friend, coworker, neighbor, etc. she hadn't realized how exhausted she was. What it took was an eight-centimeter wound to stop her and reveal the truth to her, which was hiding under the stones of pleasing others. Most likely, she thought, the bucket would not have fallen from her hands if she had stopped when it began to hurt her hands. But she wanted to finish. And, she wanted to prove that she deserved a place in the team. Prove that she was good enough. That her schoolmates would be satisfied. That Mark, with all his ever impossible demands, would also be satisfied. Again others. Her thoughts slowly turned more and more pale and quiet until she fell asleep.

Her nostrils once again were filled with the intoxicating smell of jasmine. Even before she saw her, she called out: "Shanti!" Once again, she was there, where everything was good. In the Golden Temple.

"Hanna, how are you?" asked Shanti.

"Tired," answered Hanna.

"I see," replied the ruler, "but, do you know, why you're tired?"

"I think because of too much work," said Hanna. "I want to help everyone too much. Probably ... I don't know, probably you'll unlock the answer, just like you have until now."

But the answer which followed was one she did not expect. "Because you're not selfish enough," Shanti surprised her.

Hanna furrowed her brow in disbelief that perhaps the beautiful queen had gone a little crazy.

"Selfish? But, I don't want to be selfish," she said. But, already in the next moment, she got a hunch that her answer would bring about a new mystery, that would invite Hanna to reveal its mystical meaning.
"Exactly, selfish," replied Shanti, "I was only able to become a good queen when I started becoming selfish. And, when I understood, what in fact that means. Because many locks are opened with keys, some by those least expected to be real."

Selfishness. A word which most people, in truth, don't know what it means. A word which a lot of parents present to the children as something terrible. A word, which a lot of women avoid putting into practice, and because of that, they aren't rulers of their own lives. Not a lot of words exist for which it would be so very important that you understand what in truth they mean, like this one. Do you want to know the real background of the word 'selfishness'?

"A Story You've Never Heard"

Have you ever heard the saying, "Children come first?" A lot of women put their children, partner, parents, and even their friends first in their lives. They believe that it's right. They love those that they're close to so much, that it seems at times as if they love them more than even themselves.

This is why these loving women wake up every morning before everyone else, wash and do their hair as well as doing everything else for themselves. Early morning is otherwise the only time, as later there wouldn't be time for such things. Then, they prepare their children's breakfast, get them ready, and send them off to school. Many among them then head off to work or to their own companies, where they spend most of their day. They return home in the afternoon and cook lunch for their children and husband. Then they take their children to music school, and in between would otherwise like to go and get a massage, but they don't have time, because they have to go to the store to buy groceries. When the children finish their lessons at music school, they all go off quickly to the mall to try on some clothes and shoes. They know that they'll need some new slippers for the gym. In their purses, they otherwise have a hundred dollar note, but with the money that remains, they spend it on a new shirt for their husbands, rather than on a new blouse for themselves. When they get back home, another hour of homework with their kids usually awaits them. After the completion of their homework, the children go and play while they tidy up the things that no one else seems to see. Around eight, the children get cleaned up, after which their mothers read them a bedtime story.

This goes on all week, except that the children go to swimming lessons instead of music school on Wednesdays. When the weekend comes around, these women head off with their families to the zoo, then off to the forest to collect some autumn leaves and pinecones, which the children need so they can make some decorations at school. When they get home, the children go and play. Then, when these women want to take a bit of a rest on their comfortable lounge chairs, the telephone rings. On the other end are their mothers-in-law, saying they're in the neighborhood and will drop by for a quick, two-hour coffee. Therefore, there'll be no free evening for them that day. After their mothers-in-law have left, they turn on their irons, as mountains of clothes to be ironed have gathered during the week. A look at the clock tells them that it's almost midnight when they finish ironing the last of the t-shirts.

The next day is Sunday, and once again, they won't be able to sleep in a little longer, as today their sisters and husbands are coming to lunch. They're barely able to turn off the ovens and remove the frying pans with mushroom sauce from the hotplates when the doorbells ring. And just like friendly hosts should, they greet them with huge smiles. Lunch drags on into the late afternoon. When their guests head off, their husbands go and lay down on the couches, turn on the televisions and take a little nap. Meanwhile, their wives clean up the dining rooms, wash the dishes, and feed the dogs. Finally, finally, but there's still no time for a rest. Tomorrow is a school day, and they have to get the kids cleaned up and prepared for a new school week. Around nine, the children fall asleep, and the women, after yet another hour of cleaning around the house, finally allow themselves deserved showers. When they come out from their respective showers, they're already thinking about how they hardly wait to get to their books, waiting for them on their bedside tables. But not that evening. Their husbands, who have just gotten up from the couches, having watched the evening movie, albeit half asleep, have different plans. And so, tired wives turn into tired lovers. The next morning, the alarm clocks announce a new working week. The week, once again, goes along like it does every week, but this time around with a small change - this coming Sunday, her sister and family won't be coming for lunch, but they're going, with their families, to have lunch with them.

An interesting scenario, don't you think? But that's not all. They still have to decide on the holidays, which are, first and foremost suitable for their children, and putting aside those trips, that they would go on themselves, without their children. Accepting invitations for coffee from girlfriends, who are basically not interested in how they are, but who, in truth, just want to gossip and complain to rid themselves of their own negative thoughts and feelings. And subordinating themselves to their husband's requests, if they can go this time around (just like every week), to pick up the kids from their afternoon activities, because they would rather get some recreation in. That list could go on and on forever.

And now the question: Why are the majority of these women, not progressive Queens, fulfilling their own missions? The answer is, for many among them, straightforward: Because they're too tired and/or because they don't have time. It's challenging to satisfy your own needs if they're last in line.

A Wrong List Of Priorities?

A lot of women have a list of priorities like that: First on their list are their children, then their partners, and only then themselves. Those who don't know how to say no, or don't know how to stick up for themselves, can even have more people ahead of them on their lists: People like friends, colleagues, neighbors, and some even some people they don't even know.

Why does such a list make it difficult or even impossible for women to become rulers long-term? Because such a list doesn't guarantee what it is, in truth, that they need. Every woman has her needs, which she has to satisfy. Why? So, she can function. So, she has enough energy. So, she can accomplish her dreams. So, she can help other people. If she doesn't take care of her own needs, her energy levels will, over time, diminish. Is it possible to drive a car with an empty tank of gas? No. Does such a car then fulfill its purpose? No. Simply because of its 'needs' for fuel, aren't satisfied. Everything and every person have its own needs. If a woman wants to satisfy her own needs, she must first know them, then take the time for their realization. Only then, when her needs are met, can she function and fulfill her own life. And only then will she be able to help others satisfy their own needs. A car with an empty tank cannot take anyone anywhere. An empty plate can't feed anyone. A fire without wood cannot keep anyone warm. Understand?

If you're not happy, you'll find it hard to spread happiness around. A lot of women invest their energy into others because they genuinely want to help others. If you don't take care of yourself first, you won't be able to offer quality help to others. If you don't have strong and relaxed energy, you can't be a good mother, wife, employee, or supervisor. You may really want to, but the fundamental laws of nature won't support you. Well, they'll support you, but not the way you want. If you work without energy, your results will be weak and far from satisfactory. There are thousands of mothers around the world who give all their energy to their children, while they themselves are tired and nervous. But the truth is, that no child deserves a mother who is tired and nervous the entire time. Children deserve a mother who radiates and has enough energy for all the kinds of 'stupidity' they can think of. If you want to be that kind of mother, first you have to take care of yourself.

The next time you travel by plane, carefully listen to the stewardess, who, before take-off, will give you the safety instructions. One of those instructions is what to do when the cabin pressure falls. In case it does, oxygen masks drop down from above. Then, it's vital that you first put the mask on yourself and then on your child. It's logical, right? If the parent is aware of what's going on, they can always help their child and then even others. If only three-year-old children are the ones on the plane who are conscious, then the passengers don't stand a particularly good chance of any kind of favorable outcome, do they?

It's exactly the same in our everyday lives. Too many hungry people would like to feed the hungry. Too many nervous people would like to calm down all others who are nervous. Too many mothers who put their own children first would like to teach them how to take care of themselves. But they can't. If you want to take care of yourself, you have to put yourself first. If children see their mothers doing everything for them their whole lives, they'll learn exactly that – how to do everything for others. Children otherwise don't learn by listening to what their parents say, but by observing what their parents do. If children see that their mothers first take care of themselves and then them, they'll copy that kind of behavior. And what will then happen in the future? As adults, they'll put themselves first, in a position where they'll be able to manage and improve their lives successfully. Which every loving mother wants for her child. Therefore, if up until now you've been feeling guilty, because you've sometimes put yourself first, it's time to realize that it's actually the best thing to do. That it's the best thing, you, as a mother, can pass on to your children.

Dear Queen, the time has come to readjust your priorities once again and put yourself first. By doing so, you'll put an end to an era of 'worn-out' mothers, wives, and employees. The time has come that you understand, as a matter of fact, that long-term, you're only able to help yourself and others in this way. And so, one of the adjectives which you'll use to describe yourself from now on is, 'selfish.'

Selfishness And Egoism Are Two Different Concepts

A lot of women, at the thought of becoming more selfish, feel bad, as they've been taught their whole lives that this is something that's not good. Sentences like: "Don't be so selfish," became ingrained deep into their subconscious minds. Parents, grandparents, and teachers for years and years told them that being selfish was not good. Yes, these people taught them with the best of intentions in mind, but they taught them something that wasn't entirely true.

In truth, what they wanted to say was that it's wrong to be egoistical. To be selfish and to be egoistical are two completely different things. The truth is that most people don't distinguish one from the other, so they throw them into the same basket. But, they certainly don't belong in the same basket. One of them makes life better, while the other destroys it.

Selfishness is one of those things, which will put a crown on your head. Because of selfishness, you'll be able to fulfill your dreams, raise self-confident children, and genuinely enjoy life. Egoism, on the other hand, is something that will begin to ruin your life (if, of course, you use it). Egoism means to be focused on yourself, without cultivating respect for others around you. It means being prepared to destroy something or someone for the sake of one's own interest. Egoism is not taking into consideration anything or anyone but yourself. An egotistical person does things just for himself, without any intention of helping others. Therefore, it's essential that you understand that relations between people are not destroyed by selfishness but by egoism. Egoism also destroys the planet, poisons water, shrinks the rainforests, begins wars, exploits animals ...

which all happens because someone doesn't respect things and living creatures around them.

Of course, you can also find your way to a crown by employing egoistical methods, but another expression for a queen, who has chosen that kind of path, is a dictator. I didn't come up with that expression myself but heard it from some lady who came to my workshop for self-confident women. She had lost her job, and because of that, her self-confidence had taken a bit of a hit. So, she decided to begin, once again, to work on herself, which, given the circumstances, she strongly needed.

Then, she told me a story about the place she used to work. For a number of years, she had worked for a private company as an assistant to the accountant. She personally didn't have a lot of contact with her ex-director, the dictator, as she called her, but she very well knew her reputation. There were rumors that in the desire for profit, she had crossed the line of the law on more than on occasion. Because she herself didn't have any bad experiences with her, the fact that she worked for her in her company, didn't bother her so much. All until one day, police investigators came knocking at the door.

And what happened? The director had issued fictitious invoices to her clients, then sold them off as debts to a company, which were specialized in those kinds of things. Of course, in the space of a few weeks, it came to light that the invoices were fake and that the sold debts, in truth, never existed in the first place. The company which bought them filed a criminal complaint, which led to the examination of all co-responsible persons, including the lady who came to the workshop. This lady's signature was on all the fake invoices, which she only found out about at the hearing. The director, or rather the dictator, had forged her signature, as well as the signature of her coworker and the accountant.

Because she was very egoistic. She didn't care that she threatened two innocent women with her actions, and she didn't care that she had tried to sell something with no value whatsoever. She was driven by a strong desire for her own good, and in doing so, was even prepared to endanger others. Obviously, the lady that came to me had a guardian angel, as she succeeded in proving her innocence, thereby avoiding all sanctions against her. However, even though it ended well for her, she felt rather uncomfortable, just as people feel alongside egoistical people. Egoism is an energy that does not respect, does not value, and does not love. So, take care that it doesn't play a role in creating your crown.

How to make sure you don't find yourself in egoistical waters?

Be aware that you're just a tiny part of a bigger picture.

You're not alone in the world. You're just a part of it. If you want the world to function optimally, the job of every single part of it is also to function optimally. So, make sure that you, as a part of the world, do the best you can. And don't forget that you represent only a tiny part of the big picture and that others are also important.

Spread light and not darkness.

If you hurt others with your actions, if you infringe upon their rights, if you exercise supremacy, and if you don't respect their life or existence, then your actions are egoistical. Focus on the fact that the consequences of your life will improve the world and not destroy it.

Focus on serving others.

Everyone has something that they can contribute to the world, including you. Find out how you can serve the world and serve others. In truth, it's never just about you.

Only selfish actions place the rudder of life into your hands. Only in this way will you be able to sail where you want to go. This world is wonderful, however, it also has another, slightly less beautiful side, which says that if you don't take care of yourself, then nobody will ... as witnessed by thousands and thousands of young animals, which become food for others, even before they're able to grow up.

Today's world demands action from its inhabitants. If you want to live happily and peacefully on this planet, you have to create this yourself. As a woman, you have hundreds of needs, wishes, and dreams, but your responsibility is to make them happen. Everyone is responsible for themselves. You have an obligation to your own needs, your partner to theirs and your children also to theirs. As you've already realized, if you want to create, you need energy, which you can get, only if you're selfish. Which means that you can create, only if you're selfish.

So, dear Queen, it's time to introduce some changes into your life, which will provide you enough of what you need. You'd like to be content and reinvigorated, right? So, what do you need to be able to begin to live your life in your own fullest energy? What charges your batteries?

Homework

Take a couple hours just for yourself and go somewhere, where you truly feel alive. Take a notebook and a pen with you. Settle down comfortably, then answer the following questions:

- What currently tires you out the most?
- Which area of your life is the most burdensome for you?
- What is it in your life that you truly don't like right now?
- What in your life do you most miss?
- What do you need right now?

It's crucial that you're completely honest. Be aware that if you truly do this consistently, then the answers will be able to help you control your life and to put you there, where you belong - on the throne.

Time Just For You: A Connection With The Elementary Energy.

Time just for you is something that every woman should have. Especially if she wants to redirect her life in her desired direction. When a person is alone, she hears her own truth. The truth is usually so quiet and invisible that many times it gets lost in the loud sounds of the world. Whispers, which are gently sent by the heart, are too often drowned out by the screaming demands of challenging feelings created by the ego.

But the modern world is incredibly fast and above all, very saturated. So, withdrawing yourself into solitude is often the only way that the voice of the heart can be once again heard. A person, in isolation, calms herself and withdraws from the world around her. Only then can she truly relax and begin to enjoy herself, with herself.

Queen, your life is full of people, with whom you maintain pleasant and not so pleasant relationships. It's full of impulses and messages. The whole time someone and something is influencing you. It's crucial to have a counterbalance - time just for you. The more your life is dynamic, the more you need time, just for you. Most women are tired and exhausted only because they haven't established that balance in their own reality.

The time you spend with yourself, is the best quality spent time in your life. When you do that, you're with your most honest friend, who unconditionally loves you, who stands by your side the entire time and knows you like the back of your hand. She needs your attention, and she's got answers for you.

When you're alone, you behave differently. It's not necessary to pretend, adapt, or take anything into consideration. You can be who you really are. Only then do you truly feel yourself. So, enter into your schedule a new 'obligation' entitled 'Time for me.' It should represent a part of the day or week when you live just for yourself. When you do it, do things that you genuinely want to do. Go to the cinema and check out a movie you like, go and get a massage and relax, head out into the forest and observe its beauty. Do everything that your heart desires. Go somewhere for a weekend getaway, alone. Go somewhere on holiday for a few days, alone. What's important is that you connect with yourself, because it's challenging to do that in an environment full of people. Go alone. People who truly respect you and love you will understand. The right partner will take on the responsibility for the children that week when you're alone at the seaside. He'll understand that you need a bit of time for yourself. When he needs a bit of time for himself, you'll support him in the same way. What's important is that you go somewhere. That you stop playing the role of a mother, partner, friend, daughter, and that for some time, you're just a person who simply exists. This will return you back to your elementary energy and will support you more than ever.

My wife is a writer. She writes exceptional books, which touch the hearts of thousands of readers around the whole world. For her to be able to write such books, she has to know her own heart. Because a book is nothing more than some sheets of paper covered by the truth which has come from the heart. So, a good writer must be in contact with himself. Which, in this noisy modern world, is sometimes a little tricky.

And that's why, a few times a year, she goes on holiday alone. I call this a writer's getaway, while she calls it disconnection from the world. There, she finds the peace and harmony she needs to create the books that change lives. Usually, she goes to some secluded part of a Mediterranean island, where there's no Internet or cell coverage, where she can disconnect from all the demands of her life, give in to the melody of the sea, the wind, and her own heart. And then she writes the most beautiful words ... simply because she hears them.

Here's some more advice that will help you reorganize your life and thus provide you with additional support in transforming you into a woman, who has a crown on her head and a scepter in her hand.

1. ***Actively support your physical body.***

This will demand some time and energy from you. Most women put their health last, because the body is extremely adaptable and can, before it falls ill, cope with a lot of stress and damaging energy. Most consequences show up with a delay. That's why they don't have to take care of their bodies for a long time, because, during this time, they still function normally. But not even the body is almighty. If it is burdened for too long a time, it will slowly succumb to illness. When this happens, trouble tends to show up in other areas as well. Health is directly connected to your career, relationships, and happiness. If you don't take care of it, you risk the 'domino effect.' The first task of a selfish person is to take care of their health, which is a prerequisite so that you can function and help yourself as well as others.

Think about how you can support your body. Include some recreation into your everyday routine (yoga, swimming, walking, running, or cycling), some quality food (fruit, vegetables, water, and nuts.), meditation, breathing exercises, and massages.

My wife began conducting workshops and seminars quite a lot earlier than I did. But, over time, the effect of working with people started to show up in her health. Working with people is amazing, but at times it can be quite tiring. She became chronically exhausted, the skin on her face seemed to lose its elasticity, and her energy levels fell dramatically. In the beginning, I didn't think that the consequences of working with people could be so bad, but after a few months of conducting consultations and seminars myself, I also felt it. All-day seminars began to suck the energy right out of me. And soon afterward, the demands for a change in our lifestyle appeared. We had to support our bodies if we wanted to continue fulfilling our paths. And so, we introduced a few changes: We became vegetarians so that our bodies got lighter food, we began to swim regularly, we began to do yoga, and I even began to run. We also included regular massages, meditation, and even breathing exercises into our schedules. All just to make sure that our bodies were strong because we realized that without them, it would be difficult to create anything.

2. ***Everyone should begin to take care of their own basic needs.***

Most women spend the greater majority of their time with their children. Time with them is divided into two different groups of tasks: Spending quality time with them and satisfying their needs. Spending time with children is the kind of thing all good parents just do. In this way, children learn, it helps develop their self-confidence, and they get to know who they are. In satisfying their needs, a lot of parents go too far, because they simply do too much for their children.

Children can begin to take care of many of their own needs a lot earlier than most parents think. Children are quite often very smart and very capable. So, begin to believe in them. Let them learn to prepare their own breakfast and lunch. Let them start to dress themselves. Teach them to do the laundry. Let them take responsibility for the tidiness of their rooms. Let them carry their own things. Don't do so many things for them. Sure, a lot of the time, you want to help your child, and you put their needs first, but at the same time, you're giving them a signal that you don't believe in them to take care of things themselves. The more you begin to believe in your children, the more responsibility they should take on. Let them put themselves first. Don't devote so much of your own time for them. Instead of preparing fish for them every day, rather teach them how to catch fish themselves.

Once, when I was having a back massage, the masseur was called by her eight-year-old daughter. She told her mother that she had already put away the washed clothes and that she was now going to wash the family dog. I have to admit that I was more than shocked when I heard what she said. Up until then, I thought that children of that age just played. Then the masseur explained to me that her daughter can do a lot of other things. I had the opportunity of meeting that young lady personally, and I have to admit that her energy, ability to learn, and self-confidence greatly impressed me. Children are far more capable than most adults think, and so it's necessary to give them the opportunity to express their capabilities. Do the same with everyone else around you. It's strange, but a lot of adults frequently behave like children and demand from the people around them that they do things instead of them. If this also happens to you, let me tell you that you don't need to do this. Let them learn to take care of their own obligations and let them be responsible for themselves. This will free up an enormous amount of time, which you can use for your own benefit.

3. ***Optimize household chores.***

Some houses are huge, and families who live in them are even bigger. Consequently, it's necessary to take care of a whole lot of things. Think about the chores you don't like doing, then give them to someone else. Think about hiring help. A lot of women, for example, hate ironing. If you're one of them, and despite this, you do the ironing in your family, think about hiring someone to come once a week to pick up your washed clothes, and bring them back a few days - ironed. You can do the same with cleaning the house. These days, services like this are really quite affordable. Already for the price of a pair of shoes a month, you can rid yourself of the ironing, which provides you with a few additional free hours a month or even a week, that you can then spend however you like.

Here, a lot of husbands object to their wives, saying that they're throwing money out the window. Well, in such a case, you can hand over the ironing or cleaning to them with pleasure. And so, the wives will have more time, and even save some money, because instead of the cleaning lady, it'll be their husbands cleaning the house. A lot of partners don't understand how much energy and time is demanded by these kinds of chores, as many of them are not so obvious, and so a lot of the time, they forget that a pile of ironed shirts doesn't just appear in the wardrobe by themselves.

Make a compromise that suits you both. If your concerns are finance-related regarding additional help, don't forget that you'll have a lot more time for things that genuinely make you happy. In the same way, you can devote your newly acquired time to developing your new business, which in turn will bring you even more income.

With the two of us, it was my wife that first suggested this. Once she came to me and said: "I hate ironing. I don't want to iron anymore.

And I don't want to clean the house anymore. When I do those things, I feel like I'm wasting time, which I could use for writing or expanding my business." So, we went on-line and searched for people in the vicinity who were offering help at home. We found a lady and decided, already at the first meeting, that she would come once a fortnight and clean the entire house, take the washed laundry with her, and a few days later, bring it back, ironed. That small change did so much in optimizing our time, as we had more of it for things we liked doing. Have a think about that.

4. ***Simplify the way you eat and cook.***

Yet another task that takes a lot of time away from women is cooking and preparing meals. Instead of taking some time to rest after a whole day at work, most women go straight into the kitchen. In all too many families, the 'rule' is that the woman cooks. And, on top of all that, it's not just about cooking, but also about the food shopping, preparing the table and washing the dishes, which usually takes altogether a few hours each day, especially if the family is a large one. If you want more time for yourself, divide up the tasks: Someone else should do the food shopping (or use an on-line service with home delivery); if you have children, get them to set the table if you cook, get your husband to do the dishes. Or, the other way around. Go out more often, especially if you have a day off, and you don't like cooking. Children are usually enthusiastic about that, and you and your partner will be able to enjoy yourselves. Also, look for quality restaurants with healthy food that deliver, and from time to time, simply order home delivery. If you have the possibility, you can also hire some help with the cooking.

My wife and I eat out a lot, primarily because we have a very dynamic work schedule. If both of us are at home for the day, we prepare something for ourselves that we really want. But, sometimes, we simply can't be bothered searching about the kitchen and simply order something from a nearby restaurant. It's important that you adjust your 'eating and cooking' rhythm to your wishes. Don't become a slave to food. Food is here to support your life, not that it would additionally burden it.

5. ***First, indulge a little.***

When you get paid for the work you do, your first thought shouldn't be the list of things which you have to buy for your children, your home or your husband ... no. The first thing you should buy is something for you. If you go to work for the whole month or if you work for yourself, you deserve something just for you.

All too many women do things for everyone else around them, financially, while they rarely indulge in anything for themselves. Once a lady came to counseling, who was exhausted and worn out. Many a thing had brought her to that state, but also that she never indulged in anything for herself. Her children had the latest fashionable clothes, had the latest smartphones, and the whole time they went on trips, while she modestly got by through the month only in two different cardigans and two pairs of shoes. So, I advised her to first buy something for herself. She was firmly against this idea in the beginning, saying that she had many more important things she had to pay for. Then, I just persuaded her to try. And indeed, a few days later, she bought herself a red blouse and a necklace made from some yellow-colored beads. She even sent me a photo by email with the help of her son's phone. When I congratulated her in my reply and asked her how she felt, she described it as if it were Christmas morning.

Maybe it would be the time that you also begin to feel that way more often. You know, it's not so much about the purchase itself as it is about strengthening your own feelings of self-worth and the energy of something done for yourself. The 'new handbag' which you will be holding in your hands will just additionally show you that you're worthy and that you deserve nice things. Of course, buy prudently and responsibly. Follow the financial plan you have and take care of essential things. But the feeling of realized intent is sometimes just as important as a paid telephone bill.

6. ***Stop being a 'trash can.'***

Have you ever gone out for a drink with a girlfriend, expecting to have a nice time, then come home all tired? The socializing didn't pan out in the way you thought it would, and it seemed that your friend dumped all her negativity, doubts, complaining, and gossip onto you. Yes, some people do that. Some intentionally, most unintentionally. But the result for you in both cases is the same – a complete depletion of energy. So, it's vital that you make sure this doesn't happen to you. If people around you are negative, remind them of their pessimism, because they're also projecting it onto you. I've learned that we can pass on even the most difficult and most traumatic matters optimally and respectfully, without burdening the people around us.

However, only those whose purpose is not complaining about unpleasant circumstances but are also prepared to listen to your opinions and solutions as well as actually using them in their life, can do it in this way. But, sadly, a lot of people are not like this. Many don't want to hear solutions, but only complain that they're deprived and that they're victims. In other words, when they socialize with you, they don't see it as an opportunity of spending time with a person they like, but an opportunity of throwing onto you all that they themselves don't like.

Stop being that trash can. Don't allow anyone to dump their frustrations and negativity on you. Maybe it's time to selfishly protect your energy and decide to help only those who genuinely want your help. If you start doing that, your social circle will change a little, in fact, the number of people in it will fall. Why? When they see that they can't load their burdens onto you, they'll seek out other people, other 'trash cans.' But don't worry too much about that. This just means that a few people will disappear from your life, who have, as a matter of fact, never really respected you anyway. At the same time, there'll be room for new ones – for those with whom you can hang out all night, and that won't drain you with one single word.

7. ***Say no. To the things, you don't want to do in life.***

All too many women say 'yes' when they think 'no,' which strongly distances them from their crowns. Many among them are taught that they have to please the people around them. One of the main ways is that they continuously agree with others and try to please them. Don't think too much about other people.

They're not that important so that you would hold yourself back and say yes, when you think no, just because of them. You do damage to yourself. Your task is not to hurt yourself, but to respect and appreciate yourself. So, always say no when you don't want to do something. Always say no when you're tired. Say no if something isn't in line with your values and principles. Say no if your inner voice says no. Above all, be aware of something – that you've got the right to say no, even without a reason.

That short word, made up of two letters, is one of the strongest friends of a woman who knows what she wants. So, invite it more often to socialize with you. It'll help you remove everything that doesn't belong in your life. The word 'no' actually exposes people around you and divides them into two groups: Those that are with you because they like you, and those who are with you because they obtain some benefit from being with you. When someone asks something of you, and you say no, these two types of people react differently: Those who are alongside you because they like you will simply accept your answer, and your relationship goes on as it was.

I saw how true this was at the beginning of my relationship between my wife and her friends. It was interesting to me that they saw each other only around once a year, but despite that, they managed to maintain the relationship in an extremely pleasant, honest, and respectful manner. How they did that was something I managed to figure out one day in a telephone conversation of theirs. They agreed to meet up over lunch. Then, on the day they were to meet up, a few hours before, my wife's telephone rings. Because she had her hands full at the time, she turned on the loudspeaker. It was her friend calling, and she said: "Hey, babe, I know that we said we were going to catch up over lunch today, and that we haven't seen each other for half a year, but I really can't be bothered leaving home. And, I'm not really in the mood to chat. Can we do it some other time?" When I heard her reason, the thought immediately came to mind: "You're really direct." Until then, I wasn't used to such communication, nor did I communicate in that way myself. Once, I actually rejected an offer without censuring my thoughts, and I was quickly told where I should stick my offense. That's why I later said yes many times, although I actually thought no. I looked at my wife and waited for her to say something. Her answer was absolutely spot-on: "Hey, no problem. We'll be in touch, babe."

At the time, I realized that you can always say no to the right person, and that person will still love you. Such an answer is indeed risky - risky in the sense that it removes the masks from the faces of people around you. Because people who are around you, only because they benefit in some way, won't be too pleased with such an answer. So, many of them then try to persuade you to change your answer. Sometimes it seems as if they somehow try to force you into making a different decision. And, if they still don't succeed, many of them afterward, when you stop giving them what you give them, show you their true colors. I say that a negative answer has the ability to bring to the surface the true nature of people. So, by saying 'no,' you can really find out who truly loves you. So, you'll know which relationships are real. Regarding the future of relationships with people who don't respect your 'no's,' the decision is up to you. But before, ask yourself if you actually want to have people around you who love you only when you do things in the way they want. Therefore, your task is only that you're first honest with yourself and then with others.

My dear, if you genuinely wish to awaken the ruler in yourself, it's time that you put yourself first. That position will allow you to see the furthest, and at the same time, it'll confirm what you the whole time, deep within yourself, you already knew - that you're valuable.

"The time which you spend with yourself is the best quality spent time."

Hanna opened her eyes. She sensed that she was smiling. Shanti was always surprising her.

These 'night journeys' were exceptional. She felt like she was a teenager, who in the evening, when her parents were asleep, secretly escapes out the house, then in the morning, just before they wake up, returns with a smile on her face, revealing that the night was 'completely crazy.'

And now it was morning, which will conceal the mysteries of the night. A new day was coming. Her task was to make it exceptional.

Mission no. 7:

The Crown of Love

Hanna's leg declared that it was time for healing and a better feeling. Her wound still occasionally burned, but nothing more than skin which had been touched a little too much by the burning sun on a hot summer's day. Two days of rest had done her well. A few minutes later, her body was embraced by a cold shower, which rinsed away the last feelings of pain. That morning, in particular, made her feel good.

She let the water run a little longer, like an unstoppable river along a known riverbed. It seemed to her that besides the pain, she somehow also washed away the 'old' Hanna, whom she wanted to leave behind. Otherwise, she wasn't able to describe the feeling, which for someone else was just a regular shower, but for her meant a true rebirth. It was so nice. Like the first day of spring after a long winter, which proclaims that everything will once again be in bloom. She had a feeling that the water, with every drop, was strengthening her new life and had confirmed that it was spring.

She was becoming stronger and stronger. And, for the first time in her life, she felt something else – that she had grown up. Up until then, she always had a feeling that she was just a little girl in a woman's body, but today that feeling left her without a painful goodbye. Instead, another feeling ruled – the feeling of being a woman. She smiled to herself, then hugged herself, as if she wanted to protect her newly acquired gift.

Half an hour later, she was already at the campsite. Once again prepared, to spend the last few days in the embrace of the warm sun, the fine sand, and her mysterious mummified friends.

"Good morning, guys. I'm back!" she said with a smile on her face, greeting her team, as she stepped into the tent kitchen. The guys ran towards her like a puppy does to a bouncing ball.

"Look at you, you're really here! How are you? How's your leg? Did the medication help?" the questions began to rain on her, then Hanna's palm was warmed by a cup of freshly brewed chamomile tea, which they had made just for her. Some of them, especially Peter, were truly happy that she was once again back. Hanna felt ... loved.

But there was not a lot of time for socializing, as the date was looming over their heads – the date of their departure. None of them would be there anymore the following week, so they quickly emptied their mugs, then headed out to the site.

Work went on that week without any hitches. Hanna took care of the easier things. As a matter of fact, most of the time, she took care of the notes and wrote up reports. A few times, she even ran into Mark. Despite the not-so-nice experiences that had occurred between them in the past, this time around, they politely greeted each other, and Hanna could have even sworn, that he even smiled at her for a short moment.

The excavations went smoothly, and the entire team truly worked hard. Many times, after they had done enough on that particular day, did she remember the stars, which shone in the night sky above mystical Egypt. Everything went according to plan, and Mark was satisfied. The fire had stopped on the battlefield, and there was no more sign of paralyzing fear in the face of the fiery general.

The days went by. The end of the expedition was approaching, and Boston called – the city which was home to Hanna and many of her school mates. Hanna began to feel some kind of homesickness. Not for Boston, but for Shanti. The last two months had been invaluable to her. And now she had a feeling that she wasn't returning home, but that she was leaving it. Even though Mark and his team were staying in Egypt, her airline ticket in the hotel reminded her that life had different plans for her. The time had come to say goodbye. Will she know how to live without her; she who had so very much changed her life? Will her heritage in the form of wise teachings remain with her, or will Boston once again push her to the edge of the abyss and ask her if she would like to fall or if she would she like to fly?

On the last day, they all decided that they were going to celebrate the end of the expedition. The guys brought something which resembled beer from somewhere, as well as a basket of corn, potatoes, and fish.

"To our first archaeological journey," Sam said as he raised his glass in the air and emptied it in one gulp.

It was a relaxing evening. On long sticks above the fire, they grilled corn and fish, they roasted potatoes in the hot ash, and in the air, new memories were felt, which were to change those young people forever on the journey of the greatest search for the truths of life. Hanna sat on a stone by the fire, and while weaving her memories, she enjoyed every particular moment in a dream-like state. She had a warm feeling in her heart.

"These are feelings which we want to feel in life," echoed in her mind. "That's it. I want to feel comfortable in my own skin, be surrounded by people I love and do what makes me happy." It was a perfect evening. A perfect memory was created.

"Hanna, do you have a moment?" said Mark as he approached her. "I'd like to talk to you."

Hanna nodded in surprise and followed him to the familiar small table in front of his tent. When they sat down, she expected nothing of what was to follow: "I would like to thank you for your effort and work on this expedition," he began.

Hanna, totally shocked, was unable to do or say anything, which he did not take offense to.

"I know the work wasn't so easy," he continued, "the conditions are not ideal, and so I always admire young enthusiasm, which I sometimes see, otherwise quite rarely, in future generations. Hanna, you have this in you."

Hanna, for a moment, thought that Mark was joking, or that perhaps he had been drinking a little too much of that strange Egyptian beer.

"Thank you, Mark," she stuttered. And once again, she was without words. She just observed him. Mark was sincerely grateful. Today, for the first time, since she had met him, she saw something different in his eyes.

"What's going on?" she asked.

Some inner voice told her that it would be better to ask Mark this. Hanna closed her eyes for a moment, breathed in the energy of a brave lioness, then looked at him and decisively said: "I'm also particularly glad that the offered opportunity to work on this expedition came my way, on your expedition, because as an archeologist, I highly respect you. However, you have now confused me a little. All along, I had a feeling that you didn't like me. And even the last time, after I told you about my feelings, you almost didn't say anything. During the entire expedition, on many occasions, you didn't even notice me, and a few times, you even yelled at me. The whole time I had a feeling that I'm doing things wrong. Whatever I did, it wasn't good enough ..."

"Hanna," Mark stopped her. "I really didn't mean it. I apologize to you if I hurt you in any way."

Hanna looked at him in disbelief and wasn't able to believe her ears. Mark, her boss, was apologizing to her? Even though in such cases it is fitting to say something back, she was speechless. A slightly opened mouth indicated that her brain was still processing what she had just heard.

"You know, I'm not the best with people," Mark continued. "Maybe that's why I love archeology so much. Old walls otherwise don't require anything back. And, please, don't be so formal when you speak to me. Speak to me just like you do to your friends. As I'm also offering you the hand of friendship."

Hanna took a deep breath, gathered up the courage, then asked him: "Has no one ever told you that you sometimes behave like a ..." She stopped, caught her breath, then carefully continued, "a bit of a pain in the butt"?

"Yes, I've heard something like that. As a matter of fact, a past girlfriend said that to me," Mark said, opening up and continued: "I know that I'm sometimes strict and unrelenting, but that's also how life is. You can't achieve a lot if you're not strong. As a child, I myself was also scared, but my father, a general in the army, taught me how to stand up for myself. Hard. With discipline. Without any countering. And I learned.

You know, archeology is hard work. Sometimes you focus on one idea for years and years, sometimes even an entire lifetime. Expeditions are expensive, and it's hard to get funds for them. People really don't like giving you money for something which 'might' bring success, especially something which definitely separates them from a whole lot of dollar bills. Often, we undertake research where there are no guarantees that we'll even find anything. Many times, it's all very much undetermined. And quite often, it's determined just by the archeologist himself. I've learned that I can rely on myself at any time, while everything else around me is subject to change. You've got no idea how lucky you are that already on your first expedition, tombs were discovered, that something tangible was found. I had to wait almost ten years for such an opportunity. And believe me, if I weren't strong and tough on myself, I wouldn't be here today. Most likely, I would have given up on this career. And you, you wouldn't be in Egypt right now. Hanna, I believe that I will still hear things about you. You're a special girl, and in you, I see the necessary spark, which archeology needs, for it to shine in what it gives people. Congratulations on everything. And now, I have to go; work awaits me, and you have to get back to the guys." With a slight smile on his face, he got up and left.

Hanna remained seated, and the inner butterflies flew about even faster than they had ever before. That, from Mark, the fiery general, she did not expect. His other side completely surprised her. Almost as much as his words. How could she have been so mistaken about him? What had happened? Had she not observed him well enough? Or are words, as they say, louder than the messages which hide behind them? He was, in truth, a completely different person she thought he was. Undoubtedly, it was the main surprise of the day.

She hadn't even noticed that she'd returned to the guys while she was reflecting on everything. They were throwing some kind of ball around in a relaxed sort of atmosphere, which said that the work had been done and that it was time to have some fun, to let their hair down. It was more than obvious that they deserved it. She sat down not so far from the action and just watched them. Everyone was there. Except for Peter, with whom she had talked to a few times already at university, the others she knew only by name. And in the beginning, most of them were quite rude to her, while today they were friends. A few days before, they had even done her work for her when she was injured.

She realized that she still had a lot to learn about people. Up until then, she had spent most of her time with the neighbor's cat and with her friend from university, Sara, who was a creature of very few words that didn't have much contact with anyone else. When she found out that the faculty had chosen her for the expedition, she was caught up in a wave of surprise. She, a quiet mouse, which almost no one even noticed, who had never had a boyfriend. She, who hid on even the sunniest of days. But she was on the list of people, the university's management, for some unknown reason, believed in and so wanted to offer her a new opportunity. And now she was there. On the other side of the world. Different. More self-confident. And, with new friends. For the first time, after the death of her parents, she felt that the people around her liked her. She smiled. She had friends. Without them, it would have been hard to succeed. And she had someone special. Shanti! Her best friend. Who always stood by her side. So mysteriously. So sincerely. So truly.

"Catch!" said Peter, interrupting her thoughts by throwing her the ball.

Hanna jumped to her feet, caught the ball, and threw it back. The rest of the evening they spent playing, having fun and telling jokes as well as weaving even closer friendships. Meanwhile, the desert sky, with its thousands of stars, watched over its Hanna and her 'new' friends.

"Team, let's hit the sack. Tomorrow, we're heading home," said Nick around midnight. "It's time we head back to civilization."

"Just a minute!" said Hanna, taking a torch and running towards the tomb. She had to see her one last time. When she directed the beam of light onto her, she was lying there, still and peacefully. Her Shanti. For a few moments, she just stood there and looked at her. In the following few days, Mark's team would take her into the laboratory, where forensics would carefully check all the details, to help them get more answers about

the history, trapped inside of her. But Hanna knew that they wouldn't be able to find their way to the real answers. No analysis of fibers, scanning of facial bones ... nothing would give such wonderful answers as she had gotten from her, herself. For which she would be forever thankful. Thank you, Shanti.

That last night she felt how she would miss Egypt and all the magic that had taken place there, so far from the well-known American life. That 'innocent' expedition had developed into something completely different. Not in her wildest dreams would she have been able to imagine how very important it would genuinely be for her. How much she would change her. How she would awaken the woman in her.

And her new friends ... now she had friends. She wasn't even aware of how much emptiness her heart had felt before. She realized that sometimes you don't even know what it is you miss. You feel that something is not right, but you don't know what. She was missing friends, people, other living beings. Perhaps that's why she loved animals so much. In them, she found company and a mirror of love, when on her own, she wasn't even able to recognize her own reflection. After the death of her parents, it seemed that the only two people who truly loved her had left her. From that time onwards, friendships were a hidden and unfulfilled wish. Her uncle and aunt took care of her, primarily because they had to, rather than out of any reasons of love. At school, her classmates teased her the entire time, which then also continued on at university. She was only in contact with two people. With Peter, who sometimes talked to her in the hallway, and with Sara, whom almost everyone thought of as a weirdo, because she often spoke to herself. Now she really had friends. Peter, Nick, Sam, and Josh. Even Mark.

The hotel room embraced sweet Hanna for the last time, who was staring out the window from her bed, watching the dancing of the stars above the rooftops. Her eyelids became heavier and heavier until the last reflections of the moonlight disappeared from view.

"Hey, you forgot about me," a voice awoke her.

"What, sorry?" replied Hanna.

"You forgot about me. I'm also your friend," Shanti afforded herself a wide smile. "You mentioned everyone except me. Therefore, Peter, Sam, Josh, Mark, and ... me. That would be right."

Hanna looked around and realized that she was standing in the Golden Temple. And standing in front of her was Shanti, beautiful and smiling. Her friend.

"Of course," smiled Hanna. "You're my best friend." And, with total sincerity, she added some words recognizing the love for her: "I'll keep a special place in my heart, just for you."

Shanti smiled, then asked: "How do you feel now that your life is now filled a little bit more with people?"
"Different," answered Hanna. "More dynamic. Happier. But, I realized that I've got a lot to learn about them. I saw that people change. And they surprised me. Just like Mark surprised me today. Probably everyone deserves a second chance. Just as I have, after all, also got one. With you."

"It's true," continued Shanti. "You know, if you want to rule your own life, you have to understand it. And other people are also a part of your life. So, you also have to understand them. Other people influence our lives a lot more than most people think. During the time of my reign, I was a good ruler because I knew who 'my' people were. And they knew who I was."

You're not alone in this world, are you? There are billions of people around you, most of whom you don't know, but some of them are a part of your life. As a woman of modern times, you're surrounded by a lot of people every day. Just look at your life. You meet them everywhere - at home, at school, at family gatherings, at work, at college, on the street, in the gym, and elsewhere. You chat over a coffee face-to-face with them, via camera on-line, you send text messages and email to them. And so on. In some way, you're connected with other people almost the entire day, unless, of course, you're a hermit who lives on a boat or in a cave in the middle of a mountain. Other people are strongly connected to your life, and they actually aide in shaping it, almost as much as you yourself.

It's true that people around you are only your circumstances, but in most cases, they respond back a lot faster and more intensively than others. Have you ever asked yourself why? Because, if they are your circumstances, it means that, at the same time, you're theirs. Because we're all creators of our own lives, we all mutually and usually relatively intensively influence one another. If you search your memory just a little bit, you'll see that very few circumstances can make you happy like other people can. Just like very few circumstances can hurt you like other people can. So, it's crucial to understand how they affect your life, as their influence can strongly decide if you hold a scepter in your hands or a pair of handcuffs.

A Dog's Story

Once, a young girl came to one of my workshops, which I had organized for teenagers, whose mother wrote to me a few days before, saying that she didn't know what to do with her, as she didn't have any desires or goals in life. She went to school, then the whole afternoons and whole weekends she just lay in bed, sleeping or doing nothing.

When that young girl came to my workshop, I got to know her a little and found out that she had no working habits whatsoever. Which she couldn't have even had. Because her parents never taught her. They always did everything for her, and, as a child, she had no obligations because she didn't learn to accept responsibility for herself. And, with that kind of inheritance in today's world, it's tough to survive, let alone succeed.

Her mother was, of course, a little offended when I told her the actual reason for her daughter's lack of ambition, but she then nevertheless affirmed to me that I was probably right. For her daughter, it was important that she began to take responsibility and that she understood that with her actions, she could create change in the world.

Her mother had in mind a list of things to do, which she wanted to offload onto her. Then, I stopped her. She and her husband weren't the right people to have a positive influence on her, as they had had the opportunity for the previous fifteen years but hadn't taken advantage of it. Their daughter, namely, was no longer a child, but a teenager, who was already interested in guys. From her parents, she had already gotten what she wanted. And, on top of it all, she didn't respect them too much. If her mother and father had tried to re-educate her at that point, the tension between them would only have grown and would have only led to an even further distancing of their daughter from them. The family needed other people. I advised her mother to talk with her husband, then choose an organization, society or club, in which creative and conscientious young people get together, then to go there and enroll their daughter, so that that other young people through socializing and mutual contacts could transfer their values onto her, which would consequentially begin to change their daughter's value system.

Two months later, her mother once again called. Already by the tone in her voice, I knew that things had sorted themselves out. The tone in the voice of a happy mother is otherwise very specific and hard to miss.

Together with her husband, they actually did sit down and begin to think about what to do. Then they came up with an idea. Their daughter had very much wanted to have a dog, but because they lived in a block of flats, they didn't allow her to have one. And that was one more reason for their many fights. Then, they took her to a dog shelter, where they were looking for additional volunteer help. The owner of the shelter was a woman, who with her son, took care of more than twenty dogs, which needed feeding, walking, and daily care for their stay to be as nice as it possibly could be. Both of them worked voluntarily out of love for the animals. Every morning they got up two hours earlier than usual, took care of all the dogs, cleaned their cages, then the lady went to work, her son to school, and in the evening when they got back, they once again dedicated most of their time to the animals, by taking them for walks, cleaning them, brushing them, fixing the fences, etc. When their daughter saw the abandoned four-legged friends, she immediately fell in love with them. They agreed that she could come and help twice a week to take care of the puppies.

When her mother called me, I was preparing myself for a new

seminar, which was to begin half an hour later. She said: "Michael, today's Sunday. It's nine-thirty, and my daughter has been at the shelter already since seven this morning, where they're sanding down the cages and repainting them."

What had happened? Their daughter had established a strong connection with the owner of the shelter and her son. The more she went there, the more she respected them. Over time, she began to notice that her new friends had very strong working habits, above all, a high degree of responsibility. In the wish that their relationship would become even stronger, she began subconsciously to copy their behavior. Consequentially, she also 'copied' their responsibility, work ethic, and focus. She changed because of the influence of other people. Consequentially, her life also began to change - for the better. Of course, it could have also changed for the worst - which you often see with teenagers, who fall into the wrong company, and begin to take on the habits and way of thinking of those people, whom they are associating with. Once I heard something that we are the average of those people with whom we associate. If you want your result to be high, then carefully choose who will contribute to your average.

Briami

Imagine that your life is a dish and that the people who are in it are the ingredients of that dish. Let's say that you are baking Briami, a tasty Greek dish. You need zucchini, potato, onion, garlic, a red pepper, tomato, olive oil, hot water, oregano, parsley, salt, and pepper. If all the ingredients are the right ones, fresh and clean, then in around forty minutes at two hundred degrees in the oven, they will 'change' into a wonderful and tasty Briami. And five minutes later, your taste buds will tell you that you did everything right. Well, this is what comes from Briami made from the right ingredients.

Now imagine that you swap the potatoes for rice, onion for black radish, garlic for turnip, a red pepper for beetroot, olive oil for vinegar, hot water for cold water, oregano for mint, salt and pepper for sugar and cinnamon. You put all of it into the oven, and in forty minutes, you get something. What? Well, it certainly won't be Briami. Then you can sit down at the table and eat it. Once again, your taste buds will tell you something, but not the same as they did the first time around. If you want the dish to be tasty, you have to choose the right ingredients in the beginning. If you want your life to be good, you need the right people in it. And who are the right people? Those who help you achieve what you want. Some do this indirectly: They encourage you, they believe in you, and they support you. Some do this directly: They teach you necessary things, they co-create with you, and they pick you up when you fall. But they all have something in common – you're a better person because of them.

How Do You Find The Right People?

First, be aware that all people are right. But not all people are right for you. If someone cooks pasta with vegetables, you need some other ingredients to make up Briami. So, don't judge others. If someone's not right for you, it doesn't mean that they're not right for someone else. Your task is just to find people who are important to you. So, how do you do that?

1. ***Focus on your own frequency and not on other people***

If you want to find the right people, focus on yourself, not them. A lot of women want the right partner, new friends, more business partners, etc. In short, people who would, in some way or another, enrich their lives. But, many of them don't have this. Why? Because you don't find the right people in life in a planned manner. You can't decide that you'll now meet the right partner, with whom you'll have children, as much as you can't plan to meet the right friends. The right people come into your life automatically as a consequence. Of what? Your frequency.

Every emotion and every thought has its own frequency. If you cultivate some emotion, you give off a corresponding frequency outwardly. Every person has both transmitters and receivers, which are oriented towards giving out or taking in certain frequencies. So, happy people emit and, at the same time, also receive the frequency of happiness. And sad people the frequency of sadness. It's vital that you're aware that happy people cannot accept the frequency of sadness. And vice versa: Sad people can't accept the frequency of happiness. Therefore, joyful and happy people usually have joyful and happy people around them. Disappointed and angry people have disappointed and angry people around them. If you want to find a loving and sincere partner, first be just like that. If you want that your business partners are honest and ambitious, be just like that. You can begin your relationships and build them only by focusing on yourself. It's wrong to think that you have to be focused on the other person in relationships. Your job is to focus on yourself and take care that you're the best version of yourself, just as people who are in a relationship with you have the same job.

If everyone does this, good and stable relationships develop. Of course, only if you are in relationships with people having a similar frequency.

Homework

In every relationship, focus on what you can give the person you're in a relationship with, and not what they can provide you.

2. ***Follow your heart and call soul mates to you.***

Everyone has a few, so-called 'soul mates,' or rather souls, who are on a higher energy level and are strongly connected to one another, rather than to others. They have some kind of common purpose, and because of the realization of this purpose, they often embody together. You also have a few soul mates. Although not all connections between soul mates are pleasant (lessons between them can also be very unpleasant), with some of them, you can build genuinely exceptional relationships. From them, the phrase "A knight in shining armor" was born.

Most women, well, almost all of them, want to get to know a strong soul mate, with whom they could co-create a life, projects, build a friendship, etc. When do they enter your life? When it's the right time. You can influence this by starting to work in line with your heart's desires. Consequently, you'll create the right circumstances which will begin to form around your wishes, and at some moment, your soul mate will enter your life, who'll help you finally realize your purpose or your part in it. Soul mates, who bring with them happiness and pleasant energy, usually

come at the time when you follow your heart.
How do I know that that's true? Because in this way, I met a girl, who is today my wife. Before we met, we were both looking at heading into new directions in each of our lives. We were both restless, curious, and urgently needed answers to questions, which came from our hearts. We both had a lot of energy and passion for life, as well as both of us having our own dreams.

It was time for our lives to move forward. If it wanted to happen, we had to get to know each other. Our souls had otherwise agreed that we would, at some point in life, cross paths, to help each other get to know and bridge some of life's lessons, which were necessary for our continued journey.

And then the 'fatal' moment happened when after a business seminar, we all went off to a bar for a drink. By chance, we sat down next to each other and began to talk. When our knees accidentally touched, the energy between us shot out, and because of that, we exchanged phone numbers. Yes, she's my soul mate, who came right at the time when I opened my heart.

When we left the bar late that night, I looked up into the sky. There was a total eclipse that night, and in the sky, I could see the outline of a ring. The following day, I sent my first email to her, in which I wrote that I was going to marry her. At the time, she thought that I had fallen on my head, however, I fell on my knee only a few years later, when I asked her to marry me. And the ring in the sky moved onto her finger. Yeah, that's what happened to us. Of course, it wasn't always easy. Not at all. Before we got married, we together overcame many obstacles and introduced many much-needed changes. But in the end, after all those storms, the sun always shone. And at the time, the light was amazing. So, dear Queen, if you follow your heart, your life will always be full of people who'll understand you and want to be a part of it.

Homework

Focus on growth and progress in all areas of your life. If you do this, it'll soon be filled with several soul mates who will come into your life and help you with it.

3. ***Perhaps now is not the time for other people***

In the same way that you need to socialize and interact with others, you also need time for yourself and peace. A lot of women want to fill the emptiness they feel in their lives with other people and run away from their responsibilities because they expect that the other people, who come into their lives, will sort our theirs.

If you've found yourself in a state where you feel very lonely and not connected with other people, consider if this is possibly happening for a reason. 'Apparent loneliness' can be a hidden blessing, which tells you that now is the time when you have to step away a little from other people and establish a stronger connection with yourself. In a noisy environment, where there are dozens of people 'throwing' their energy about, it's otherwise difficult to hear yourself.

I saw this once with one of my very good female friends. There was a period in her life when she had an almost obsessive need to find a partner as soon as possible and marry him. After a few unsuccessful dates, she found a guy with whom she started a relationship, and from him, in the space of a few months, had almost forced him into marrying her. Of course, the relationship didn't last, and they broke up. She became practically depressive, and it seemed that she was losing herself. The people she was searching for and from whom she so wanted to fill the emptiness in her were nowhere to be found.

Then, she began to work on herself. Instead of pointless drinks in the evenings, she began to spend time at home, meditating. She also began to eat healthily and started to become active. Over time, she began to like doing what she was doing, which was also evident on the outside. And guys began to arrive on the scene, who, in comparison with the others, were hovering around her. She didn't need other people at the time, just peace and time for herself, so she could once again find out who she was and what she wanted. Now she knows, but she heard the answers in the silence.

Perhaps you recognized yourself in her story. If within yourself, you have strong feelings of loneliness and fear of being alone, it's essential that you're alone because these feelings mean that you've so strongly distanced yourself from yourself, that you no longer know how to have fun with yourself - which is your most important job. Do you know what the difference between being lonely and alone is? Being lonely means wanting someone alongside you who would fulfill your life, which in other words means that within, you don't feel fulfilled. Being alone only means that in your physical surrounds, there are no other people, which means more peace. Thousands of people all around the world every now and then escape out into nature, where they return to their own elementary energy, to monasteries, where they meditate, on trips where they go alone ... all for the purpose of taking some time for themselves. Being alone and at the same time, happy is a state of the soul, which shows that you've genuinely accepted all parts of yourself and that with them, you are calm.

Homework

Take a few days, just for yourself. Go somewhere, alone. Do things that make you truly happy. Go out into nature and talk with it, meditate, etc. Turn off your phone often and be unavailable. Listen to the silence, more often.

Follow the described steps, and your relationships will undergo significant change. As a Ruler, you'll begin to gather together your loyal advisors and supporters who will help you manage your kingdom. It's genuinely possible that the throne on your left, which is reserved for the king, will be taken (unless, of course, it's already been taken).

Honest People

If you've got people around you who are honest with you, know that this is one of the greatest gifts you can receive from them. They will honestly give you their opinion on the things you ask about, thereby providing you with the possibility to see the real picture so you can then improve or fix things. Other people have different information about you than the information you have about yourself. So, they can also help you find different solutions than those you would find if you only searched yourself. Consequentially, in your own life, you can improve a lot faster. One of those people in my life is my wife. You could only wish to have her for a friend. She is honest and loyal. She knows how to give praise, and she also knows how to clearly tell the truth, even if it's uncomfortable.

ADVICE:
Focus on people who are honest like you and whom you trust. Then, ask them for their opinion about you or your circumstances, where you want more information. Approach them and say (for example): "Dear Sarah, you're my friend, and I love you. I value your opinion, so I would like you to tell me what you think about (here specify the thing, person, circumstances which you are interested in). Please, tell me honestly and clearly." Then they should tell you. However, be careful: Irrespective of what they tell you, even if they give you their opinion on something you don't agree with or even their opinion which is completely different from yours, you mustn't be offended or even angry at them. If the answer is honest, you have to accept it as it is. Irrespective of their answer, your relationship with them mustn't change. Don't forget that you asked them for their honest opinion. If your attitude towards them changes because of their answer, then you're not a good friend.

The magic of these answers lies in the fact that they are usually true. These people otherwise have different information about you or the circumstances in question than you have yourself because they see things from a different perspective. Added to which they are less emotionally involved, and because of that, are consequentially more objective. If you want to get ahead in life, surround yourself with honest and smart people, then ask them often for their opinion.

Truth: Demotivation

Sometimes the truth can be a little unpleasant, or even brutal, and the person who hears it can feel bad, because of it. In such a case, it probably hasn't been delivered properly. What does that mean? That the truth had the opposite effect on the person than was desired. When you ask people for their honest opinion, you usually do this because you want to improve yourself or your desired circumstances. Therefore, you want the truth to lift you. You want your life to be better because of it. Which does not happen if what you hear knocks you down. In that case, your life doesn't improve. All you've done is additionally burden it. In other words, the truth doesn't liberate you, but it demotivates you.

And now a fundamental question: ***"Do you socialize with people who support you or with people who demotivate you?"***

Let me explain it to you with the following example: A woman gains a few pounds, which leads to a fall in her self-confidence. Then, one day, she asks her husband: "Darling, have I put on some weight?" Her husband looks at her and says: "Yeah, it's true. You're a little fatter. It's time that you lose some weight." That was actually the truth, however, with his answer, he's created a new truth: That his wife now feels even worse than she did before. Therefore, her husband's response, otherwise valid, had demotivated and crushed her.

People usually want to help others improve their circumstances by telling them the truth. But, if we don't deliver the truth in the right way, we don't help them improve. All we do is make things worse. If we return to the woman's husband: An emotionally intelligent man, who only wants the best for his wife, will never demotivate her with the truth or additionally take away her power. Instead, he'll try to find out how he can deliver it so that he lifts his wife's self-esteem and her level of energy. For example: "Darling, don't worry. Kilograms sometimes come, and sometimes they go. In either case, I love you. Otherwise, next week I'm planning to go swimming. How about going with me?" Can you see the difference between both answers? With his first answer, her husband demotivated her and additionally took away some of her power, while in the second, he calmed her down regarding the situation which was worrying her, helped to lift her self-confidence, then offered her a solution to her challenge. The task of sincere people who love you is not just that they tell you their opinion, but also that they take care that you feel good regarding your circumstances. You want people you love to feel good, right? If it's necessary for this to happen that words are thought about before they are expressed, this means a little extra work with which we can create much better relationships.

All the more, people around the world aren't doing this. A lot of them just don't think what they say. But like everything, this also has consequences, which for a lot of women aren't all that pleasant.

> If a woman doesn't feel confident, she won't be able to fulfill her ambitions.

> If a woman doesn't feel attractive, she won't want to have sex with her partner.

> If a woman doesn't feel intelligent, she won't be bold in her decisions.
>
> If a woman doesn't feel safe, she won't trust herself and the world around her.
>
> If a woman doesn't feel loved, she won't open her heart.
>
> If a woman doesn't feel free, she'll never truly express her own potential, etc.

Therefore, it's obvious just how important the way we 'deliver' the truth is. The difference can be a completely different life. And, a completely different woman. A lot of people here say: "If someone doesn't want to hear the truth, then that's not my problem. I've said what I needed to say." This is true, however, there is also something true here: Always, when someone says something about someone else, they are saying something about themselves. So, it's not always about 'what,' but above all, about 'how' it's said. Because some people take care that others are motivated after the conversation and feel better, while others are frustrated and feel worse. My dear, if you want to live as a proud woman, surround yourself with people that make you feel better. Regarding the rest, decide for yourself.

Homework

> Think about the people in life that 'lift' you, and the ones that push you back down. With those that lift you up, strengthen the relationship even more, and make sure that you 'lift' them back. Get those who demotivate you to read these lines.

A Smile Of The Heart

In your life, there are a few angels whose purpose is to offer you help, the right word, or sincere love. These are people who have decided to support you and help you fulfill your mission even faster. You can recognize them by the smile that appears on your lips when you see them. You feel amazing around them. Your heart trembles when they approach you. You want to shake their hands or even hug them. You love them, and they love you. You know you can always call them. These people are a part of your heart, and without any kind of hesitation whatsoever, you can give them the key to it. These people are at your disposal. Always. For anything. They don't judge you, and they accept you just as you are. You don't need to pretend in front of them. They know who you are, and they see your essence. These people are your supporters and earthly angels. These people listen to you, and they also hear you. These people help you achieve your crown and are happy when you're happy.

How do you recognize them?

- sometimes they call you just like that; just to hear from you and to see that you're okay
- you feel that you can trust them with whatever it is because, despite everything, they never judge you
- when you need them, they always come to your aide
- they know what you like, so they often make use of that knowledge, just to make you happy
- when you're down and out, they offer you a hand and uplift you

- if they do something that hurts you, they apologize
- they believe in you and encourage you to follow your dreams, even if they themselves perhaps don't understand
- they're sincere in their happiness for your successes and wish even more of it for you
- a lot of times, they let you know, of their own accord, that they love you
- you're prepared to give them the spare key to your house

Think, which people in your life put a smile on your face? When you answer this question, call them and tell them that you love them.

Tears Of The Soul

Another group of people exists, who don't put a smile, but put tears on your face.

Every tear that flows down the face of a woman is a reflection of her soul. The bigger the tear, the bigger the cut into her soul. Who makes you cry? In this way, Ruler, you can see who cuts into your crown. Tears are the companions of the deepest and 'most challenging' feelings. Sadness, fear, disappointment, and despair are a group of four that travel alongside them. Some people break your inner happiness with their words and actions. They don't respect you or your decisions, and so they don't care how their words or actions affect you. Through their egoistic eyes, they only see that they're right or things from their point of view, while at the same time they don't even realize, that while they've been stomping around, that they've walked over someone – you.

How do you recognize them?

- they only call when they need something from you
- you don't interest them, but only what you can do for them
- they often offend you, which is a consequence of a low level of emotional intelligence
- usually, they want to win in a conversation, because they want you to consequentially lose
- often they demotivate you with their advice, scare you or even try to stop you
- they try to subordinate you
- they don't respect your wishes, demands or boundaries, which you've set up
- if they don't understand your dreams, they laugh at them
- they do things which hurt you, even though they know that
- they carry out any kind of physical, sexual, verbal, emotional or psychological violence (***)

Think, who's putting out the fire with your tears? When you answer this question, you decide that you won't allow it to happen anymore, then begin to set boundaries with these people. Where necessary, withdraw from their lives or remove them from yours.

Tears are visible, difficult emotions. And people who see your tears but do nothing don't deserve to be in your life. Don't hide your tears. Show them. But show them to people who put a smile on your face, as they, in difficult situations, will also stand by your side and advise you what to do. But, be careful: If you're the victim of any kind of violence (***), contact the competent authorities who will help you resolve your situation (counseling, hot-line, a safe house, the police ...).

How can a woman stop her tears? I once met a girl who attended one of my courses. When she sent me the application form, she wrote that she wants to obtain more knowledge and that she's looking forward to the course. Then, at the door appeared a lovely, smiling girl, full of optimism and faith in life.

If she hadn't told me about her previous experiences herself, I would never have thought that she had had them. She was around thirty-five years of age and a single mother with three children. A few years before, she left her partner, who had abused her in all sorts of ways. Because of the trauma she experienced in the relationship, she lived for a long time under the influence of many fears. But she nevertheless didn't allow her tears to put out her fire. She fought and fought, searching for how to heal her soul and her heart. During the course, I admired her, as, within her, she had that fighting spirit, which she had used to successfully tear herself away from the claws of her past. Today, a few years later, she is a free woman who does everything she wants in life. She enjoys life to the fullest, taking advantage of it every day and, what is most important, is surrounded by people who support her.

Dear Ruler, know that real tears are already the last phase in the process of being hurt. Things don't need to go that far. Your energy already warns you far earlier that someone has infringed upon it. So, pay attention to your true inner feelings and work in line with them, as you will save yourself a lot of tears ... and save them for a nice evening out with your girlfriends, while eating chocolate and ice-cream, telling jokes until your stomach hurts. And in doing so, you will cry tears of laughter.

So, Queen, the people in your life are the pieces of your puzzle, who will help you put it together. If you want it to reflect the charisma of your truth and your heart, then let them be the right ones. Allow your heart to choose them. It knows how to do this.

"Obviously, it is so important how we 'serve' the truth. The difference can be a completely different life. And a completely different woman."

Hanna was confused for a moment. "Where's Shanti? She was just here ..." What's going on? She looked around for a few seconds, looking for her friend, then realized that she had woken up. "Oh," she thought, "it's as if my dreams have spilled over into reality."

She lay there in bed for some time and just enjoyed waking up, albeit rather unusually, then got up and said: "Well, it's come. It's time to leave." She didn't know what to feel. On the one hand, she was happy to return to Boston, as she liked the city and wouldn't have to deal with the Egyptian heat, which her body didn't cope so well with, while on the other hand, she realized that she was leaving a mystical place, in which she had got to know herself and her new friend of royal blood, Shanti.

Mission no. 8:

A Chameleon of Discoveries

Hanna laid her suitcase onto the bed, which testified to the fact that she was leaving Egypt, then took out her list of things she had brought with her on the expedition. Lists were her way of functioning, providing her with a feeling of control, ensuring her safety in an uncertain world. They calmed her down. And she never ever forgot anything. She ticked off all the things and put them into her suitcase. Already, when she placed her last shirt into the suitcase and went to close it, she remembered something else – the stone from the tomb. She went over to her bedside table, opened the drawer, and from it took out the mystical beauty. Not any ordinary geological stone, but something which she had found in the corner of the tomb on the ground when she was cleaning, which she wanted to take with her as a memory of her first expedition.

For most people, it was just an ordinary stone, but to her, it symbolized the beginning of something new, something different. It reminded her of the time when she transformed into a woman and changed for good.

A few minutes later, she was already going down the broken stairs of the hotel into the lobby. The guys were already there. They were laughing at the tops of their voices and looked like wild teenagers who were heading off for the party of the decade.

"Hanna, good morning!" Josh greeted her. "We thought you had slept in."

"Good morning," Peter looked at her all serenely, approached her, and like a true gentleman, helping her with her suitcase. Then, he offered her an energy bar and said: "Eat something. So, you won't be hungry. I think it's your favorite."

"Peter, how did you know?" asked Hanna surprisingly.

"I noticed coincidently, that you always had them with you, along with dried cranberries, in the tent kitchen." Hanna looked at him and gave him a big, warm hug. She hadn't felt so special in such a long time. Her thoughts returned to her nightmares, and she knew that Peter was one of those special people who could paint a smile on her face, out of pure joy ...

"Time to leave, team!" said Nick, interrupting her thinking, as he noticed their ride to the airport had just arrived. Each of them took their own suitcase and put them into the trunk. Even before they had taken their seats, Hanna looked around and asked: "Where's Mark?"

"He's not here. Already first thing today, he went to the site. He just left us a note at reception saying, 'Wishing you a safe flight home.'" replied Sam.

"That's a shame," said Hanna, "I wanted to say goodbye to him."

"Well, obviously, you don't have the same wishes," said Nick abruptly and somewhat sarcastically.

Hanna looked at him, surprisingly. "What the hell is going on with you?" Did you get up on the wrong side of the bed?"

"Hanna, I can't be bothered," he replied. "We're getting on this plane so that we'll be home as soon as possible!"

"What's up with him?" Hanna quietly asked Sam. As if she was afraid of announcing out loud the fact that there was tension in the air that then might bring about a new spate of bad relations from the ruins.

Sam motioned with his hand and said: "Nothing. That's Nick."

"What do you mean?" replied Hanna, confused.

"We've got to go, we don't have a lot of time," interrupted Sam as he gave the driver fifty Egyptian pounds, and a few minutes later, they were already driving towards the airport.

"Next stop - Cairo International Airport," said the driver, attempting to be humorous, happy that he had got some money in advance, but his attempt at humor fell flat on the cold wall of somber faces. Hanna firmly grabbed onto the door handle and, with fear in her eyes, looked at the road, as she very quickly noticed that their humorous driver was not driving in line with the road regulations. He was dangerously overtaking, braking, honking his horn and yelling at the other drivers in Arabic.

"This is a little different than it is back home ... well, at least we don't have to worry about being late for the plane," attempted Josh to cheer her up with a sour smile. But, she didn't hear him. She had lost her affection for driving at the death of her parents, and of 'such' driving, she had her own opinion, and it was anything but rosy. She closed her eyes and hoped they would arrive as soon as possible. Around an hour later, five young pale-faced archeologists stepped out of the creaking van, glad to have arrived at the airport in one piece.

"That was some ride," Hanna said in a seemingly encouraging kind of way, stepping towards Nick, hoping to fix the bad start to their final day. But Nick just looked at her, then took his things and, without a word, left towards the entrance of the terminal. Hanna looked at Sam in astonishment, who had witnessed everything.

"Once again, I'm asking myself what have I done wrong?" she asked, confused.

"Nothing," replied Sam. "You haven't known him that long. We've known each other for a number of years. That's just the way Nick is. When he doesn't need you anymore, you're no longer important to him, and someone he just doesn't want to have in his sacred space."

"What do you mean?" replied Hanna, confused.
And Sam explained to her that part of Nick's personality: "Nick's usually nice when he knows that you're of use to him and that he needs you. When he gets what he wants, he shows you another side of him, which is entirely different from what he first showed you. Do you remember the day when Mark announced that he would put us in his report as an official part of the team, and not just as interns? Do you remember how from that day onwards, he began to behave differently towards you from the way he had previously, by showing you some kind of affection? He needed you so that we could finish the work at the site in time so that Mark could give him the reference that had been promised."

"Excuse me?" replied Hanna, who simply couldn't believe what she had just heard. "No, not Nick. He's probably just having a bad day." Sam smiled and said nothing more.

After more than a half an hour of waiting for their flight to be called and for finally checking in along with their baggage, they all spread themselves out on the seats by the gate for the flight for Istanbul, where they were headed, and where they would transfer for the plane that would take them to Boston.

"Still almost an hour and a half till boarding; I'll take a bit of a nap," decided Hanna, throwing Nick a quick glance, then attaching her headphones to her cell phone, before partly laying down on the terribly uncomfortable seat and closing her eyes. The fast pace of the last few weeks had obviously

been more taxing than she thought, as she began to fall deeper and deeper into ...

She looked all around, and everything glowed in a scarlet-red color. Fluffy clouds surrounded the magnificent landscape in which she had found herself. "Where am I? Have we already taken off?" Then, before her, she saw the well-known door that led to the Golden Temple. In anticipation, she opened it, and there she stood, her Shanti.

"Hello beautiful, how are you?" she said, speaking with a respectful tone, indicating to her that she genuinely cared about her.
"Confused," said Hanna, a little sadly.

"Let me guess," said Shanti, "Nick, right?"

"Yes," replied Hanna, "I don't know why he changed so suddenly. I thought we were friends ..."

Shanti spoke in her wisdom: "You know, Hanna, life has many faces, just like people. All these faces, unfortunately, are not pleasant and smiling, and even when they are, its often just some kind of acting in an insincere kind of show. I myself have had the opportunity of seeing a lot of them. As a Ruler, I also had the power to bestow land, titles, and authority. Many times, people, in the beginning, behaved pleasantly and honestly, but upon getting power, they changed face. Their masks fell and revealed some things, which were sometimes difficult to accept. Some people changed very quickly and showed their true colors. One of my personal advisers called them chameleons because they knew very well to merge in with the environment when it was necessary."

It's interesting how some people are so very similar to chameleons and how a lot of them, like those exceptional reptiles, are able to change their 'outer color' with regard to the environment in which they are in. The only difference, in truth, is that chameleons, among others, change their colors to balance their body temperature, while people do so for some reason to hide their own truth. Regarding this, today's world is very complicated, as every person can hide their true colors and put on false ones. So, a lot of the time, you don't even know who in truth is standing in front of you.

Dear Queen, do you know how to recognize a chameleon? Do you truly know those who surround you?

Why are these two questions so very important? Because in intimate relationships, friendships, or relations with business associates, etc. you're strongly connected to them. These people are continually shaping your life, and as such, they're also changing it. So, if you want your life to be the way you've planned it to be, it's wise to know who the people are around you. All too many women are married to men they don't really know, and all too many women have people around them who take advantage of them, etc. There are a lot of such cases, but they all have the same result – the removal of power. So now it's time for the masks to fall, but before they break apart on the ground, let me explain how they even arose.

People change, whether they plan to or not. You, your partner, your friends ... everyone. But it's important to understand the kind of change taking place, above all the intention behind it, as this will provide you with an exceptional starting point for the further building of the relationship. Therefore, people make use of two different changes: Sincere and fake ones.

A Sincere Change

Sincere changes can sometimes demand a lot of energy, but they pay off.

When I met my wife, she was a completely different person to the person she is today. I can't say that she was a bad person, but on the other hand, she wasn't overly friendly either. She had an extremely exhausting character, which she sometimes added jealousy, screaming, and obsessive control to. A few years before that, she got injured in a car accident, and because of that, she was angry at the whole world. At the time, she had to give up her one love: dancing. It seemed that there was an out of control hurricane inside of her, which every now and then uncontrollably escaped and ripped through everything in its path. Being alongside her was sometimes truly tiring. Every month, countless verbal attacks and 'bouts of energy' flew my way, which over and over-tested my love for her. I have to admit that at some stage, I even asked myself if my girlfriend was quite possibly a bad person. I knew that she was wild, but even wildness has boundaries somewhere. And in those circumstances, it was more than necessary for some kind of limit to be set.

Then, a few difficult life lessons came knocking on her door. Around that time, we broke up, temporarily, and not long after, her mother died from cancer, leading to her being alone. She was forced to face up to herself. In some moments, she tried to 'resolve' manners, even with suicide. But, she didn't succeed. At the time, I moved in with her, because I saw that being alone, she wouldn't succeed. Although we weren't a couple, I stood by her side.

Then, she decided to choose life. She began to climb out of the deep hole, into which she had fallen. She changed jobs, started attending seminars for personal growth, filled her free time with meditation, read books, began to eat more healthily, and worked on her emotions and thoughts, etc. She was really trying. On this path of self-healing, she even discovered her life's mission: Writing. She began to change, slowly at first, then faster and faster. Today, she's an entirely 'different' person to the one I met at that time. The change in her is so huge that some people from the past don't even recognize her. And what's most important: Her change was sincere – no masks, no later revelations, no pretending. She is what she is. She's remarkable.

People who are sincere in their change say what they think and do what they say. Their words are in sync with their emotional responses, which are expressed via the body. When you talk to them, you are emotionally calm, as you intuitively know that they are speaking the truth. Why is it here so crucial that you follow your inner feelings? Because every person has a natural system of recognizing energy. Just like you can naturally recognize whether something is edible or not, by the way it smells, you can also feel via a recognizable social system, if a person is 'edible' or not. In other words: You can recognize if the person in front of you is showing his true colors or is a chameleon.

False Change

Some people don't really change. Perhaps they do look different on the outside, with forced smiles and by dressing differently, etc., but on the inside, they're still the same. Sometimes people don't want others to know who they actually are, or that they would think they're something, which in fact they're not. And so, they pretend. The real reasons for why they do this are many, but most often, there are two:

- The first is that they're not character-wise or morally strong or stable enough. And so, every change which isn't in line with who they truly are rocks the weak foundations of their personality. A lot of people like this function via strong feelings of helplessness, fear, or even despair. And, as you already know, frightened or desperate people behave differently than calm ones do. That's why a lot of people in such circumstances subconsciously manipulate, which is usually driven by a force for survival. When they fall into difficult times, they have a too-weak character for them to find a suitable solution. And so, they resort to methods that arise out of manipulation. In other words: They begin to pretend or lie to somehow find their way out of difficult circumstances. Although most of these people are not 'bad people,' their weak nature actually forces them into misbehaving. The result for the surroundings is usually the same as if they had done it deliberately – someone gets hurt. For them and those in their surroundings, who are negatively affected by this, it's important that they understand that a weak personality is no excuse for any kind of manipulation at all. A person like that has to accept responsibility for his actions and also his character.

If you have such people in your life, put some distance between them and you to protect yourself, then from a different perspective, help them sharpen their personality and to grow emotionally (all the tips in this book).

- The second reason why people change into chameleons is planned manipulation. If people from the outset manipulated out of a feeling of helplessness, they're now manipulating you out of a position of power. These are people who calculate the possibilities, then plan to do what is best for them, irrespective of the consequences for other people. Their moral awareness is usually very low. They have a strong egoistical personality, which makes them capable of making decisions that can hurt others or even harm them. Usually, they help so that others owe them a favor. They're capable of socializing with someone just for the sake of obtaining benefits, often they communicate with lies, and they also have very weak values which they very quickly adapt to their current needs. So that on Monday they can hate someone, then on Tuesday, they find out that the person could do something for them, and because of that they're already friends with them on Wednesday. They consciously manipulate, which represents a reason for most of the sadness and fear which people experience in relationships: The reason for most disagreements and conflicts between people, the reason for the end of stories which could have been exceptional, the reason why wars happen, the reason for the killing of animal and plant species, the reason for the destruction of the planet, etc. And the list could go on, and on. If manipulative chameleons have power in their hands, they can be very dangerous. Look back in history, and you will find dozens of rulers, male and female alike, who manipulated with their power, which turned them into dictators. Then, look at the consequences of their actions. Some of them are still very painful.

If you have such people in your life, remove them from it, as they can harm you with their actions. And something else: If they're in your life, they're most likely also manipulating you, because in the opposite case they wouldn't be with you.

Therefore, Queen, your life also includes other people. Your task is to know who is sincere and who is a chameleon that changes colors. Let me give you some advice and insights that will help you with this. With these insights and knowledge, you can ensure that your relationships will be truly sincere, added to which you'll be able to save yourself from a lot of unnecessary quarrels or disappointment. Once I heard a saying which best describes the things I'm about to describe. It goes: "When people show you who they are, believe them."

1. ***Take a look at what people are like when they are standing on the podium.***

   People show their true colors when they're at the peak of their power, not when they're fighting for survival. Power and success expose people for who they are. At the time, they don't need to adapt to anyone. They have everything they want, so they can be who they are. Without needing to explain anything to anyone. Usually, when success comes very quickly, the tendency to please others falls just as fast. They no longer need to please others, because their desired success is already there. Some people are the same, whether that be in times of defeat or in times of success.

But not all. As a matter of fact, there are a lot whose masks get ripped off and have their true selves shown, all because of success. From that came the phrase "money corrupts people." Money doesn't corrupt people, but it opens them up to others, so beautifully. Why do so many people have such an opinion about money? Because almost everyone knows or has heard of a chameleon, who was at the time, when they were without money, completely 'normal' and kind, and then money turned them into a person who didn't care about anyone else anymore. If you want to know what a person is truly like, look at him when he is standing on the podium and has everything he needs, or rather, everything he wants.

I learned this lesson once, when I had the opportunity, over a long period of time, to observe the rise and then fall of a young, businesswoman. The lady began to realize her ambitions already as a teenager. She was beautiful, smart, and presumptuous. And she had a strong desire for success. For a few years, she was very successful because she was active in all areas. However, she achieved a lot of her success with egoism, contempt, and manipulation.

Then cancer came into her life. It stopped her in her tracks and made her a little humbler about life. And she really did change. Her conversations became more emotional, and it seemed that she had calmed down; she apologized for some things she did in the past, and a few times, she even cried. She revealed her true feelings in front of everyone, and in a moment's notice, she touched the hearts of many.

But not the heart of my wife, who is like a 'lie detector' for people. Through the years, I've learned to simply listen to her when it comes to others. If she mentions that "smoke" is coming out of somebody, then soon, sometimes even a few years later, a fire appears. And for that woman, during the period of her fall, my wife said that she's just faking it. She didn't believe the woman's tears. And soon, it turned out that she was once again right. Once again, she was on the rise and her strength began to once again increase, the promotion of her disease contributed well, the cancer disappeared, and with it also did her compassionate and warm personality. For her, there was no more room, as her good old egoistical character had taken it up – her true self.

Every success in life brings with it a certain power. You very well know the meaning of power on this planet. It means that you can create or you can destroy. It means you can do whatever you want. If you, therefore, want to know what a person is truly like, look at them when they have everything they want. And you will see their true colors. Then, just believe what you see.

2. ***Look at whether the attitude is 'business' or 'loving.'***

People often hide their true motives why they're with someone in a relationship. If people would truly express their inner feelings, a very large number of couples would break up as well as a very large number of friendships. Thousands of women are with their partners only because they have children with them or because of real-estate, while thousands of people socialize with their friends only because they benefit in some way from being with them. Even though they should be relationships based on love, it's not like that, but about normal business relations, they're in because the opposite side in exchange for what they bring guarantees them something in return. So that there are a lot of partners in relationships with someone where the spouse earns the money and takes care of them. Not because of love, but because of money. And so, a lot of people are friends with others, only because they know influential people and hope that through them they'll get to meet them. Not because of love, but because of social networking.

Once I ran into an acquaintance with whom I went for a drink, which led to a discussion. He told me that he had been in a relationship for some time with an older woman who was the head of a department of a larger company and who financially supported him, took him on her travels, and generally provided him with everything he wanted. Given the fact that they had been living together for a few years and were officially a couple and were on the outside visibly happy, I asked him if they were perhaps planning to marry. He looked at me in astonishment and said: "Are you crazy? What would I do with such an old woman my whole life? This will last at most a few more years, then I'll leave her." When I asked him if she loved him, he answered. "Do you think she would pay for me to go to America, Asia, and elsewhere if she weren't? Of course, she loves me. A lot." Then I was interested in whether he thought it was morally questionable that he was taking advantage of her so. He replied: "I give her my youth and vitality; she gives me money."

Dear Queen, learn to recognize if the relationships you have with people around you are business-based or loving. In that way, you'll know when and how far you can count on people. Because these two types of relationship strongly differ from one other: A director of a company knows that he can count on his employees from eight in the morning to five in the afternoon, no later, as their business agreement usually doesn't determine this. A husband knows that he can always count on his wife because that's what they promised each other.

But, sadly, a lot of times, things lead to dishonesty among people, because people don't know any longer the kind of relationship they're in. A lot of people think that they're in a love relationship, but in truth, they're in business one. The difference between a love-based and a business-based relationship is motive. The motives behind business-based relationships are clearly stated in a contract or agreement, the motive of love relationships is simply love. Business relationships usually aren't problematic, as the collaboration ends immediately when the subject of the agreement comes to an end. Love-based relationships are problematic, because a lot of the time, it's not clear what the real reason for the 'collaboration' is. Many ladies thought that the reason was love, until their husbands waved from their cars, in which someone younger than themselves sat on the passenger seat. And many men also thought the same, that the reason was love until the collapse of their company also meant the collapse of their relationship.

How can you find out what the true motive is?

If you have already suspected that something is wrong, you're probably right. Where there is smoke, there is usually fire. The most effective way to find out what kind of person you're in a relationship with is to take everything away that you provide them. And so, you remove all the possible reasons why they're with you. If they leave, it was a business relationship. If they stay, it's a love relationship. This is good to know before you get married. The lives of people are otherwise diverse and changing. People find themselves facing different challenges and tests, so it's good to know, in the case of disease, emotional falls, financial crises, or a simple change in life, that people are there because of you. And that they will also stay.

This is yet another of those exceptional feelings, which I am ever so thankful for in my marriage. My wife loved me at the time when I was confused, irresponsible and a young dreamer without anything, and she also loves me today, as a grown man on his way, fulfilling his life's purpose. And vice versa. We have never asked ourselves about one another: "What if he/she is with me only because ..."

3. ***Look at what their fundamental values are and compare them with their words as well as actions.***

Fundamental values represent what a person truly believes and what is truly important to him. Everyone has them. Typical values are family, honesty, love for animals, health, money, influence, etc. Everyone has a few of these kinds of values, and around them, they try to build their lives. No value is better, or worse, but between them, they're very different. People form their lives around their values – everything is channeled towards realizing and confirming them. And so, all our actions and words somehow lean towards that which confirm what we believe or what we are fighting for. Words and actions, as a matter of fact, come from values and, as such, should both come from the same energy. As it is with people who are honest, but not those who manipulate. The difference between words, actions, and values are particularly frequent and expressive in chameleons. With them, words very often differ from what they do, just as their actions frequently differ from what they believe in.

Once I was in some restaurant having dinner. Right when the waiter brought me what I had ordered, a large group of people came to sit down at the neighboring table. They sat down, took the menus, then each one of them ordered their meals. I wasn't listening, but my ear caught the word 'vegetarian.' Because I'm a vegetarian, I instinctively looked toward the group of people just as one of them, a woman, was explaining to the waiter that she didn't eat meat. So, she ordered a salad, then explained to her friends that a few days before she was watching television and saw how badly they treated the animals at one animal husbandry farm and how she felt sorry for them. The words, which came out of her mouth that evening, which consumed just vegetables, were so very compassionate and nice. At times, others at the table, who were eating meat, were most likely confronted with feelings of guilt. However, her words did not align with something – her leather bag and her snakeskin boots. The words of that woman were 'vegetarian,' but her values and actions were surely not. If they were, she wouldn't buy animal products. Just another chameleon. Funny.

Compare also necessary actions with non-necessary ones.

Everyone has otherwise some maneuvering space for action.

Once some young girl asked me if I could help her find a job. She said that she really wanted to work, that she would like to be more independent, and that she would like to create herself a career. I called a few people I knew who worked for a company and told them about her. Around three weeks later, a friend called me back who was the owner of a smaller company, dealing with the preparation of public tender works. She said that she was currently not looking for any new staff, but she was prepared to offer that young girl some kind of practical work in her company, of course for an appropriately smaller amount of money. She offered her work for four hours a day, for the same amount of money which she got from the government, in the form of unemployment benefits. She said that the young girl should look at it as a trial period, in which she would learn about the business and that later both of them would see what kind of opportunities would exist for continued employment.

When I told the young girl about the offer, she rejected it flatly. She said that if she could lie on the couch at home for the same money, she would rather lie on the couch. Once again, I had come across a chameleon. Her words about working and the wish that she would create a career simply were not in-line with her values, which were obviously laziness, free time, and money. The story, later on, got two different conclusions: The female friend, who offered her experience in her own company, took on another young girl for 'practical work,' who, after half a year working in that company, was offered a full-time position. The young girl, who asked me to help her in finding a job, was still without work, as she wasn't prepared to do any more than was necessary. The opportunity to work at the company belonging to my female friend was a good one, even if it only amounted to getting some experience. And it was good for something else: For exposing the differences between words and actions.

How do you recognize the true values of a person?

- You simply ask a person what's important to them, and they'll most likely tell you. People like talking about things that are important to them. So, you should pay attention. The things they talk about with passion, come from their true values. What really matters to a person represents a fundamental starting point, around which you can build their profile.

- So, take a period of time (for example, two months). During this time, listen carefully to what the person says, above all, what they do. Their words and actions should be consistent with their fundamental starting point. If they're not, the person in front of you is most likely a chameleon.

- In the next phase, just find out where they're pretending.

4. ***Recognize fake chameleons.***

Chameleon colors are almost always expressed with intended or unintended lying (in the second case, it's about denying themselves). But, in both cases, the result is a lie, so it's important that you learn how to recognize it. You can recognize it by an interrupted flow of energy. If a person speaks the truth, his energy flows throughout his body: Creative energy transforms into mental, mental into emotional, and emotional into physical. Everything flows smoothly, without any unnecessary twitches or stoppages.

If a person is lying, it means that they want to censure some energy about themselves. Usually, their words. What happens next? Their creative energy and their thoughts are still the same, but now they've created another thought. A false one. The body is confused, as it doesn't know which thoughts to express – those, which come from true creative energy, or those which come from false creative energy, which leads to a shutdown in the energy flow of the person and consequentially, to confusion in expression. 'Confused' changes in energy are visible, so you can simply detect them if you're attentive to them.

Here there are some of the most frequent changes in energy, which happen when people lie.

Most people who lie, while lying:

- ***Change their tone, speed, or way of speaking:*** Because lying chameleons know that they'll say something that's not true. They consciously attempt to get others to 'buy' their story, and so they consciously interfere in the conversation, which is by itself automatic, so it changes in a moment when they want to consciously control it;

- ***Look down to the left:*** Eye movements are one of the most accurate indicators of a person's true inner state. Due to their sensitivity, they almost immediately respond to all internal mental control. Their responses are expressed as unconscious views in certain directions. Ninety percent of people (right-handers), when lying, look for a moment to the left and downwards. The look lasts a few tenths of a second and is very quick. Of course, sometimes people look down to the left because something falls into their sight of vision, so look for a pattern. Ask them a few questions, then watch to see where they look. If they look to the left and downwards at least three times, it's a very probable sign that they are censuring their answer or that they are lying;

- ***Become nervous:*** With liars, a subconscious fear is created that others will find them out, which is shown as nervous movements, the swallowing of saliva, the curling of hair, the biting of nails, wandering looks, etc. Consequently, their heart rate rises, and then the flow of blood in their bodies increases. The result of that is a changed skin tone on the face, a more prominent lower lip, increased perspiration, etc.;

- ***Use of phrases such as:*** "I swear that ...", "If I tell you honestly ..." : most people don't use these phrases because they don't think that their words would be untrue. Usually lying chameleons use them, who try to additionally consolidate the 'trueness' of what was said;

- ***Exaggerated the explanation of things:*** Lying chameleons try to take care of the trueness of their lies by citing a lot of unimportant facts, which relate to their lies because they want to consciously take care that their scenarios are even more believable;

- ***At some point, mix things up:*** A lot of people don't have a good memory, which is a prerequisite for lying. Consequently, they forget about their lies, leading to differences between the stories they told, and the ones they previously told. You can expose ninety percent of chameleons if you listen to them carefully. As a matter of fact, they will do it all themselves ...;

- ***They avoid a direct answer:*** When you ask them a direct question, they don't answer clearly and directly, but unclearly and confused. Most people have a moral compass, which in situations of lying nevertheless triggers unpleasant feelings, during which they try with confusing answers to protect themselves. Just like lying, chameleons often answer with things that have no direct connection with the question, and in doing so, want to create a relieved feeling that they have nevertheless given some kind of answer.

5. ***Take into account extreme circumstances.***

People can, in extreme circumstances, change in an extreme manner, which also changes their colors. But they're not chameleons because of this.

> A few years ago, one of my female friends was cheated on by her, at the time, boyfriend. When she found out, she went from smiling and fun-loving into an angry girl and a nervous wreck. Even though she truly loved her boyfriend, what he did triggered in her feelings that were so testing, that she was no longer able to feel her love for him and express it as she had before. She became something like a hungry puma, which was prepared to bite off the hand that was bringing it food to eat. Her boyfriend's act of cheating on her changed her overnight. But those changes were not proof that she was a chameleon, but with them, she faced up to the betrayal and sadness, which came as a consequence of the end of the relationship. The phase lasted a few months, then she began to calm down, emotionally, and once again, find stability within herself. Her smile returned once again to her mouth, her eyes once again shined the sparks of hope, which proved that she was looking for beauty in the world. Yes, that female friend changed her thoughts and words in a significant way for some time, but despite this, she was not a chameleon. Extreme circumstances (disease, separation, the death of a loved one, the loss of a job, betrayal, a state of war, the fight for life, etc.) sometimes bring out extreme colors in a person, so always look at the big picture and their circumstances so that you won't cause any ill-will to anyone.

Dear Queen, your love and energy are precious. The more important your mission, the more precious they are. Therefore, take care, that you only share them with those, who in truth, really deserve them.

"People show their true colors when they are at the peak of their power, and not when they are fighting for their lives."

Hanna was awakened by the rather loud but almost indistinguishable announcement, given in English, albeit with a strange accent: "All passengers flying to Istanbul, please note that the gate is open and the plane is ready for boarding."

"Where am I? was her first thought, but in the next moment, she saw Peter's face in front of her: "Wake up sleepyhead, get up, let's go. They've opened the gate."

"Oh right, the airport ..." Quickly, she looked at the clock and couldn't believe that she had slept for almost fifty minutes. She grabbed her bag with her personal items, looked for her passport and ticket, then got into line. Passengers around her began to gather, and she estimated that there would be around one-hundred and twenty on the plane. She observed them, but this time differently than she normally did – she tried to otherwise determine if any one of them was a ... chameleon.

Mission no. 9:

The Steel Bird of Dreams

Hanna excitedly watched the happenings on the plane. She had not flown a lot before, only a few times in her life. But she loved planes. They seemed so mighty to her. They were similar to strong steel birds, which confidently conquered the sky and flew exactly there, where they wanted. In them, she saw freedom, the possibility that she could escape somewhere, to a better life. When she sat down in their mighty hulls, she felt how, inside of them, they brought out a feeling of adrenaline in you, because she believed that you can achieve everything you want in life, and become one of them, those indestructible birds.

And today, that feeling was particularly strong. It beat inside her like a universal heart, full of love and life. She didn't know if it appeared because of Egypt, because of Shanti, or because she was simply happy that she was going home ... it wasn't even important. But she knew something – that she had changed. Egypt had changed her. On that plane, no longer was that Hanna sitting there, the one who had come two months before. The one who was never noticed, who wiped the board and was the last to leave the classroom, without her classmates noticing, that she even existed. And so, that insecure girl disappeared, the one who had countless wishes drawn up in her head, but lacked the courage to admit to them, let alone make them come true.

No, here sat a different Hanna. For the first time in her life, she was calm and confidently looked at life in front of her and believed that she would succeed. Thoughts buzzed around in her head like a swarm of bees, which announced that from the seemingly unimportant pollen, it would create the golden food of the gods. They were so strong that at some moment, she even slightly shrieked. Sam, who was sitting beside her, grabbed her hand as friends do and explained that there was no need to be afraid of flying and that everything would be alright. But it wasn't a shriek of fear of flying, but the shriek of an awakened woman, who was preparing herself to open her wings and fly into a dream life.

The call for all passengers to fasten their seat buckles sounded throughout the flight cabin. The stewardesses checked once again to see if all the hand luggage compartments were properly shut and if all the passengers were securely buckled up. Then, one of them stood alongside the entrance to the aircraft, while the other at the emergency exit in the middle of the plane and the security protocol demonstration followed, in the event of an emergency landing. Hanna listened intensely, and for a moment, it seemed to her that the stewardesses were talking just to her. As if life was giving her some kind of instructions on how to proceed forward. In the part where the two stewardesses were simulating how to correctly put on the oxygen mask, she remembered the dream about selfishness.

She smiled, then said: "No, life. Here I am. Prepared for the starting gun, which will propel me into action. And God, if you really do exist, I want to let you know that I'm starting my new life! And you are warmly welcome to help me."

Although planes filled her with enthusiasm, the thought that they would soon leave solid ground, nevertheless left her with a feeling of anxiousness inside. Trust in the unknown. Trust that it'll safely reach its destination. Simple trust.

Already in the next moment, the lights were turned off, and the plane began to slowly reverse. Then it turned around and made its way toward the runway for takeoff. Ten minutes later, they got permission from the control tower. They set themselves in the middle of the runway and slowly made their way along, then at some moment, the engines kicked in and roared in power. The pressure pushed them back in their seats, while the pilot added even more power to the steel bird. The plane accelerated and accelerated until, at some moment, it lifted off the ground and began to fly. Hanna felt how a part of her life had been left behind, while before her, a new world was opening; a world of endless possibilities.

"What are you going to do now?" Sam asked her when the plane leveled off, and the lights above their heads, warning them to remain fastened in their seats was turned off. "What's your dream?"

Hanna thought for a moment, then passionately said: "I would like to live the way I have always wanted to live. I would like to feel that spark inside myself every minute of my life. I don't want to be a shadow in the background anymore. I want to radiate in colors, strong colors." Upon saying so, her eyes grew slightly brighter, while her cheeks turned bright red.

"Wow," replied Sam in surprise, "I truly didn't expect an answer like that. Bravo, Hanna!" he replied, with a sour look on his face at the same time.

"What's the matter, Sam? You can tell me," said Hanna, when she saw the look on his face.

For a few moments, he hesitated, then he confided in her his story. In truth, he never wanted to become an archeologist, nor did he want to go to Egypt, as these were the wishes of his parents, particularly his father, who was a renowned art historian and lecturer at a prestigious university. His parents had created their own picture about him, which Sam had to play out whatever the cost if he wanted to remain a part of their hearts and, above all, continue to receive their financial support. When he returned home, he was to begin working as an assistant for one of his father's friends. His father expected that his son would be his pride and joy, about whom he would be able to then talk about at a number of parties with the city's 'creme de la creme,' which he so regularly attended.

Sam told Hanna how he had never had the childhood he wanted to have. How he always had to wear the clothes his mother said he had to wear, how he never dreamed of bringing a girl home, how he had to go to the school his father said he had to go to, and how the two of them were blind to the fact that their son was unhappy and how they never asked him what he wanted. In the embrace of the 'forced-upon' dreams of his parents, his heart died along with his dreams. He was ashamed that still in his thirties, he still lived at home and drove his father's car. The cage, in which he was trapped, was becoming narrower every day and threatened to hurt him, faster than he thought.

Hanna listened to him with compassion and realized that Sam was sharing his innermost feelings with her. With his every word, she knew more about her new friend. They were so caught up in the conversation that they didn't even realize that the plane was already approaching Istanbul. Only the call for all passengers to return to their seats and once again fasten their seat belts before landing 'awoke' them from their conversation. When Hanna fastened her seatbelt around her waist, she sensed how it clamped her to her seat. She immediately knew that those were the feelings that Sam spoke about, leading him to feel trapped and powerless. At that same moment, she promised herself that she would never allow anyone to control or determine the way her life and dreams panned out in any way whatsoever. She would never allow anyone to domineer her in any way, even with the explanation that she's better off and safer because of it. Sam's story was just another confirmation that the time had come for her to take control of her life and to direct her steel bird wherever it wanted to go. She truly wished the same for Sam.

The plane landed, and not long after, the group of young archeologists was already on the bus, which collected them on the tarmac and took them into the airport terminal. When they arrived at the connecting flights area, a few of the guys wanted to buy some famous sweets, made from Turkish honey, but there was no time. Their plane from Egypt arrived in late, they had to hurry to catch their connecting flight to Boston. A little over an hour later, they were already in the air, and ahead of them was a ten-hour flight, their last on their way ... home.

Hanna sat in her seat and stared out absently ahead. She just wasn't able to get Sam's story out of her head. She thought that people, at least from thirty onwards, arranged their lives so that they basically lived the way they wanted to. But that day, she realized that a thousand different truths hold true for a thousand different people. Her decision to fulfill her life's dreams rose up like an ostrich's head out of the sand; when, of course, an 'ostrich' decides that it no longer wants to be afraid of that which it sees in front of itself. She didn't want to sit next to someone on a plane in seven-year's-time and, like Sam, tell them of the cage she was in, and the unhappiness that went along with it. She sympathized with him but nevertheless decided that she wouldn't follow in his thorn-ridden footsteps. Perhaps she really didn't know what she wanted, but she knew what she didn't want. And she didn't want to be unhappy. That was for sure.

Then, she took out her notebook. She always had it with her, and in it wrote down all her thoughts and poetic verses that came to mind, from time to time. She had had it for a very long time.

"It's surprising how many things can go in it ... as if the sheets of paper were in endless supply ..." She was surprised as she flipped through its pages. One of the pages in the middle, with a coffee stain on it, caught her eye. It immediately took her back to the café, two hundred meters from the university, in which she, on many occasions, in her first year of studies, and in the company of her thoughts, spent time after her lectures. Then, on the edge of the page, she noticed a message of congratulations, written rather quickly: "Hanna, congratulations! :) You passed your first exam :)"

"My first exam ..." she thought. Her mind went back to her first year at university when she battled through pages and pages of textbooks, full of anthropological theories, during which she spent many long night hours. It seemed to her that they were the only ones who wanted to spend time with her. At the time, she had no idea that the next time she read that message of congratulations would be five years later, eight thousand meters in the air, on her way home from her first archeological expedition. And that, from Egypt!

She looked out the window of the plane. Beneath them lay a never-ending carpet of snow-white clouds. And so, as the scene caressed her eyes, the feeling that she was following her dreams touched her heart. She had almost graduated. Only one more exam and she would get her degree, which would be the icing on the cake for all her hard work. And then, she would become an archeologist. She was twenty-three years old. She had her whole life in front of her. The whole world lay before her like a loyal canine friend does at the feet of its beloved master. And thousands and thousands of years of history had created secrets, which she would be able to now discover for the rest of her life. The secrets, which promised to show her the horizon few got to see. Everything interested her ... old Greeks, Romans, Indians, Egyptians, Mesopotamians, Incas and old Chinese dynasties, etc. She wanted to discover things hidden, learn about mythology and explain it, awaken ancient cultures and knowledge, travel around the world, explore museums, libraries, read records, visit temples, pyramids, tombs ...

When she came to the word 'tomb,' she stopped. Thoughts in the form of her mysterious friend immediately flooded her mind – Shanti. In her heart, she felt a strong love for her and deep gratitude, that she had somehow ... gotten to know her. She could have talked to her for days and days. Or better said nights and nights. Oh, how she loved her. And oh, how she would miss her.

The plane gently rocked her like a little child, then laid her down to a cradle of dreams.

"Hello. Did you call me?"

"Who's that?" Hanna questioningly looked around, while already in the next moment she noticed, that she was once again sitting in the Golden Temple. "Shanti?" she replied, surprised. "Is it really you? Are you really here?"

"What, you don't recognize me anymore?" replied the beautiful Ruler with a smile on her face. "Of course, it's me. Welcome back. Again."

"I thought that I'd never see you again," replied Hanna relieved.

"Why?" asked Shanti.

"Because I left Egypt and because you were there ..." said Hanna, trying to express her joy. Then, she just ran to her and hugged her tightly.

"There's no way I would leave my girlfriend. I'll always be by your side, Hanna. Always. Don't worry, I'm not going anywhere. You know, love doesn't die because of the distance. It dies only in hearts that forget to love. But my promise to you is that I'll love you forever," said Shanti warmly, comforting her.

Hanna felt tears of joy trickling down her cheeks. She knew that Shanti was telling the truth. Then, she wiped them, sat down in front of her, and said: "Shanti, I feel that I've got to change my life. I'm heading home, and I know that things will be different from now on. I don't feel the way I used to anymore. Something has changed. As if I'm somehow different."

"Of course, you're different," replied Shanti. *"You were in Egypt. There, you experienced a part of your dreams, and they changed you. Dreams aren't what most people think they are – quite often, they awaken us, as opposed to putting us to sleep.*

The Street Of An Average Life

The greater part of terrestrial society is somewhat cloned. Many otherwise don't have their own identity formed. Most people are similar to others: They eat similar food, they have the same hairstyles, they talk about similar things, and they live similar lives. Quite boring, right? Why is that so? Because most people don't have dreams. Well, at least they don't think about them. Most people don't use their own heads, so they don't see their own images and wishes inside of themselves, but only what some influential individuals and organizations want them to see. Because so many of them don't have their own leadership, with which they could compare the external images and so judge whether they are suitable or not, they're left with nothing else but to accept and begin to live in-line with them. But where is that uniqueness that parents used to describe their children when they were three years of age? It's faded.

Have you ever asked yourself what is it that puts the most power to the hands of a woman? A woman is strongest when she's aware of her dreams and when she makes the decision to fulfill them. At that moment, from a cute little girl, who hugs her little rag doll, she changes into a mighty Ruler who holds a scepter in her hand.

Yes, every Ruler has a scepter. And every woman was, at least once in her life, a Ruler - at the time when she was born. Yes, that was when that little girl knew what she wanted. And that she also knew how to express it, sometimes even demand it. She occupied herself with things that interested her and made her feel happy. She only associated with people who she loved. Her heart was happy, and her face was smiling. If she wanted something, she simply asked for it. And usually, she got it. In society, she stood upright and wasn't embarrassed. She felt good, even if she ate the last cookie on the table. Before she fell asleep, she read books about beautiful fairies and wizards. When she fell asleep, she dreamed peacefully. Yes, she was a mighty Ruler. She looked forward to every new day. She saw a miracle in everything. Every turn marked a new adventure for her. Every tree was there for her to climb. Every animal was there so that she could pat it. The young girl knew what she wanted and what she didn't, the kind of food she liked and didn't like, and the kinds of dresses she liked and didn't like.

Yes, all little girls were Rulers in the beginning. Then, the young girls began to grow up and change. She began to notice that the world around her was huge, and above all, different. She realized that she had to learn a lot about it. And she began to become aware that she was also just a part of it.

The more she grew up, the more she began to assimilate to the world around her. It seemed as if the world had started to spray her with grey, which began to slowly cover her vibrant, natural colors. She started to meet people who told her what was right and what was wrong. What is becoming and what is not. The kinds of dresses she has to wear for different types of situations and how she has to behave in the company of others. A lot of the time, she felt that she doesn't want to do what others demand from her, but that she would rather, instead of offending them, offend herself: She suppressed her own truth and accepted theirs. Her actual dreams, how she wanted to live, began to be banished by the instructions of the world around her, which insistently directed her to what was right and what was not. Her scepter was becoming smaller and smaller, and with it, so too was her strength fading. Her voice was no longer so powerful and content. Her words were no longer so encouraging and cheerful, and slowly, they were being replaced by routine responses.

Then she grew up and asked herself what it was that she wanted. But already at that time, the picture of her dreams was somewhat blurry. It seemed to her as if she didn't see so well anymore. She felt that there was something there but didn't know what. But now she was grown up and had to decide to do something. Every woman should otherwise do something. That's her job, right? She has to provide for herself and create something, which she'll call a grown-up life. So, she took what others offered her. Life began to come together: She found a job which she took, just because of the money. She got married to her boyfriend, with whom she otherwise felt good around, but she didn't feel any real passion for. Once, or sometimes even twice per year, she went on holiday, and every second Friday, she got together with her girlfriends over a coffee. That's what her life had become.

The years went by, and the lines in her face grew deeper. And so, one day, as she was walking along the street, she got caught up in a crowd. She looked around and just couldn't find herself anymore. As if she had got lost in it. She was almost the same as everyone else. Between her and the strangers around her, there was practically no difference. And, it seemed that everyone around her had also received the same instructions for life as she had. And most of them had begun to behave in accordance with them. She became aware that she had become just another face in the crowd, walking down the "Street of a Mediocre Life." Then she looked at her hand and noticed that the scepter in it had disappeared. Instead, she was holding an empty wallet and an ID card of someone who was supposedly her. Then, she realized she was lost. The little girl in her that climbed up trees and believed that everything was possible had disappeared, and with it, her charisma, which was in truth, the entry ticket to her dream life.

And now a question for you: Is that a story about you? Have you lost yourself in a world that's not yours?

Thousands of women are in relationships with people they genuinely don't want to be with; they've built careers in which they're unhappy; they live in houses they don't particularly like; they do things that don't harmonize with them and live lives, that in truth, they don't want to live. Thousands of women have gotten lost in the grey gloominess, where they no longer see the light of the sun. But look, the life of a flower only makes sense when it begins to bloom. Only then does it become what it has actually been existing for. It's time to see yourself as a flower and your dreams as a blossom. When will you open yours? When will you make sense of your life? I've got an answer for you – unlike a flower, you're not limited to time. You can blossom ... at any time. But it's important to know that you can only do this now. Tomorrow doesn't exist. All that exists is now. So, stop where you are and rein in things as only you know how to.

Choose Wisely

Now, take a look around you. You'll see that you're surrounded by thousands of different directions, opportunities, tools, information, environments, solutions, etc. which are here with just one purpose – to help you make your dreams come true. You live in a world of limitless opportunities. Never in history have there been so many possibilities like there are now. And you're here. So, simply choose. You know. You've done it thousands of times already. Choose again now. Choose left or right. Left takes you somewhere, right takes you somewhere else. But regardless of the possibilities, know that it's your decision what you choose: Something which will make you happy, or not. Will you choose your dreams or the dreams of someone else? I advise you to choose wisely, because, at the end of the day, it'll be your choice. There is no such thing as not choosing. You always have to choose something. As a matter of fact, you don't have a choice. So, I advise you to choose what you want, yourself, because in the opposite case, only one other possibility remains: That you choose what others want. But then you won't realize your dreams, but you'll realize theirs.

You can become whoever and have whatever you're capable of thinking of. A bold statement, right? But how very true. A person, alongside intuitive ideas, also receives the ways to realize them. If it were impossible to realize them, it wouldn't make sense that you would receive them in the first place. Intuitive ideas are, otherwise, the potential of the soul. They represent one of the many possibilities the soul has. When your soul monitors your life, it adjusts the possibilities at the same time, which it then sends you in the form of intuitive ideas. Every intuitive idea and every dream you have, has, in the background, its own energetic purpose. Believe me, the soul does not involve itself with meaningless things. All dreams come with a purpose and are, therefore, completely meaningful and, above all, realistic. So, take a moment for yourself and make sure that you listen to your heart, which is whispering your true dreams to you. Of course, as soon as you begin listening to your heart, your conscious mind will try to impose itself by explaining why something isn't possible and will send you thousands of examples of 'proof' why you're better off listening to it. But, it's time that you understand what the purpose of your heart is, and the purpose of your conscious mind. Your heart, in truth, directs your life. Your heart accepts the energy of happiness and fills your life with purpose. Your mind helps you to seek out solutions and ways in which it can accomplish tasks, which your heart has set. Understand? If you want to live happily and fulfilled, let your heart create energy and allow your mind to manage it. Your heart is the owner of your life, while your mind is its director. The heart has the mission while the mind has the strategy.

How To Get The Cheese From The Mousetrap Of Your Dreams

Dear Queen, fulfilling your life's mission demands from a person that they're aware of themselves, but above all, that they're faithful. When all this is combined with the energy of authenticity, reality begins to be perceived by most people as 'dreams come true.' Now that you've embarked on your journey, make sure that you remain on it, which is very simple if you follow the map, drawn out by your heart. A lot of women, when they decide to embark on their journey, consciously or subconsciously, fall into a trap set by society. A lot of them think that realizing dreams goes according to plan until sooner or later, they realize that they're caught in a trap. Even a mouse, caught in a mousetrap, is calm and happy in the beginning, as long as there is cheese to eat. It gets into trouble when it discovers that it can't get out. So, take care that you don't get caught up in the mousetrap of your dreams. Follow these steps to get your cheese, and avoid its fatal prison bars:

1. *HOW TO GET THE CHEESE: Never Choose Your Dreams Based On What Is Good (Only) For Others.*

A woman who loves her surroundings is often inclined to adapt her dreams to those around her. And not because they demand it, but because she herself thinks that it's right. Such a woman often thinks: "If I love him, I'll choose what he likes." If you do this, stop. Don't change your personal dreams to fit in with anyone. You don't have to. A lot of women do the kind of work they do and have the jobs they have, just because they think it's expected of them. A lot of women voluntarily give up their wishes for food, sport, and travel because they know that their partners have a different outlook on those things, and they try to please them. A lot of women fall pregnant just because their partners want to become fathers, or even because their parents want to become grandparents. Many thinks that they're good wives, mothers, and daughters because they do these things. Know the following: If you've got some kind of role in your family, that doesn't mean that you have to change your dreams or even give up on them in any way. The lives of others around you is their thing, their responsibility. Don't give up on your dreams just because people around you have a different outlook on them than you. Don't pay so much attention to what others think.

Of course, other people are important to you, and you love them. Help them, by all means, and stand alongside them, but you're always responsible for your own circumstances, and they for theirs. You can choose your dreams, which are only yours, even if they're completely different from the dreams of your partner, parents, or children. People who genuinely love you will never demand that you give up on your dreams because of them. Those who are close to you don't have to understand your dreams; their job is to just accept them. Why? Because they're important to YOU.

I once saw an excellent example of this kind of acceptance of dreams in a young girl who came to me for individual counseling. She had a severe identity crisis. At the time she was eighteen years of age and wanted to become financially independent. She was a very talented hairdresser, and her biggest wish was to open her own hair salon. When I asked her what was stopping her, she replied that it was her parents.

Because I didn't quite understand, I asked her to explain. Her mother and father, already for a number of years, had successfully managed the family business, that had a long tradition in the field of viticulture and winemaking, which they had taken over from their parents. Many times, they proudly emphasized that the company had been in the family for many generations, and it was apparent how much it meant to them. Because the young woman was an only child, she herself, somehow accepted that she would continue the tradition. When I asked her if that's what she wanted, she said no. Then she explained that it was her mother, as a matter of fact, who sent her to me for counseling.

Upon completing high school, she began to become more and more involved in the family business, which was a little strange as far as her mother was concerned, as until then, she had never shown any particular interest in it. When the two of them spoke, her mother realized that her daughter had taken the burden of tradition upon herself of her own accord, as she didn't want to be the one that 'ruined everything.' Because she felt some kind of obligation to those before her, who had created it. Because she thought she had to, as a good daughter, to otherwise think and do things in that direction. The counseling session was really good, as I saw how deep someone can dig themselves a hole by trying to please other people. I talked to the young girl about those things. The truth was that she didn't have to take on anything, even though their family's long-standing tradition would come to an end. In the end, she admitted that her mother had told her the same and had sent her to counseling so that she would hear it from a third person. The conclusion or beginning of the story: Her parents supported her and offered her help in starting her own hairdressing salon.

TEST: HOW DO YOU KNOW IF YOUR DREAMS BELONG TO OTHERS?

Imagine that those people disappear from your life. Would you now, that they have gone, still do what you thought you had to do before? If the answer is no, then you've got dreams just because of them. If the answer is yes, then those dreams are yours and are true.

2. *HOW TO GET THE CHEESE: Never Allow Other People To Determine Your Dreams.*

Your dreams are yours, and their dreams are theirs. It's very important that you know this because some people have a very strong tendency to impose their dreams on others, so they could, in some way, control or manage them. They feel that it is their vocation to tell people around them what they should do. And what do you know? They usually have solutions for them. These kinds of people often put pressure on their loved ones and project their troublesome emotional patterns of behavior on them via their wishes or demands. When you tell such people your dreams, they quickly override them with their vision of what they've prepared for you. And so, a lot of women do what their partners say they should, or even have to do. And so, a lot of women live just like their parents told them they should. Above all, some parents have a tendency, a lot of the time, to load onto their children their own ambitions and from them demand that they fulfill 'their' dreams and achieve their standards.

I will never forget a woman who was all worked up and angry and wrote me a text message in which she accused me that I had brainwashed her son and ruined many years of work for her, as well as his upbringing. When I read who it was about, I smiled.

A few days before, a young man came to one of my, at the time, seminars faced with a huge challenge, about a lack of confidence. He just wasn't able to decide which university to go to. When I worked with him, I realized that most of his challenges came from his very possessive and commanding mother. It was even so bad that she forbade him to attend a university far away, only so that he wouldn't move out of home because she wanted him to continue to live with her. And so, she put him down in all possible ways and forced upon him, the whole time, her way of thinking and her principles.

When I explained this to her son, that his mother was the source of most of the 'difficult energy' he was carrying around, he changed in a moment's notice. In short, I later found out that he had enrolled in a university a few hundred miles away, moved into a rental apartment with some other students, and found some part-time work in a nearby bar. He told his mother all of this the day he moved out.

Upbringing (and also other forms of relationships) is not just about giving suggestions and passing on convictions from parents to children but is encouraging the discovery of a child's own path, without imposing the parent's outlook on them. Parents can't tell their children what's best for them because, honestly speaking, they don't know. Yes, they're their parents, but that doesn't necessarily mean that they have the knowledge of what's best for the child. Here, parental authority comes to an end. This is something that children have to discover for themselves. And so, they have to choose what's best for themselves in their lives, or rather, what they think is best. The role of parents is to encourage them to do this. If parents don't understand what their true role is, then it's possible that they program their child in their own image. The expectations of other people (particularly parents) can be very insisting on the thinking of people. Programming usually begins already in childhood, when parents load their dreams onto their children during their upbringing. The child then grows up to be a person who has already 'loaded' programs of who it wants to be, or rather what it should be. But, at the end of the day, it doesn't want its own, but the dreams of its parents.

Never allow anyone to determine your dreams. Always determine them yourself. Why? Because you'll be the one living them, not them. You'll get up early and go to work, and you'll accept the responsibilities and rewards for your efforts, not them. So, follow your own inspiration and your own leadership, then take care that you also allow other people around you the same.

TEST: HOW CAN YOU TELL IF YOU ARE TRYING TO FULFILL THE DREAMS OTHERS HAVE SET YOU?

If, when you think about your life, you feel a wish to rebel, you're most likely fulfilling the dreams that someone else has forced upon you or dreams that have been determined by others. If you feel peace, then they're yours.

3. *HOW TO GET THE CHEESE:* ***Never Copy The Dreams Of Other People.***

You were born unique. One and only. Your true nature is so unique and special that it's not comparable to anything else. Why do you then think that your dreams are any different? Dreams are one of the most precious things you can have. Only one variation exists: They're yours. People will try and copy your dreams, and maybe you'll try and copy theirs. But no one will succeed in creating such unique energy as the original.

Never copy the dreams of other people. It's not that you won't succeed. It's possible that you would. But, in doing so, you won't receive that true inner fulfillment that a person feels when they fulfill their dreams. True dreams come from the heart of the person who created them. And your heart creates dreams which differ from the dreams of others. Trying to realize dreams which aren't yours is the same as trying to love with a heart that's not yours. Impossible. Your soul, just for you, has prepared hundreds of masterpieces, which are just waiting to be turned into reality. The world is an endless museum made up of the dreams of millions of people. If you look carefully, you'll see that there's an empty display case, waiting for your masterpiece. Just so you won't misunderstand, the dreams of others should inspire and encourage you to believe that it's possible. But from then on, awaken the master in yourself and create what only you can create, which in truth will awaken the ruler in you. So that you'll leave your mark, which will add a new grandness and a new charisma to the world.

The world is extraordinary and wonderful. But, it's that way because of the thousands of people who dared to dream by adding their shades of color to the picture. Inside of you is a flame of dreams, which warms you, protects you, and gives you hope. But your responsibility is to take care that it never goes out, otherwise you'll be cold, and you'll only able to warm yourself if you move towards the flame of someone else.

Every day, thousands of people warm themselves by the flames of others. My wife is an extraordinary writer and lecturer and holds workshops for authors as well as meditation sessions. She's very good, and a lot of people come to see her. But, every now and then, someone comes along who tries to copy her work. Some even lack originality to such a degree that they also copy her descriptions and the entire structure of her workshops as well as her guided meditations. And then, they publish her products on their own web sites and present them as their own. But the truth is, that 'their' workshops and meditation sessions aren't, and cannot be anything special. Because they were created by their minds, not their hearts. It's true that these people are trying, and so attempt to create their own dreams somehow, but the fact remains that they were created from energy which came, if truth be told, from my wife. Are they then 'their' dreams?

Queen, if you want to rule over your own unique life, your task is to create your own model, upon which you will build your dreams. When you do this, the thing you create will shine in the light, which the world has never seen before. And the empty display case in the museum of the world will get a new artifact, with your signature underneath. And museums usually have, after all, originals on display. That's why they're so invaluable.

TEST: HOW DO YOU KNOW IF YOU'VE COPIED THE DREAMS OF OTHERS?

If the model, upon which you design your own version of something, was created by other people, then most likely, you're copying. If you can begin creating your dreams without the suggestions of others, without external influences, then they're unique. Yes, sometimes someone's purpose is to improve on something that already exists. If you want to find out if it's yours, then look to see if your product or service has some kind of added value. If it has, you've upgraded the dreams of someone else. If it hasn't, then you've copied them.

4. *HOW TO GET THE CHEESE: Fall In Love With Your Dreams.*

Real dreams are so very special because they awaken feelings within you that cannot be awakened by anything else: Feelings of extreme happiness, pride, love, and drive. A woman feels her true dreams in every part of herself, which energizes her throughout the entire process of their creation. A woman who knows her true dreams and also follows them is seen as if she knows something that others don't. And in truth, she knows – she knows how it is, when inside you feel the true essence of life. For you to feel it, the dreams have to be truly yours, which means that you 'decided' for them with your heart.

There are a lot of women in the world who could be Queens, but because of the 'wrong' types of dreams, they're trapped like slaves. A lot of women are very smart, ambitious, and hardworking, and many among them are also strong and focused on following their dreams. When they achieve them, a lot of them don't feel the powerful emotional rewards of pride and success, which they should feel. Why not? They worked for them and sometimes even slaved over them! These feelings are not there because these ladies decided on their dreams with their minds, which upon realizing them goals does not demand euphoric emotional response, but just a short confirmation that the task has been completed. Most people try to decide on their dreams by using their minds because they've been taught that they can do everything they need to with it. It's true that with your mind, you can understand, analyze, decide, and even create, but it's important to understand that the energetic composition of your real dreams is not the same as the energetic composition of all the other information around you. Your dreams are unique and special, so you can't manage them in the same way as all your other tasks and responsibilities. Take, for example, math and poetry – you only need to understand a math book, but if you read poetry, comprehension alone is not enough.

We live in a world built on the foundations of the mind, in a world where someone has mentally explained everything that goes on around it. But the mind represents just but a small part of the entire reality. If we want to understand the world in all its grandeur, we

can't just evaluate it with the mind. That's why a lot of people don't understand painters, writers, musicians, and other types of artists, as they work in accordance with things that are dictated by their hearts. They paint, articulate, and display their energy in a different way. An artist can devote months and months to painting, and during that time, feel nothing but pleasure and happiness. Perhaps his art doesn't have a lot of market value, but he doesn't do it for the money, but because he feels it in his heart. The most beautiful books are written from the heart, just like the most beautiful songs. In museums, most of the paintings you see were created from the heart. The most precious energy is created by the heart, which is confirmed by the fact that you've probably already seen thousands of billboards created by the mind in your life, but most of them you don't even remember.
What is the additional reward for following your heart? Over time, the mind also joins it. With most people, only in the beginning does the mind trigger different dreams than the heart. If you're unrestrained regarding the dreams of your heart, then your mind in time has no choice but to connect with your heart. When the mind of a woman joins her heart, all conditions are created for her to become a Ruler.

The heart is powerful, and the mind has difficulties understanding it entirely, so sometimes, you won't be able to explain your dreams. And it's not even necessary – it's enough that you feel them. When I met my wife, my mind said that it wasn't the time for a relationship. Later, it said even a few times that she wasn't the right girl for me. She was otherwise so different, and in so many ways, I couldn't even imagine how we could work together peacefully. However, my heart had the last say and said: "She's the one." And every new day confirms that it was right. Listen to your heart.

TEST: HOW CAN YOU TELL THAT YOU'RE DECIDING WITH YOUR HEART AND NOT YOUR HEAD?

If you don't need more and more justifications, as well as proof, why you should do something, then you've decided on a dream with your heart. If you're continually looking for confirmation and proof that you've decided correctly, then you've decided with your head.

5. ***HOW TO GET THE CHEESE: Stay In Contact With Your Dreams.***

Dreams are made up of several different energies. Make sure you're aware of all of them. Use your senses to stay connected to them, that you'll be able to see, hear, smell, taste, and touch them the whole time. Most people forget their dreams or don't fulfill them because they lose contact with themselves. In the first phases of implementation, there are often no results. And the bigger the dreams, the longer it takes for the first results to be seen, and the longer it takes to reach that what they've set out to do. That's why a lot of Rulers quit before they even get to put the crown on their heads. As if they would have somehow forgotten why they're doing what they're doing. If you stay connected to your dreams the whole time, the whole time you will see them, hear them, feel them, etc. and you'll never distance yourself so far from them to forget them. So, do everything in your power to stay connected to them.

Believe that you can do this in many, many ways. One of my female acquaintances started her own company a few years ago. One day she realized that she was unhappy at work and that it wasn't giving her what she wanted out of life. And so, in the evenings, she began to build her business. She started to deal with networking. The first few months she was learning about the business, and because of this, there weren't any tangible results. But, she didn't give in. She knew what she wanted and didn't let her eyes stray off the target even for one second. She had a dream which she knew she could reach with that business. She wanted to create enough passive income to be able to leave her job. And instead of going off to work in the mornings, she would go off to yoga. So, one day, she hired a photographer, who took a very specific photo – of her doing yoga, with a clock in the background on the wall, showing nine o'clock in the morning. Then she copied the photo and hung them up everywhere – on the wall at work, in her car on the dashboard, and on the inner side of the front door to her apartment. Every morning, when she got up, she put on her workout clothes, sat down on her yoga mat, and felt the feeling of her dreams. Then she got dressed and went to work. When she had built up her business in the evenings, she never allowed her dreams to sneak away from her. She worked and took care that her dreams remained alive. After two and a half years, she had created a big enough business that would ensure her enough passive income to be able to turn off her alarm clock and begin to live in the way she had always wanted to live.

You know, Queen, every dream has its path. And some paths are shorter, while others are longer. Sometimes on the way, you have to adjust or even change direction. And at such times, it's imperative that you know where you're going. And above all, why.

Write down your dreams!

In the beginning, your dreams are just intuitive-mental energy. They come true only when you make them happen, right? In other words, when the mental energy somehow materializes. Check out this trick: When you simply write down your dreams, you begin their process of materialization, as they start to take shape and form some kind of appearance. They're no longer just some thoughts, but now they're already some words written down, which actually exist. Therefore, they've already begun to become real, somehow. Now you've got proof on a piece of paper. What happens to the brain when we see them? It begins to believe. When the mind truly believes, it supports you with all its capabilities and helps you find how you can actually make your dreams come true.

TEST: HOW DO YOU KNOW IF YOU'RE STRONGLY CONNECTED TO YOUR DREAMS?

Because at every turn, they remind you that they're coming into your life. If the day goes by without you thinking about your still unfulfilled dreams, you're not connected enough to them.

6. *HOW TO GET THE CHEESE:* *Avoid Dream Stealers And Spend More Time With Those Who Are Enthusiastic About Life*

People, with their presence, often influence you a lot more than you think. This includes not only the more than obvious fleeting actions and words but also the subtlest touches of energy, which you may not consciously be aware of but are recognized at some deeper levels within you. Other people have the power in their hands to slow you down or to encourage you. Now, it's your job to recognize who's who, and then wisely choose with whom you associate. As a Ruler, you otherwise need people around you who are going to support you, while at the same time, it's good that you know how to also recognize those who want to take your crown.

LOBSTERS AND THE GREATEST CEMETERY IN THE WORLD

Some people somehow want that you won't succeed in realizing your dreams. They tell you that you won't succeed, that you're too young, that you're too old, that it's not worth it, that it's too late, that it's stupid ... and that it's better that you give up. Most of them, of course, don't tell you directly, but you can see it, more than obviously, in their skeptical, cynical, sarcastic, and even rude responses. Are these people bad? No, they're not; most of them are even quite okay. Why, then, do they do that? Why do they try and stop you right at the time when you usually most need their support? Because they see things only from their own perspective and are trying to direct upon you their true inner feelings.

Look, dream stealers are usually those who live a life they're not completely satisfied with. Most of these people in their youth had real dreams, but for many different reasons, they didn't fulfill them. Because of that, they've become bitter. When they meet someone who is enthusiastically fulfilling their dreams, they remember at the same time that they once gave up on their own. The dreams of other people don't give them hope and don't provide them with enthusiasm for new possibilities but frustrate them and remind them that they surrendered and gave up. And these feelings are not pleasant. And so, they instinctively want as few of these triggers around them as possible, triggering such feelings. The simplest way for them is to steal the dreams of others because, in doing so, they won't feel bad about having abandoned their own dreams. It's simpler to otherwise convince others that they won't succeed, than for them to succeed themselves.

Just like lobsters do. Lobsters are cooked alive. But usually, at least two of them are cooked in an open pot at the same time. Why? Because if a lobster is alone in the pot, it can climb or jump out because of its strong tail, while if there are two in the pot when one begins to climb out, the other pulls it back, which they continue doing until both are cooked. If they would allow each other that one finds its way out of the pot, and then the other, both would be able to 'survive.'

No, dream stealers work in the same way. Because they didn't fulfill their own dreams, they try, consciously or subconsciously, that others around them wouldn't also fulfill theirs. Avoid such people, as they're dangerous for your dreams, as they can pull you into the water and not let you go. The only place where such people let you go is the largest cemetery in the world – the graveyard of dreams.

Because, of course, if you don't intend on burying your dreams, avoid them.

TEST: THINK, IF YOU'VE GOT DREAM STEALERS AROUND YOU.

If you do, talk to them and make sure that they encourage you and that they stop projecting their dissatisfaction onto you. If that won't work, think about whether you want to continue having them in your life.

ENTHUSIASTS WHO ENCOURAGE

People who you're looking for are enthusiasts – enthusiasts for life who express the energy of happiness, joy, curiosity, and encouragement. These people have in themselves passion, the desire to discover the world, the wish to learn. An excellent example of enthusiasts is adrenaline 'junkies.' Have you ever met one? Their eyes shine when they talk about their latest jump from a cliff, their most recent deep-sea dive, their latest descent from a mountain, etc. In their words, you feel the passion and will for life. An excellent example of enthusiasts are also entrepreneurs who build their stories of success, for which they move the boundaries of the impossible, resolve the unresolved, and invent a new reality. I myself know a few such people. They're exceptional. At some moment, they sit down at the table, drink tea, and already in the next moment on the napkin in front of them, they draw out a new idea. Look out for them, then surround yourself with them. These people live their mission and will help you realize yours. They are warriors who don't have warrior markings painted on their faces, but the colors of a smile and enthusiasm. These people have another exceptional capability: they're strong encouragers. Because they've tasted the sweetness of success, which they themselves created, they know how tasty realized dreams can be and what's necessary to do for them to be realized. And so, they understand you, Queen. They understand your wish for fulfilled dreams and respect your path.

TEST: THINK WHICH PEOPLE IN YOUR LIFE ARE ENTHUSIASTS.

Then, connect with them and try to spend as much time as possible with them. If you're looking for a second opinion, ask them for theirs.

So, Queen, it's time to join the club of people who dare to dream. The club that creates the greatest number of Rulers, male and female alike, in the world. The club whose members are rewarded with a crown. And yours has already been formed.

"Your heart is the owner of your life, while your mind is its director. Your heart has a mission, while your mind has a strategy."

The plane shook about strongly. Hanna immediately opened her eyes and felt that they were losing altitude. As if they were free falling. Seconds later, it once again stabilized, but it was still shuddering and reminded everyone on board that they had passed over their fate to it when they entrusted it with their lives. A loud beep reminded the passengers that they had to fasten their seat belts. The pilot's voice could be heard through the speakers. He calmed them with the explanation that they had found themselves in some turbulence, but that everything was in order and that flights across the Atlantic ocean were often spiced up by turbulence like that due to air masses mixing up amongst themselves.

"Spices and things like that. Certainly, in bad taste," thought Hanna. "That came like a bolt of lightning." Although she was a little shaken up, she quickly calmed down. It wasn't so bad. With a bit of relief, she looked at Sam, who was also on the same flight, sitting next to her. The relaxed expression on his face calmed her down even more. Obviously, he wasn't afraid of turbulence. She looked at her watch, and it seemed that it wasn't showing the right time.

"What's the time? Obviously, there's something wrong with my watch," she said, looking at it.

"Show me," said Sam. "No, your watch is fine. It automatically changed to the time zone, we're currently in."

"Of course, the time difference," remembered Hanna. "Istanbul is seven hours ahead of Boston."

"It's funny," smiled Sam. "In fact, we're flying into the past."

When he uttered those words, something distracted Hanna. Even though he was joking, she knew something inside herself ... that she didn't want to fly back into the past. No, the past was a closed chapter in her book of life, which she didn't want to read again. She wanted to open a new one. She wanted to head towards the future. There, her dreams were waiting for her.

However, already in the next moment, she remembered that she was (almost) an archeologist. And archeologists dig about the past. The irony of it! How do these two things go together? For the first time, she asked herself the point of what she was doing or, rather, what she wanted to do. For a moment, her book of life hit her on the head and told her to finally decide what it was that she actually wanted. And then she discovered something which she had never thought about before – that archeologists go back into the past so they can easier understand the present, which can then create a better future.

"Wow," she thought. "That sounds great!" Her thoughts were already flooded with headlines from well-known newspapers predicting the stories of a young archeologist who had discovered the secrets of ancient civilizations, and whose understanding and knowledge had improved the world. She felt so good at that thought! She didn't just want to be some anonymous researcher, locked away in some archives that nobody had ever heard of. She had already had enough of that. She wanted to be seen, she wanted to be strong, and she wanted to be successful. With her work, she wanted to change the world for the better. She wanted the spotlight, which would illuminate the future of many. Hers also.

"What's happened to me?" she asked herself at that moment. She had never thought of herself in that way ... in such a big way. Otherwise, she had always wanted to be a part of something bigger, but never on the front lines of battle. She had usually thought of herself as someone supporting in the background. Obviously, this had also changed, as now she wanted

more – she wanted to be seen. Shanti was obviously right when she said that everyone who gets a taste of their own true dreams, changes. There were still almost five hours until they reached Boston, so once again, she opened her pocket notebook and at the top of an empty page wrote:

MY HEART'S DREAMS:

- *I want to travel the world,*
- *I want to write a book which would awaken people,*
- *I want to become a renowned archeologist,*
- *I want to lecture young researchers,*
- *I want to 'have' at least one large 'life discovery,'*
- *I want to marry a guy I love and have children with him, and*
- *I want to be happy and fulfilled.*

When she completed the last line, she felt calm and, above all, fulfilled. She could have sworn that for a moment, while writing, she actually felt what it would be like to be her after having fulfilled all those dreams. And that feeling suited her so much, just like mysterious Shanti and her perfectly made dress suited her. The feelings were heavenly. She knew that her life would one day be like that. Without any doubt in the world. She felt that finally, beautiful things were coming her way as well as that horizon, which announced a new sunrise of happiness. When she once again read what she had written, she was ... oh, my God ... happy. Happiness existed. It's not just an expression in romance novels, which are read by desperate housewives.

Proudly, she rested her head back, looked at the ceiling of the steel bird, and smiled with satisfaction: "It's time to change my life to the way I want it to be." Then she allowed herself to dream about the beautiful colors of life. "Boston, here I come!" Boston was ready to greet the new Hanna.

Mission no. 10:

A Marionette

Just like she had the previous four months, Hanna that evening, around one a.m., locked the door of the fast-food restaurant. "Finally, some fresh air," she thought, breathing in and out deeply, trying to rid herself of the energy which was described as food on the menus. The smell of deep-fried onions and French fries almost made her vomit. Every night, because of it all, she took a few minutes, to sit down on the bench beside the dumpster, breathed in the cool, fresh air, looked up into the night sky and enjoyed the peacefulness, which rarely caressed her life, but danced in the wild rhythm of serving customers, which she did to keep her already cranky boss in a good mood. She was forced, the whole time, to have a smile on her face and satisfy every whim of her customers, so in those moments, she usually just wanted some silence, to forget all the demands, which didn't care, that she too was just a human being.

The stars touched her eyes and somehow soothed her. They seemed to be a million miles away. And, so unreachable. She reached up with her hand towards them and tried to grab them. But she knew she couldn't. Inside of her, once again, she felt that pain. The pain, which awoke her every morning and which she felt, every evening when she lay down to go to bed. The pain reminded her that she wasn't happy. And that night was particularly difficult as if her heart had broken like some fragile Chinese porcelain. Two hours before, the manager of the restaurant told her that she would only be able to work there for another two weeks. After which, they wouldn't need her anymore. Just like that. He told her that she was being made redundant due to the optimization of business procedures.

"Optimization for whom? For sure not for me ..." she thought.

She was angry, almost furious. But not at her boss. Not at the restaurant. Not at the customers, whom she served every day and allowed that they pull her strings of humility, just like a marionette, which she had allowed herself to become. She was angry at herself. How could she have let that happen? How could she have even gotten there? How could her 'Egyptian story' be turned into one about a marionette, full of despair and without any will for life?

She felt so helpless. Already for a few months, she was in no way able to motivate herself to do anything, and so, she hadn't even been able to pass her final exam. As if life had shown her everything she wanted, then quickly took it away, and in doing so, seemed to laugh in her face in the knowing that her strings wouldn't allow her to ever reach them again. It seemed to her that everything she achieved was of no use to her at all and, as a matter of fact, that she had nothing at all to show for herself. She looked up into the night sky as if hoping that something up there would answer her and finally begin to paint on the empty canvas of her every day.

At that moment, the peacefulness of the stars was disturbed by some flashing lights, which slowly started to descend. Another plane which would land that night at Boston's airport, and in it, some people who had set off to see the world. In her thoughts, she sailed off into time, more than half a year back, when she was also one of them. She remembered Egypt and her long flight home, which promised that everything would change.

Her memory was obscured by the image of a wonderful woman – Shanti. Oh, how she missed her. She hadn't seen her for such a long time. The last time was actually on the plane. She felt some warmth on her cheek. Her first tears were followed by second and third ones, all until her entire face shimmered in the moonlight, reflecting off them. What had happened? How could she have gotten so lost? Where was that enthusiastic Hanna, who returned from Egypt all full of vigor? Where were those dreams now, which filled her like an everlasting source of energy and which didn't allow her to be less than that, which she was truly capable of? Where was that Hanna with the ponytail?

Even though she still had her hair in that same ponytail, she didn't feel the same. Quite the opposite; she felt tired, and it seemed to her that the source had dried up. She watched the plane ... just a little more, and it would land and kiss the ground. Then, something bothered her ... for a moment, she froze, and a whirlpool of recognition caught up in a word, which in no way wanted to leave her thoughts.

The ground. She was numb. The expression on her face gave away the shooting star of important thoughts. "How the hell hadn't I understood that before?" she began to ask herself and her inner marionette in disbelief. In a quiet conversation with the night sky, she had otherwise come to understand that her plane of dreams in truth was still on the ground. And that it hadn't even taken off yet. What the hell was it still doing there?! Planes are meant to touch the clouds, not the ground.

Although she still didn't quite understand what was going on inside of her, it seemed that this realization had shone some light into her tunnel of horrifying darkness and showed her the way towards the shining exit. As if a little of the forgotten energy had once again begun to water the dried up cells. Her eyes began, despite the long shift she had just completed, once again to radiate, and the expression on her face also changed. Once again, she had hope. In that dark night, the sounds of thin marionette strings breaking could be heard.

"Hanna, that's it. Your plane hasn't even taken off yet. You're sitting in it, but you're still on the ground and hoping that you'll see a wonderful sight through the window," began the words of her own mind, preaching to her like some authoritarian teacher. "It's time to wake up and take action!"

She grabbed her backpack, which hid some remains of food from the restaurant, as usual, which then she had for dinner, or at least something similar, jumped onto her bike and headed off for home. With every push of the pedals, the strength in her grew like a sleepy dragon, that had lifted its head, indicating that it was time to show its incredible strength. With every new bend passed, it seemed as if she was riding through worlds of her memory, which were uttering the words that she had written down in her small notebook half a year before. The time had come to once again open it.

Hanna, under the watchful eye of the hidden dragon, arrived home to the building in which she lived, an apartment building with approximately one hundred and seventy apartments. Well, if two hundred and seventy square feet apartments, in which its tenants lived, could even be called apartments. She got off her bike, picked it up, and then almost ran up the stairs with it. The stench from the timeworn walls hit her, and it was clear that the hallway had not been ventilated for a very long time. The walls were yellow, not from paint but from a mixture of dirt and mold. However, she was unable to afford anything better and had to be satisfied with what she had. And now, the threat loomed over her that soon she wouldn't even be able to afford it. But now wasn't the time for such thoughts, but for her little notebook, which once again, bestowed on its owner the gift of dreams.

She put the bike down in the hallway in front of the door, hurriedly opened it, rushed into her apartment as if it were on fire, and began to dig around amongst the piles of things which were hiding somewhere that she so urgently needed. "Who would have thought that so much stuff can fit into such a small apartment," she thought when after ten minutes of searching about in drawers and cupboards, she finally held her beloved notebook in her hands. She opened it and flipped through it, page by page, until she came to the part which was written "MY HEART'S DREAMS."

She sat down on the edge of her bed and began reading. Every newly read word awoke in her a new memory. Slowly, the old image of herself returned, the image of a confident young woman with drive and determination. In her, once again, that Hanna began to awaken. The one which Egypt had so strongly left its impression on. Her memories started to awaken ... the tomb, Nick, her ponytail, the cut on her leg, dreams and her ... Shanti. When she remembered Shanti, once again, a pearly tear slowly ran down her cheek, out of sadness and joy. Oh, how she missed her. And how she very much wanted to once again look into those eyes of hers. Although she knew that she had seen her only in her dreams, they had been nevertheless so different, so real.

Sadly, she closed her notebook, went to the bathroom, took out the things which held her ponytail in place, and brushed her hair. She looked at herself in the mirror. Her memory brought her back to that morning when she decided to change her hairstyle. That was when she began to change from a frightened, young creature into a strong woman. But today's reflection acknowledged that the ponytail was just a cover for an insecure young girl, who felt as if she were standing on the last station of the land of "Despair." The dark circles under her eyes reflected back in the mirror and represented the sad fact that she wasn't happy. She knew that something had to change.

And now was the right time for that. In her, something was still smoldering. The fire in her had not gone out completely. It could still warm her heart. And that night, after a long time, she once again felt that smoldering. Despite the grueling past few months, she gave a slight smile to the tired image in the mirror, then dragged her weary self to bed. She knew that the day to follow was going to be a new day. And, she also knew that it would be a day just the way she wanted it to be. She decided that she would use all the strength which the muscles of her fate could give. And, with that thought in mind, she quietly fell asleep.

All around her, a dense fog spread, in which nothing could be seen. Already in the next moment, a mysterious wind blew which dispersed the mystical fog, and before her eyes, the magnificent Golden Temple was revealed. Hanna couldn't believe her eyes. She was there, again! Impatiently, she ran through its doors and with a look, searched for ... her. She immediately found her. She was sitting on her golden throne, calm and beautiful as always.

"Shanti, finally!" Hanna cried and ran to embrace her.

"Hello, Hanna," smiled the Ruler, and returned her hug.

"Where have you been so long?? Do you know, how many times in the past months I have called you?" said Hanna, almost desperately.

"Here I am. And, you didn't call me; you called yourself," replied Shanti, mysteriously.

Hanna asked, slightly confused: "What do you mean, myself?"

"You got lost, not me. I've been here the whole time, ready to come to your aid whenever you might have needed me. And now you need me," replied the Ruler.

"But, Shanti, I needed you much earlier ..." replied Hanna, almost reproachfully.

"As a matter of fact, you didn't," said Shanti. "You didn't need me for the things you did and thought about upon returning home."

"What do you mean?" Hanna was perplexed.

"The day, when you returned home, you fell into a crack, which a lot of people who dream fall into, and later on, they're never able to make their dreams come true. You began to dream, but at the same time, you lost your sincere desire for work and growth," answered Shanti.

"But I wrote down my dreams! The dreams I wanted for myself!" replied Hanna, slightly rebelliously.

Shanti continued: "That's true, but then you got stuck in the quicksand and you weren't able to move your legs. You got caught up in your daydream and weren't really moving, which would put into motion the hands of the clock of your charismatic future. You got stuck in the false conviction that you were fulfilling your dreams just because you were aware of them. But you weren't. Awareness is not enough. You know, my crown belonged to me because I was the legal heir. But a crown on the head of a woman does not mean that she is a queen. Queens are not born. They are made. With work."

Every single woman has dreams. Every one of them, deep down inside, in truth, knows what she wants. Her inner 'little girl' bubbles over at the wish and thought of what she could become as well as what she could have. Every woman is capable of imagining her dream life and everything else that goes along with it. Why? Because dreams are free. They don't cost anything. They're here. Everywhere around. You can see them on every corner. If they don't see them themselves, then huge corporations make sure that they do. They show them the most beautiful and ideal pictures, which of course, they want to incorporate into their own lives. That's how their wishes are created every day, every hour, every second. The whole time, new information is finding its way into their heads and creating ideas about a beautiful, better, and possibly even a different life. As a matter of fact, this is how women wind up getting a whole lot of ideas about what they want. But you can't live just from ideas about dreams, can you? No, not at least on this planet you can't. Try this, the next time you go and put gas in your car at the gas station. When the sales-person asks if you would like to pay by card or by cash, reply: "You know what, I don't have any money, but I have an idea about it. I reckon that'll be enough." It would be interesting to hear their answer, wouldn't it?

You know, the whole thing about dreams, in truth, is a little more complicated than what we see at first glance. But not because of the dreams themselves, as they are otherwise very simple. They become complicated because of the dreamers – the people who dreamed them. If they want their dreams to come true, they have to harmonize a number of different areas of themselves and their lives. Dreams are just ideas in themselves. They are only able to become real when we connect them in the right way with the world in which we live and work.

However, it's possible for every dream to come true in many different ways. This is one of the wonderful things about this world. It gives us tremendous room to maneuver, that we ourselves decide on the style of life we want, and the way we go about it. And precisely because of this freedom in choosing the way we realize our dreams do dreamers get caught up in illusions about making them happen. That's why so many potential Queens actually never make them come true. Because your dreams are too important for you not to make them come true. It's time you get acquainted with your illusions, and truly understand what's necessary for your plane of dreams to take off:

The Illusion Of Daydreaming

When people find their way to their dreams, in a moment's notice, thousands and thousands of unbelievable thoughts and feelings are triggered in them, making them feel exceptional. Why does this happen? Because your heart draws your attention to your real dreams, which then trigger in you feelings of happiness, excitement, and longing, which are similar to the feelings of being in love. Well, as a matter of fact, they are feelings of being in love. Being in love with your dreams. But, for you to be able to understand them, you have to somehow define them, which you usually do by trying to understand them. When you continue to think about them, other feelings and mental images appear, which means that the energy anchors even more into reality. So far, your life on the outside hasn't changed at all, has it? Only some of your feelings have changed, which you will feel, as a matter of fact, at the time when you make your dreams come true. They have been given to you in advance for some insight to let you understand why you're doing what you're doing so that you'll be able to create enough motivation in the present.

So, you already have some of the feelings now. You feel them throughout your whole body, and they're so very real. And, whenever you think of them, you also feel them. And now, the time has come to roll up your sleeves and physically make these dreams come true. And now comes the not-so-fun-part. If you want to otherwise make your new dreams come true, you'll have to change your actions, habits, and way of thinking in your life, which is something that's no longer so pleasant.

Most people otherwise don't like change. They don't want to change. They don't like that they have to act differently, because the thought of such change arouses discomfort and resistance in them. And many of those people would rather avoid that part of fulfilling their dreams. And they do – they stop acting on them and rather return to daydreaming, which doesn't demand any change from them, instead of providing them with the exceptional feelings of fulfillment and a kind of inner happiness.

Some do that for a very long time. Well, until their stomachs start grumbling. Then they usually find out that daydreaming won't fill the refrigerator. If they want to eat, they'll have to do exactly what they previously wanted to avoid – roll up their sleeves and get down to work.

Once, a young girl came to me who was a 'professional' daydreamer. Already at my door, she loudly greeted me and then strongly shook my hand. When I looked her in the eye, I saw sparks in them. She knew what she wanted. And, because she didn't have what she wanted, she didn't know what she was doing wrong. After twenty minutes of explaining what she wanted to achieve and experience, I realized that she had no problems with dreaming, but the actual execution of it all. Specifically, her daily habits represented a challenge to her, which in some way weren't in sync with her vision. When I told her that she had to change some of her habits so she could make her dreams come true, she wanted to convince me that she could somehow, nevertheless, succeed. She thought that she was different from everyone else and that she could succeed just by dreaming. No, sadly, the unemployment office, her bank account, and list of unfulfilled dreams were not of the same opinion – already for the past ten years.

A question for you: Have you ever got caught up in the illusion of daydreaming? Or do you think that thinking about your dreams is the same as making them come true?

The Illusion Of A Free Lunch

A lot of people expect that certain things belong to them. They believe that it's enough for them to exist, to get them. Well, they're right about something: That only their illusion of it exists to them. Nothing in this world is free. You have to pay the price for every single thing. Every dream has its own price. Usually, the bigger they are, the higher the price. Things don't belong to people just because they're 'cool.' If they would really be so 'cool,' they would otherwise already have them. That kind of thinking in this world can be extremely dangerous. Especially because it's subject to the law of exchange, which says that every energy has to somehow return. If you get an apple, give a banana in exchange. If today, we just take and don't give anything back, tomorrow there'll be nothing for you to take. Understand?

Modern man, with regard to this is completely delusional. He was born in nature and realized that in it, there is a lot of wealth. Then one day, he decided to take control of it. And he began to exhaust the natural resources, cut down forests, pollute the water and air, decimate animals, etc. He took and took from nature. And is still taking. And gives almost nothing back. And he doesn't obey the laws of exchange. And one day, there'll be nothing left to take. And what will happen then? His wonderful dreams will come crashing down like a house of cards, as there'll be nothing left, from which to build.

A question for you: Have you perhaps ever got caught up in the illusion of a free lunch? Do you expect something in return for nothing?

The Illusion Of Affirmations

This illusion is one of the most common illusions, where people who dream know that it's necessary to do something for the realization of their dreams, but at the same time don't understand (or don't want to understand), how the entire process of their creation works. So, they make a plan, which is far from perfect, with regards to how they are going to make it come true, but it's actually a little similar to a situation where you would want to drive a car, but don't have any wheels.

Let me first tell you what affirmations are – affirmations are planned and created messages (usually positive), which someone uses to support and fast-track the creation of their dreams. Their purpose is to reprogram the mind of the person to create the appropriate energy, which would make their dreams come true more quickly. Affirmations are usually written in the present, sometimes also in a future tense, but it's important that the person believes in them.

FOR EXAMPLE:

A young, ambitious businesswoman wants her company to expand its business abroad. Within the framework of striving to achieve this goal, she also creates an affirmation, or rather, a thought which would additionally support her way of thinking and, consequently, her actions: "I am successfully and ambitiously running this company." With her, it would just additionally support her mental system in achieving her goal. But, a lot of people at this point fall into the illusion of affirmations. Why? Because an affirmation is just a part of the process of creating dreams.

The normal process of creating dreams goes something like this:

1. The person first finds out what they want.
2. Then, they take care that they see the vision of their dream come true in their minds. Therefore, they dream a little.
3. Then, they make a plan, how to make the dream come true – which includes changes on all levels: on the physical, mental, emotional, and spiritual.
4. Then, they roll up their sleeves and begin working on all

these phases: On the physical level they take care that things actually move; on the mental level, they take care that they start functioning with appropriate thoughts, affirmations, information, and words. On the emotional level, they take care that toxic emotions such as anger, hatred, sadness, etc. do no longer lead them, but positive ones such as passion, happiness, love, etc. And on the spiritual level, they take care that their faith, fundamental convictions and general understanding of themselves are in harmony with each other.

If a person takes into account all parts of this process, they can, in some time, expect the fulfillment of their dreams. A lot of people decide to shorten the path somewhat and try to cut a few corners. Their process or better put, their attempt at creating their dreams looks something like this:

1. First, find out what they want.
2. Then take care that they see the vision of their fulfilled dreams. Therefore, that they dream a little.
3. Then they make a plan, how to make the dream come true – which includes changes at all levels: at the physical, mental, emotional, and spiritual.
4. Then they roll up their sleeves and begin working – however (usually) only on one level - the mental. And then they thunder into the abyss, as they otherwise haven't understood that the road to their dreams is, for certain reasons, one full of twists and turns – to bypass the abysses which lie beneath it.

Most people in the process of creating dreams work only on the mental because it is the simplest. It's very easy to otherwise repeat positive affirmations and nice thoughts. It's very easy to imagine happy relations, a successful career, a high level of self-confidence, etc. But this kind of approach doesn't work. Why? Because if we want to fulfill some dreams, we have to take care that all the levels are aligned. In this case, only the mental level develops because all the other levels are not harmonized, and the energy of their affirmations cannot anchor itself or be consequentially fulfilled. Which means that their dreams are not fulfilled. If you want to fulfill your dreams, use affirmations, but as an addition to the basic process, not as a fundamental part of it. Affirmations without the actions of people will otherwise not realize dreams, even if we spend a lot of time imagining and really want something. On the other side of the world, there are a lot of people who have succeeded without affirmations. How? By working.

A question for you: Have you ever been caught up in the illusion of affirmations? Do you want to make your dreams come true only by thinking about them?

Now that you know those illusions about taking action, which many women with dreams fall into the abyss of unrealized dreams, you can avoid them and take care that you don't find yourself among them. Now you can take care that every day you are making your way closer to your crown, which is waiting for you somewhere, to undertake the necessary work and to make the necessary changes. Dear Queen, you choose your path in life, so choose the one that will actually take you to your dreams.

Down To Earth Dreams

Imagine that dreams are some kind of energy that come from the Universe and that you cannot see, but you know nevertheless exists. They can appear practically out of nowhere, just as they can also, mysteriously, disappear. Thousands and thousands of dreams, thoughts, ideas, inventions, and wishes ... come into contact every day with many women on this wonderful planet. And, also with you. The only signal you get that the energy is with you are the extraordinary feelings, which you feel in your heart and the interesting images you see in your mind. Therefore, these dreams, in the beginning, exist only in you, but not yet in your physical life. If you want that they also exist there, you have to ground them. In other words, you have to take care that they come true.

How to do that? By taking action. That you do everything in your power to make them happen. That you use all your thoughts on how to do it, all gadgets available to you, all information, the people around you, etc. In other words – that you give it your all.

A good example of this is top athletes. I know a few of them myself. These girls devote and invest most of their time, energy and, in the beginning of their careers, also money, into their sport. And then they give everything they have to achieve the results they want, by putting the rest of their lives to the side, including nutrition, free time, socializing, fun, etc. All are subordinate to their goals. They train 'in the heat of the sun,' and they train 'in the pouring rain.' They train physically, and they train psychologically. Then, they find experienced professionals (coaches, physiotherapists, doctors, nutritionists, psychologists, masseuses, etc.) and also begin working in conjunction with them. All so that they would make their dreams come true. Professional athletes know what is important if they want to succeed and achieve their goals. They know what their dreams demand. So, in accordance with their plan, they train and train – they work, and they work. They are otherwise professional in making their dreams come true. Just like you are. You also have all the talent and possibilities inside of you to achieve everything you want. However, it's up to you. The Universe believes in you, which is why, already from the start, it sent you a dream. However, do you believe it? And more importantly, are you prepared to prove it? If your answer is yes, here are some key steps that will become a red carpet to lead you to your throne.

1. STEP: *Jump Into The Water And Swim.*

A lot of women who decide to change their lives, think about it too much and don't take enough action. Many want to learn to swim on land, which is impossible. If you want to learn to swim, you have to jump into the water. Before doing so, check to see if the water is deep enough; the rest you will work out as you go. Don't try and learn everything necessary for the fulfillment of your dreams before you actually begin to start fulfilling them. In that way, you'll never even start. You can't learn everything in the beginning, just as you can't get all the answers. Most of the things that are necessary are things you'll learn in-between, while you swim. So, stop procrastinating. Start as soon as possible. Start now. When "you jump into the water," you'll already begin to make your dreams come true. Do you know the difference between someone who has a dream but doesn't make it happen and someone who doesn't have a dream at all? Nothing.

2. STEP: Take Advantage Of All Opportunities – That's What They're For.

Making your dreams come true is, as a matter of fact, your responsibility. You decide on them, and you do all the necessary work as well as reap the rewards. So, decide that you'll do everything in your power to make them happen. Most people don't make their dreams happen because they limit themselves to social rules, for example, to an eight-hour workday. If you take a closer look at successful businesswomen, who follow their dreams, you will see that in some phase of the fulfillment of their goals, they work a lot more than eight hours a day, as well as also working over the weekends. They truly put in the effort and grab hold of everything available to them to help them climb to the top – they upgrade their knowledge, learn new skills, get to know like-minded people, connect with them, research new work opportunities, think about innovations, how they can speed up things, optimize, simplify, etc. ... they use all resources that are available to them.

3. STEP: From a Gray Mouse into a Colorful Peacock.

If you want to make your dreams come true, focus and show the world: "Here I am, and here are my dreams." A lot of women dream of a different life, but when you encourage them to say it out loud, they blush and step backwards. They become ashamed and don't want to talk about it. How can they then possibly make it happen? Be aware that you're the main energy carrier of your dreams. You are their face. So, get out there and speak about them, and show them to the world! And what'll happen if you do this? The world will notice you and offer you help. Dozens and dozens of singers were discovered because that once 'ordinary' girl made a video which she then uploaded onto the Internet, and which then fell into the hands of the right person. However, there are a lot more such girls who have the voice of an angel, but the world will never hear because they hide behind four walls. Expose yourself. Promote your dreams. Who knows, maybe the next person who crosses your path will be able to help you make them come true.

4. *STEP: Be Flexible ... Like Chewing Gum.*

Chewing gum changes shape, doesn't it? You can stretch it in all directions, or you can stick it into a crack, as it is incredibly adaptive. That's how you have to be. Learn how to adapt. If your dreams demand that you quickly turn to the left, then immediately turn to the left. A lot of people don't make their dreams come true because they're too rigid. The world demands some kind of different approach from them, but they would like to do things 'the old way.'

Sometimes you can see some older woman who hasn't kept up with the times. Many among them have not learned the rules of the new age, so they don't understand the world in which they live. As a consequence, they're also incapable of making their dreams come true.

One day I was standing in line at an ATM, and there was an older woman in front of me. She took her bank card out, and then she just stood there. When I asked her if everything was alright, she replied that she didn't know what to do. She said she used to go to the post office where she had a savings account, but that now her son had ordered a bank card for her, but he didn't tell her how it worked. I reassured her that it was a lot simpler than it looked at first glance, then advised her to go to the bank, where they would explain everything to her. The lady didn't move ahead with the times. She remained caught up in the past, and as a consequence, she wasn't able to function anymore. Make sure that this doesn't happen to you. The world is changing very quickly, so change with it. Observe it, try to understand it, ask, and be curious so that these changes won't surprise you too much, catching you unaware, as you'll always know, 'how' and 'what.'

5. *STEP: Don't Forget to Have Fun.*

Most people who dream give up before they get to the end of their goal, because they don't have fun while pursuing their dreams and because the whole thing becomes overly stressful as well as completely uninteresting. It's not very pleasant if you have to invest your time, energy, and money into something that doesn't make you happy, and so, you very quickly lose your motivation. It's true that you have to have a responsible attitude towards your goals, which doesn't necessarily mean that you can't have fun. Look at fulfilling your dreams, like playing with children - you take care of them and make sure they're safe, but at the same time, you still have fun. In this way, you'll never run out of energy, as the fun 'system,' which is self-sustaining - uses energy, but at the same time creates more. If you have fun while fulfilling your dreams, so too will the line between work and play be a bit more blurry - you'll begin to have fun, while you're working. Which is entirely different from just 'plain-old-boring-work,' right?

6. *STEP: Obstacles Along the Way in Truth Don't Actually Exist.*

A lot of people who dream quit because of the obstacles they come across on the way. It seems that the holes in the ground in front of them are too wide to jump over or go around and that they're too high to be climbed, etc. For some strange reason, most people want to separate the path from the obstacles on it, in the same way they would like to separate a hole in the road from the road itself, which is impossible because the hole doesn't actually exist – that's just a part of the road itself. There are actually no obstacles in the way. It's just that kind of path. From where, then, is the thinking that the path to the fulfillment of your dreams has to be smooth and peaceful? Surely not from nature. Nature has the richest and most colorful environment on the planet, but nowhere will you find smooth and peaceful paths - no mountain wall is straight and without cracks, no sea without waves, no rainforest has naturally walked paths, etc., so such paths are not even the paths, that lead to your dreams. Along some, you'll be able to walk faster, along others slower. Some holes you'll simply jump over, while others you won't be able to, so you'll have to find another path. But, there are never obstacles. That's just the path.

7. STEP: A Strong Body for Strong Dreams.

Fulfilling any kind of dream demands physical effort from you. And once again: The bigger the dreams, the greater the effort they require, which then creates the need for a strong body. A physical body is the main tool for fulfilling your dreams. It allows you to physically move, it allows you to actually do some tasks, as well as translating all mental, emotional, and intuitive energy. In this way, all the energy that's needed for fulfilling a specific goal flows through the body. That's why it's important to be able to accomplish the goals you have. Some goals will possibly demand from you that you have to run a marathon, that you take five trips a month, that you have to read a new book every week, that you have to work sixteen hours a day ... and if you're not in good enough physical condition, you won't be able to get the job done. So: If you want to really take care of the foundation of your dreams, make sure that your physical body is rested, strong and healthy. Eat fresh and nutritious food, drink enough water, get enough sleep, stretch your body by doing yoga, swim, run, dance, etc. Spend a lot of time out in the fresh air, or go and have a massage, etc. Make sure that you'll be healthy and flexible.

I saw this very clearly in myself. When I began doing seminars and workshops, my body was in good shape for a twenty-five-year-old ex-athlete, which meant that I was able to do all the usual things without any problems. Then, I began to do multi-day seminars with larger groups of people. I'll never forget my first two-day seminar - I needed four days to recover so that my energy levels came back to where they should have been. My body was exhausted, as the whole time, it had to translate high levels of mental, emotional, and spiritual energy, which literally 'burned me out.' At the time, I decided to initiate concrete change, with yoga, running, and my diet, etc. Today, my body is strong and steady. With it, I can fulfill all the dreams I have. Yes, sometimes, I'm tired, but I never find myself in circumstances where I would be physically incapable of functioning. Take care of yourself. At some point in your life, you'll be grateful.

8. *STEP: The Most Important Step - Don't Give Up Until You Reach Your Target!*

You know, there are thousands of ways you can fulfill your dreams. Your job is to find the one that best suits you. And whichever one you choose, decide on that path to your dreams, and never give up. If you're active and are moving forward, you'll always have the possibility, but if you stop, you won't have any chance, anymore.

Thousands of women around the world live average lives, which they don't like because they've given up. Because they gave in and lost hope. And many among them had big dreams, with which they could have changed the world, which never saw the light of day because they accepted just one decision - to give up. Know that as long as you persist and strive, you'll still be in the game, and you'll still have a chance of 'winning.' If you want your crown strong enough, where you'll reign over your own life, instead of looking for excuses, focus on finding solutions. Quitting is usually just an excuse.

Here, of course, two scenarios exist, where you can give up without feeling guilty: When you make your dreams come true, or in the case that you realize that the current path is not quite the right one - of course, in that case, you need to find the right one. Queen never stop on your path to your dreams. You're a lot closer than you think. Know that when you became aware of your dreams that you were already half-way there. Your crown is not as far away as you sometimes think.

Three Cat-Burglars

These steps, dear Queen, can help you achieve your dreams faster and with greater ease. Just about every one of them is important, so think about how to include them in your journey to your crown. But beware - your crown is an extremely valuable thing, and there are often lots of cat-burglars around, who want to steal it from under your nose and make sure that it will never find its way to the top of your head. Many women who embark on the pursuit of their dreams don't know what these cat-burglars look like, so they don't even recognize them. Therefore, in the lines that follow, you'll get a detailed description of all three, so that you'll be able to recognize them in an instant if they want to cross your path. These three cat-burglars are called Laziness, Procrastination, and Self-sabotage.

The First Crown Cat-Burglar: Laziness

This one is responsible for most burgled crowns. It slowly approaches you, sits down on your legs, and makes them so heavy that you can't even move them. Then, it slowly grabs your arms and your whole body, all until you give up and don't move anywhere. If you want to get up, it slowly whispers in your ear: "You can't be bothered." At first, you resist a little, then you begin to slowly believe it. Have you ever met this cunning cat-burglar? Has it ever crossed your path? You can only escape it by setting a trap, which is called disciplined action. Laziness is rather slow, while disciplined action is a lot faster. That's why it'll never be able to catch you again. It's just not fast enough.

The Second Crown Cat-Burglar: Self-Sabotage

This cat-burglar is an evil aunt, which, when you're at the bottom, first picks you up, then pushes you so that you fall back down. It was the one who baked you all those desserts, which you ate when you lost all that weight. It was the one who made all those calls, accepting invitations to wild parties, which you got just as you were studying for your upcoming exam. It first helped you create something, then destroyed it. Self-sabotage always comes to visit when you take on new decisions and are already forging new habits, then it awakens in you a false feeling that you can stop and reward yourself with a small indiscretion, which in truth will push you back and ruin all that good work done. You can only run away from self-sabotage if you take care that your values and convictions are stronger than the temptations which it offers you. You can fight it successfully with advanced types of combat and by telling your best friend all about your decisions. When self-sabotage comes to visit again, your friend will shut the door and take care that its offered temptations don't find their way to you.

The Third Crown Cat-Burglar: Procrastination

This cat-burglar is very cunning, as it can very elegantly convince you that you have all the time in the world. Its words are so sweet and convince you that you're in no hurry. In the end, you believe that you're actually immortal and that all your dreams and goals will always be waiting for you. It even convinces you that time doesn't count, so it takes you by the hand and takes you to the comfortable armchair of the present, from which you truly see how your future is all the more shorter and the possibilities for fulfilling your dreams are all the more smaller. Maybe you know this cat-burglar? Has it ever wanted to take you by the hand and slow you down? If it ever gets close to you and wants to slow you down, you can save yourself by writing down the tasks you have to do every day in the morning, then by not going to sleep until you have done them all.

So, Queen, now you have all the necessary tools that people who fulfil their dreams need. Every Queen. Now, roll up your sleeves, activate your brain, use your talents, and make your dreams come true. The whole world around you is here to support you. From now on, unrealized dreams are only a vague memory from the past, which you can erase every day and replace them with new images of the crown on your head and scepter in your hand.

"You are not born a Queen, you become one. By working on it."

Hanna opened her eyes. Even though it was already morning and that one of the sun's rays was shining through the crack in the blinds directly into her eye, one light that morning was even stronger. The light of a sincere desire. She wasn't even aware of how very much she needed Shanti. These past months she had been feeling so alone. Just like she had most of her life.

The relationships with her classmates after the expedition had cooled down somewhat, as each of them had chosen their own path. She didn't even see Peter anymore, as he had already completed all of his obligations at university and had gone to New York, where he took a job in a well-known museum. She was happy for him but missed someone believing in her when she wasn't able to do it herself. Although she was aware that she was responsible for her own life, the feeling that someone was standing by her side was nevertheless an important pillar in her House of Happiness. And today, Shanti once again appeared. Beautiful, friendly, and strong. Just as she always was. She was once again there. With her, which filled Hanna with tremendous inner strength. She felt as if she had once again found herself, after having been lost and wandering the desert of missing dreams, looking for a drop of water, which would bring those dreams back to life. She jumped out of bed, almost ran to the bathroom of her small apartment, and stared into the mirror.

"Hanna, that's enough!" thoughts flooded through her mind. "Your life is like a broken mirror and doesn't even closely resemble what you want. You've let yourself go, you eat unhealthily, you don't even know where your dream of archeology has disappeared to, and every morning you wake up grumpy, and above all ... alone. Look at yourself, you're no longer a child, you're a grown woman! What are you doing with your life? Everything else except what you should be doing. You have so much promise, but promise can only get you so far. Of course, you can do whatever you want with your

life, but don't drown in your own tears and don't expect that complaining will save you. Did anyone force you to start working at the restaurant again? No. You decided. Did anyone convince you not to apply for work at university? No, you didn't apply for it, and you didn't send it. So, what do you want now? Consolation? OK, I can pat your hand and sympathize with you for what has happened, but it won't change your life. But I can also tell you what I see - I see a woman who can do what needs to be done. Now, you've got two options: You can go back to bed with greasy hair and get all angry at yourself and everyone around you, or you can get yourself together, put your hair into a ponytail and start a new chapter in your life. So, what are you going to choose? Your bed or a magic fountain pen?"

Hanna stared at herself in the mirror as if she was hypnotized. She didn't know what had just happened. It seemed as if her reflection was talking to her. For the first time ever, she was so openly and directly confronted by someone. And above all, by someone, she knew like no one else in the world - by herself. She looked straight into her own green eyes, which were sparkling. Sparkling with life.

Mission no. 11:

The Signpost from a Dead-End Street

Hanna went for a run that morning, like every other for the past two months. The cold March wind clung to her face, but after having run six miles, her body was blanketed by a pleasant warmth. First, she ran to Boston Harbor, where she usually did some jumping-jacks, pushups, and stretches, drank a cup of hot chocolate at the nearby canteen, then once again ran back home. But not that morning. That morning, the chocolate just didn't appeal to her. Instead of some sweet indulgence, she sat on the bench by the harbor and gazed out to sea. Running usually cleared her mind, but today, despite the freshness of the morning, there was a real hustle and bustle going on in her head. She was restless. She gazed out towards the harbor, where some brave sailboat owners were sailing out into the cold sea, trusting that they would also bring them safely back. She watched how the white sails so simply and easily cut into the air above the water's surface. "If only it were that easy," she said to herself.

She didn't know what she was doing wrong. She was looking for an answer in the vast Atlantic Ocean, which stretched out behind the airport that proudly stood before it. Over the past two months, she had completely changed her life, and convinced those hands, which Shanti spoke of, which were finally moving things on the clockface of her life. She began to take better care of herself; every morning she ran, she began to eat more healthily, and she even tried to meditate. She began to clean up after herself, her apartment was 'spic and span' the whole time, and she diligently did all she had to at the new restaurant she began working at after she was made redundant at the old one. And, she also changed most of her bad habits.

But something gave birth to more and more worries every single day - the fact that for two months there had been no response from the university. Finally, she sent a letter to the head of the university, requesting a position as an assistant for archeology, but hadn't received a response. Despite the fact that Mark wrote her a really good recommendation. She also sent dozens of e-mails to archaeological societies, museums, and similar organizations in several cities, even one three hundred miles away in New York, asking if there were any vacant positions for lecturers, researchers or even reporters, but all the replies that came back tore her soul to pieces, and were like the last one she received: "Dear Madam, thank you for your inquiry. We are currently not looking for any co-workers, but we will enter you in our database and will be happy to invite you to apply for a position when a suitable opportunity opens up."

She was really trying. In her spare time, she read about the well-known work of archaeologists and researchers, learned about all kinds of things that were at least slightly related to archeology, and even created a blog where she wrote down her findings and point of view. Nothing. She even created her own profile as a young archeologist on all possible social networks and started connecting with other people in the field. Nothing. She called journalists and newspapers to see whether she could write professional or even popular scientific articles. Nothing. She seemed to be wasting hours and hours a day on something which would never lead to blessing the fulfillment of her deepest desires. And now, everything was pointing to the fact that she was wasting her time on something that would never eventuate. She had nothing concrete in her hand. Nothing that would comfort her, letting her know that she was on the right track. She felt lost. And most of all, frightened. The signpost of life, like so many times before, had also this time led her down a dead end.

She was barely earning enough at the restaurant to cover her rent and food. At the end of the month, two-hundred, hard-fought dollars remained, which she had to carefully consider how to spend, if at all. While all of this was going through her head, she wasn't even aware that she had been sitting on a bench all drenched in sweat from the run for more than twenty minutes, and that she was seriously cold. The cold began to wrap itself around her, and she felt something else in her bones: Fear. What should she do if she doesn't succeed? It's one thing to have dreams, but to make them come true is really difficult, requiring an iron will. Yes, she wanted it more than anything, but she wondered if she would be able to make it at all. It seemed terribly difficult at times.

She started to cry. Warm tears streamed down her face, and at that moment, she felt like someone was missing in her life, to hug and reassure her that everything would be alright. She needed a friend, who's shoulder she could rest her head on. Far away on the horizon, a sailboat with a white sail was drifting along, all alone. It cut through the waves like it wasn't afraid of any lonely voyage. It left just a small trail behind it in the vast ocean. Hanna felt just like that - alone in the middle of the big world. Absentmindedly staring out into the distance, she was suddenly awakened: "Wait a minute, once upon a time I felt that ... but where?"

Her brain forced the rusty wheels of her memory into action, and she began to search from where this déjà vu came: "Exactly! In Egypt, during the first weeks of the expedition. Exactly."

Her thoughts carried her away to the hot desert. She remembered how she walked away from it, a proud woman. "Well," she told herself, "if I could do it then, then I can do it now. My butterflies of transformation haven't yet said all they have to say."

Then, something else came to mind - a conversation with Mark. The memory of it became clearer and clearer, all until the fog of oblivion finally vanished. Word after word began to dance about in her mind, so vividly in fact that it seemed as if she was actually standing in front of him again and listening to the words he said to her on the last night of the expedition.

She couldn't believe how vividly she remembered him, and the echo, as real as she was herself, that told her: "And quite often, it's determined by the person himself. I learned that I can rely on myself at any time, while everything else around me is subject to change."

It was only then that she realized what Mark had wanted to tell her, which then instilled in her a new desire and lit the almost extinguished fire of love for her own life. Although she hadn't understood things more than five minutes earlier, inside, she felt a touch better about herself. She still didn't know what she should change, but the energy within her once again lifted the head of the sleeping dragon of will and courage. She got up off the bench, almost thanked it for being her confidant for a moment, stretched a little, then ran back. The sun had already warmed the landscape, although Hanna's breath was still visible in the cold air as it exited her mouth. That day, she absentmindedly traveled the world of her thoughts. Usually, she liked to talk to the diners she was serving, but today she just stuck to the usual polite phrases, which gave her more time for what she had to learn.

In the evening, she came home tired, unaware that a number of guardian angels were hovering about her, enabling her to arrive home safely. Even though she had worked the whole day, the feelings she had from that morning still did not leave her. One part of her was still eager to work through and explore all the possibilities, while the other part was tired, not to mention scared, like never before. The memory of Mark's words gave her new hope, which was, however, constantly shattered by the truth that she was investing in work that she didn't want to invest in.

She put on her pajamas, went into the kitchen, and, five minutes later, slipped into bed with some hot chamomile tea. It was one of her favorite moments of the day - when she was finally able to close herself off from the world and hide in the safe refuge of her blanket. In the background, some relaxing,

Tibetan bowl music was quietly playing, which, during recent weeks, she had been unwinding to after busy days, and to which she had all the more often fallen asleep. Despite having a few unresolved things in her mind and an uncomfortable feeling of fear in her muscles, her body began to relax and sink into a state of deep relaxation. The warm chamomile did what it does best, and the heavenly drink once again began to work its magic. Just like her mother used to say.

It was getting harder and harder to keep her eyes open. "Will I make it?" was the last question she asked herself as she said goodbye to the day, then put her empty cup on the nightstand, pulled the blanket up to her chin, and fell asleep.

Once again, her nostrils were aroused by the intoxicating scent of jasmine. Taking one step at a time, she walked down a paved path made of white stones, which wound around the Golden Temple, leading to a beautiful garden, encircled by breathtaking blue azaleas. Hanna looked around and knew she was around somewhere. The jasmine had given her away. And she really was. She was sitting on a golden bench at the end of the white path. Beautiful as ever. Shanti!

"Hello, Hanna!" Shanti said.

"Shanti!" Hanna said out aloud and ran to her like a child who had lost her mother in the crowd for a moment and then saw her again. "Oh, how I've missed you."

"How are you, my dear friend?" Shanti continued.

"What should I say ..." Hanna replied. "I don't know what I'm doing. I thought I was doing everything right, but the finish line is nowhere to be seen. And instead of the joy in fulfilling my dream, I feel doubts and fears."

not. Dreams are really never really about that; those things are just a wonderful addition at the end of the journey. A nice extra reward for all the effort. The real results of dreams that have been reached are something else - the realization of oneself: A strong character that the dreamer develops along the way, the solid and pure values he forms, and the insights into the depths through which he must go if he wants to express himself the best, etc. This is what the soul seeks out during the experience of what we call on Earth 'The Realization of Dreams.' Many of the women I've worked with, came face-to-face with the true purpose of their journey for the first time, during my workshops. Once they understood what they were really looking for, they were simply able to face up to, and deal with, all their difficult ordeals.

So, it's about experiencing. Experiencing everything. The good and the 'not so good.' What do I mean by 'the not so good'? Already a millennia ago, people determined that the only things that are pleasant are those that are good and desirable, for example: Feelings of happiness, love, joy, acceptance, enthusiasm, etc., and for some reason, they began to reject all other feelings, such as, for example: Doubts, fears, disappointment, anger, etc., which have always been avoided and even labeled as bad and unwanted. Because they simply didn't understand why they were important. But know the following - unpleasant feelings are just as important as pleasant ones. Why? Because it's only the presence of all emotional aspects that we're able to see the complete and true picture of a person and the circumstances in which he finds himself. Only then can we find out who we are and understand what we are truly capable of.

Sunrise

If you want to understand your 'light,' then you also have to understand your 'dark.' How do you know if something is good if you don't know what's bad? How can the day begin if there was no night before? A day without a night would not even be a day. How can you know what faith is, if you've never doubted it? To understand all things, both aspects are necessary, just like the light and the dark. Even though most people reject the dark, they learn the fastest in it. It's easy to work 'in the sun' - it's warm, and everything is clear. Working in the dark is a little different because it demands that you work harder. A lot of things that are taken for granted in the light, no longer exist in the dark. The dark no longer offers you a clear picture, so you have to adapt to it somehow, to continue on working. This means that you're somehow 'forced' to develop those parts of you that you would not need to develop in the light. The dark requires that you learn to act differently; that you learn new rules. Because that's the only way you can survive in it. Only in this way you can light a fire that will keep you warm so that you can hold out until morning when the sun will shine again on your life and give you your light.

And when morning does come, you'll be different. Your outlook on things will be different, your strength will be different, and your confidence will be different. Everything about you will be different. Stronger. The night will polish you, sharpen you, and awaken the best in you. I know a woman who, as she put it herself, had many 'dark nights of the soul.' Sometimes, it seemed as if her life was nothing but darkness, without any light. A loss of health. Bankruptcy. The death of her mother. An attempt at suicide. A few years of pure darkness, surrounded the energies of fear, doubt, disappointment, etc. Then dawn came. And with tired eyes, she saw the glow for the first time in a long time. But that was when she was strong. What made her a winner was not the day, but the dark, cold night. And from that moment onwards, she has been able to appreciate and enjoy life. That woman is my wife.

And now a question for you. Is a night, full of fears and doubts still 'bad'? Or is it perhaps a blessing that can help you become what you're truly capable of becoming, looking at things from a different perspective? Decide for yourself. But don't forget that a day without night does not exist.

Pain - Friend or Foe?

The wisest leaders know their nights. They know their fears and doubts and also understand them, which gives them the power to accomplish whatever it is they want. And so, they're unstoppable. Yes, doubts and fears are important. Exactly the same as courage and faith.

FOR EXAMPLE: You want to feel good in your body, right? You probably don't like it when something hurts. Then comes the physical pain, which ends that period of feeling good. Or did the pain come as a friend, rather than as an enemy? You know that pain is uncomfortable. You know you want to get rid of it as soon as possible. What then, is pain? A friend who lets you know that something is not quite right in your body, as a reminder that you have to do something better. That's what pain really is - a blessing from the Universe that helps you become better.

People don't know how to cope with their doubts and fears because they fill them with emotional and even physical pain. Because they instinctively want to avoid pain, they instinctively avoid doubts and fears. But they can't escape them. Doub and fears are the basic building blocks of every person's emotional system. They can't be removed, just as you can't remove your gut from your body. It's simply a part of you. And a part of you is also doubt and fear.

So, dear Queen, it's time to open your doors wide and invite your doubts and fears in for coffee and cookies; take the time to get to know them and accept them, which will lead you to a better understanding of yourself. The better you understand yourself, the freer you'll become.

Fears

Ego - The Blacksmith ff Fear

Some human behavior is really simple: For example, that you're not afraid of things you understand and vice-versa, that the things you don't understand, create feelings of fear inside you. Why? Because of ego. When you embody yourself in your life, you develop a kind of system - a 'lower self' that helps you to adapt and survive in your new environment. Ego's first task, in other words, the 'lower self,' is to protect you from anything that might endanger or hurt you.

Ego's second task is to provide you with information about your environment, based upon which you make decisions.

As a baby, you didn't have a developed ego. Simply because you had no experience of the world you were born into. So, you didn't know how to recognize real danger. But then you started to experience things and found out that some of these things are useful to you, while others are harmful. So, you started to develop some unpleasant feelings, including fears, in relation to those things which hurt you. Over time, however, your ego began to gain importance in your life. You began to move away from your soul and follow your ego more and more because it had the necessary information for you about 'how' and 'what.' Your ego grew stronger, and it became an increasing source of information for you.
However, the ego is very 'egoistic.' If it becomes really powerful, it wants to rule over all other systems. And so, it usually acknowledges only what it already knows, that is, what you've already experienced. It protects itself from all other and unknown things by ensuring that you don't touch them or bother them. This makes you fearful of them. If you think back, you'll realize that over time, you've developed and acquired more and more fears. Therefore, adults have more fears than children. Because their egos are more developed, which then try to turn them away from the things they don't know. That's why people are afraid of things unknown.

"Fight or Flight"

The ego is basically a very good thing. In fact, it's your very good friend - if you understand it. If you don't, it can turn from a good friend into an annoying grump. As a friend, it helps you stay alive and unharmed. Who do you think triggers a responsive reaction when you accidentally touch something that you shouldn't on the hotplate? Your ego. It's developed a defense system we call 'fight or flight,' which simply means that when your ego senses danger, your body physiologically adjusts in an instant to be ready to fight, or to escape from that danger. That's when your heart rate increases, blood circulates throughout your body and fills your muscles in your arms and legs, enabling you to fight, or run away. In other words: So, you can stay alive.

The feelings that arise within the body are what we've called 'fears.' In the past, when there were still predators that were a threat to humans, this was great. With fears, our egos made sure we weren't eaten by 'dinosaurs.' These days, this same ego response protects you so that, for example, at the last moment, you get out of the way of the roof tile which the wind has lifted from the roof, or the car, whose driver has lost control and is hurtling towards you. But these days, there are no dinosaurs around, nor are there so many life-threatening situations. But our egos are still with us, and they still do their job. Unfortunately, most people, most of the time, do themselves a disservice. Why? Because it no longer tries to protect them from justified dangers, but also from unjustified ones.

Look at how it works: The ego wants to protect its protector from danger, in this case, you. And what's the danger for it? Everything it doesn't know. Because of all the things it already knows, it doesn't need to worry because it knows they're no longer dangerous as it already has some experience about them. It knows how to survive around them. The challenge, however, is in the new things it doesn't yet have in its memory, or the things it knows nothing about. New things that happen ... for the first time. That's why you're afraid when you start achieving your goals and dreams. Your soul wants something new, and it wants new experiences that'll bring new meaning. New dreams and goals, however, require new approaches, new people, and different actions - all things that your ego has no information about. Therefore, they're perceived as potential danger. Therefore, it preventatively triggers fear. But, in the vast majority of cases, it does so totally unjustified. This fear, in many people, is so intense that they stop and never end up realizing their dreams. The ego honestly wanted to help, but because people didn't understand what was really going on, they gave up on their dreams rather than face their fears and therefore understand it.

A lot of women, all around the world, are terrified of apparent fears. But often, this apparent energy becomes real. A frightened woman always makes decisions that are built around circumstances that only confirm her fear. And so, a frightened woman usually forms a relationship with a partner she consciously or subconsciously fears, starts a job where she faces challenges that scare her and acts so that she is more susceptible to injuries and disasters, which only add to the confirmation that the world around her, is really dangerous ...
And now Queen, a question for you. Do you want to live in fear? A world not driven by fear is far more charismatic and beautiful than one that is. Understand that you, too, deserve peace and a life that will encourage you, not frighten you. So, it may be time to talk about your fears and deal with them. May they help you fulfill your dreams, not the other way around. It may be that in the beginning, your fear appears to be truly frightening or even scary and facing it might even shake you up. But when you look behind the veil of your ego, you realize that the truth is completely different; most of all, it's very bright.

The Veil of the Ego

It's all about some kind of invisible headgear that you have either worn yourself, or that's worn by some others to hide the truth from those who seek it; that is, from yourself. The best way for your ego to stop you is to deprive you of hope when you need it the most. When you work, you grow, you make decisions, and you look for solutions. That's why it's important for you to understand when it's day and when it's night. Closing yourself off to a windowless room during the day and turning off the light doesn't mean that it's nighttime. You already know how to act when fear legitimately protects you from life's dangers. It's written in your cells. That's when you respond instinctively. But it's important to know how to act when you're overwhelmed by fear that's not real. Fear, which in truth is ... veiled by your ego.

So, how do you remove the veils from your ego and deal with the fear?

1. **Calm yourself down and accept it.**

   Fear is a part of you. So, accept it and relax. Admit that you're scared. We live in a rather strange society, which says that it's weak to show that you're afraid, that's why so many people try to hide it. Outwardly, they show that they're strong, while inwardly they're shaking. But everyone who has a heart feels fear. It's one of the most basic emotions there is, and there's no heroine around who doesn't feel it. It has scared presidents, Olympic champions, and even rock stars ... so, you've also got the right to be scared. Because it's human. People are sometimes afraid. And you're a person. So, you, too, can be scared. So, never try a suppress your fear, because you can't. Instead, allow yourself to be scared, and it's right to do this. The moment you accept the fact that you might be scared, you'll be able to calm down, and then more than half of all the unpleasant sensations in your body, and even your mind, will subside.

Once, a woman came to me for counseling because of her 'fears', after having found out that her husband was cheating on her. She was totally lost. You could even see it on her face that she didn't know what to do. Her husband was her first and only love; she never thought about other men, nor did she want anyone else. When she found out what was going on, she was crushed. She felt like a bird that had had its wings broken. She was scared. Very scared. She didn't know what was going to happen - whether they would break up, how the children would accept it, what they would do with the house, whether she could ever trust again, etc.

For the first thirty minutes, she just cried. It seemed that she had found herself in a flood of fears. If she wanted to find her way out from it, she had to let herself go. It was time for her to recognize all her emotions. And, in the next hour, we did exactly that - raising the awareness of her fears, talking about them, and even writing them down. At the end of the session, she was quite calm and even smiled at me. She no longer had that uncomfortable feeling in her chest, and she was able to speak normally. Because she no longer resisted her fears, they no longer pressured her, and she could breathe more freely. Even though it was just the beginning of her journey, she was at least calm enough to deal with her situation.

2. **Find out what your fear is telling you.**

Fear is an emotion and just one of many. You have emotions so that you can perceive the world around you on other levels, not just at the level of the mind. Emotions provide you with valuable information about yourself and the world around you. Fear, also. If you understand what fear is able to teach you, you can become one of the most powerful rulers out there. Its teachings are extremely valuable, so much so that they can even decide if you'll become a Queen or a slave. They determine if you'll be happy, or if you won't.

That's why it's so important that you learn how to recognize what the fear you're feeling is really telling you. In most cases, it's that you don't know anything about the matter, or the person. So, it's now your job to round up all the necessary information and insights regarding the circumstances or the people who are causing it. Explore. Ask. Delve deeper.

Some advice: Sometimes, you'll find it difficult to think objectively under the circumstances, as your system of judgment will be filled with fear. So then, it makes things even more objective. Imagine seeing yourself through the eyes of a friend. In that way, you'll see things far more objectively.

When the lady, whose husband was cheating on her, found out at our next session what her fears were telling her, she was more than surprised. They told her she was heavily dependent on other people, especially her husband. She was afraid she wouldn't be able to survive emotionally, or financially, without him, so, of course, she was scared. Because she was aware of the consequences of divorce. Her fear told her that she had to take responsibility for her emotional stability and her financial independence.

3. **Replace fear with action.**

One of the best things about fear is that the more you act, the less you're afraid. And vice versa, of course. Energy triggers action, which is the opposite of fear, and usually stops it. That's why we often say that fear paralyzes you.

This lady really wanted to sort her life out, so she immediately rolled up her sleeves. She started looking for a job where she had long-term prospects for promotion, and she took up playing sports. As she herself said, she found that she was 'hanging' onto her husband too much. So, she made a conscious decision to start taking charge of her life and deciding on everything related to it. It seemed as if she somehow had to grow up. At first, it was quite difficult for her, but eventually her confidence began to grow, which in turn made her more and more emotionally independent and bold in her decisions.

At this point, she canceled our sessions for a while. It was only after about a month that she called me. When she next showed up at my door, there stood a completely 'different' woman than the one I had first met. When I asked her how she was, she replied, "I've got so much work to do on myself that I don't even have time to think about my husband." She was half-joking, but there was also a lot of truth in what she said. Because of all the things she had going on, there simply wasn't enough time for her to be thinking about her fears. She realized that activating and using her creative energy relaxed her. She also told me during our session that she was thinking of going back to school.

There were so many of these activities that it even crossed my mind that she wanted to run away from her actual situation, that is, the unresolved relationship with her husband. When I mentioned this to her, she replied, "Right now, I'm not prepared to discuss his infidelity with him. I feel that what's important right now is that I do what I'm doing." I listened to her and realized she was right. She had been harnessing her strength and was becoming more and more sure of herself, every day. The fear in her eyes was slowly disappearing. As a matter of fact, I admired her how strongly she was able to focus on herself. If you've ever loved, you know how much energy you send to the other person in a relationship. For her, however, it seemed as if the part of herself that had taken care of her marriage had simply been switched off, at least for some time, and that then she was devoting herself to that other part that had been asleep for years and years, which was then starting to awaken and that would turn her into a ruler. All this was going on because she had taken the initiative to become active.

4. Use tricks to focus better.

Magical tricks? If you can cast a spell, you can also do these. But the tricks and things I've got in mind will 'trick' your mind into focusing on the right things and positive things.

When you're confronted with fear, it's very important to keep your mind positively balanced. Fear in itself triggers negative feelings and thoughts that you sometimes have to deal with. But the easiest way to deal with them is to replace them. To make sure that strong, positive thoughts and feelings find their way into your energy. As a human being, you're unable to feel conflicting emotions at the same time. You can't possibly feel fear and peace at the same time. Either you feel one or the other. So, stop focusing on eliminating fear in your life, but on attracting joy and all the associated energy that goes with it. In this way, fear will only be able to stand by and observe how you go on a merry-go round of joy and happiness.

How to do that? When you feel scared, fill your thoughts and emotions with beautiful things:

- Smile. As soon as you do this, cellular memories of joy and happiness are activated inside of you. As a result, serotonin (the happiness hormone), dopamine (the feel-good hormone) and endorphins (pleasure hormones) are released. Once activated, your whole body responds to them, which in turn changes your perceptions, your feelings, and your thoughts. Yes, a smile is much stronger than you think. So much so that it can even bring the strongest fears to its knees.

- Play some relaxing music. It'll lower your cortisol (the stress-producing hormone) so that you can begin to calm down. Calmness is just the opposite of total fright, wouldn't you agree?

- Dance, and have fun while doing it. Movement activates your muscles. Muscle fibers are the most susceptible to the accumulation of fear. That's why most people experience the most uncomfortable feelings of fear in their stomachs and thighs. By stretching and moving, you activate these muscles, which, in turn, change the energy and, as a result, remove the fear created stress.

5. **Surround yourself with the brave.**

Do you know why people love hanging out with each other so much? Because they share their experiences, thoughts, emotions, energy, and... fears with each other. Yes, you've learned about fears. From people who have had and still have a huge impact on your life. As you may have already come to realize, babies don't have a lot of fear. They're not afraid of the dark, of snakes, of people they don't know, of a lack of things, or of thousands of other fears that prevent us, adults, from living to the full.

But, wouldn't you know, twenty or even thirty years later, a fearless baby grows up and turns into an adult woman who's no longer fearless. All of a sudden, she's afraid of the dark, of snakes, of a lack of things, etc. ... but why? Because they taught her to be afraid. Parents, teachers, and some other important individuals raise children and teach them how to live, survive, and succeed. But in addition to a lot of well-intended advice, they inadvertently pass on their fears to them. That's how kids somehow take it on. Not only in their childhood but later on, when they're adults.

You can't choose your parents and teachers, at least from the way we see things down here on Earth. But you can choose your partner, friends, coworkers, and acquaintances. Choose them wisely. Why? Because they'll transmit their energy to you when you socialize with them, including their fear-based energy. That's why it's important that you're surrounded by people who dare to dream, who are active in pursuing their dreams, and who have goals that they achieve. Of course, even these people aren't without fears; they have them just like everyone else, but they understand them and overcome them. Because of this, they'll rarely project their fears upon you, if at all. They'll usually help you to understand and resolve them. However, if you're surrounded by people who have no dreams and who aren't proactive, you run the risk of adopting their way of thinking, occupied by their demons. Because fear is most easily fueled by fear, such people will inadvertently (or even intentionally) awaken in you ... fear. Consequentially, over time, not only will they be frightened, but you will too. How do you recognize them? They're usually complaining and blaming the world around them. And most of all, things aren't going the way they would like them to in their lives.

During our session, the lady who was on her path to awakening was quiet the whole time. When I asked her if she was okay, she said she was simply thinking about the people she spent time with - her best friend was just as scared as she was, just like her mom. What worried her most was that she seemed to be passing on her frightened way of life to her younger daughter, whom she thought up until that point was just a little shy and introverted, but then realized that in fact, she was scared. As was her own 'little girl. ' Only then did she realize how great an impact fear had on her life. That was the point when this lady started to change with lightning speed - she seemed to have woken a protective bear within her who wanted to make sure her cub was safe.

6. **Accept information that supports your dream.**

Today's world is full of information. Thousands upon thousands of terabytes of data are generated every day. Changes are happening all around the world, reported on by TV, newspapers, internet media, and books, etc. The extremely influential media serves the public a lot of nice information, but unfortunately, even more messages which intimidate. They don't give hope to most people, but fear. That's why it's important, dear Queen, to break free from the negative messages. It's extremely difficult to maintain a vision of dreams and motivation if you're "bombarded" every day with images of disasters, wars, manipulation, and other dispiriting things.

Many systems of influence have found fear to be an excellent tool for controlling the masses, so they make good use of it. Decades and decades of intimidation have resulted in the subconscious of most people being filled with fear. They have it written in their DNA.

That's why fear sells so easily. People are interested because they have it in them. When they see those messages, they are basically confirming themselves. But their path leads them downwards.

You, my dear, are going upwards. You need messages that'll give you wings and carry you up to the clouds, right where your dreams are. You need information that'll help you create a better tomorrow and will fill you with positive energy. Some will tell you that this kind of thinking isn't realistic and that you need to know what's going on in the world. It's true that it's good to know the world around you, but you don't have to take on the fears of others that are a part of this information. Fears, which again, are not yours. To do this, you need quality based media (books, websites, movies, etc.) that'll provide you with clean information without unnecessary emotional clutter. Look for them. You'll recognize them because their influence will energize you and help you strengthen your hope and happiness.

Oh yeah, you want to know what happened to that lady? Only nice things. She's proof, yet again, that the Universe supports you in ways that are favorable to you, but only if you act. She and her husband resolved their marriage. Her husband was running away from her, because, for the past ten years, she was no longer the girl he had fallen in love with. She had become a dependent and passive woman who hung onto him and choked him the whole time. However, after the challenge that came into their lives, she was forced to face up to herself. She had to take responsibility for herself and once again become the person she actually was - joyful, happy, and courageous. The changes she made very quickly showed her another reality, as a few months later, her husband invited her to dinner, where they apologized to each other - he, because he ran away, and she, because she had let herself go already many years before and given in. It was time for a fresh start. Together.

Fear is an Indication That You Have a Dream!

By now, you have come to know many of the positive roles that fear plays, but now it's time to get to know another - fear is an invaluable indicator of dreams. Where there's fear, there are also dreams and desires. Fear never appears in people who are not active or in people who don't have any dreams. Why would it? It won't stop them from doing anything. Fear only appears in those that dream. So, be proud of yourself if you have fears. Because it means you want to move forward, to seek an even better version of yourself, to earn more. If you don't have any fears in your life, then it means only one thing - that you're not living. Do you know who's not afraid? Bodies in the pathology department. That's why you never want to live a life without fear. They can be so scary and horrible, but they'll always remind you of one thing - that you're a person who makes your dreams come true.

A Period Of Suspicious Demons

Every Queen on her path sooner or later finds herself in doubt. That's when all her inner demons awaken in all their grandeur, bombarding her with thousands of reasons why she won't succeed. They touch everything: Her dreams, her courage, and even affect her by triggering physical fatigue within her. Her thoughts become confused, and her image of the future becomes blurred. All this just to take away her hope.

Doubt is a silent killer. In the beginning, it looks rather small and insignificant. It appears as a fleeting thought: "What if it doesn't work ... and what if I don't succeed ..." and then it slowly anchors itself into your thinking and begins to change it. Whenever it hits, hope is diminished, just a little...

In the beginning, it's hardly noticeable ... until, over time, her whole mind has been taken over. And doubt slowly begins to eat away at every new idea, all until she gives in and loses hope for the future. Many women have had dreams, but they gave up on them because they were cloned under the pressure of doubt. Queen, it's time to find out what doubt really is. It's not what you think it is. Doubt can be, like fear, an extraordinary friend. "You doubt that?" Ha, haha. See how quick it is?

Doubt is, in fact, the Universe testing you to see if you really want to fulfill your dreams. We all know that life has its ups and downs. It's very easy to live and be active when you're on your way up when you're on top. But, what happens if you fall to the bottom for some reason? Nothing special, I would say; that's just a part of life. Yes, most people think like that. Until they fall to the ground. However, once they're on the ground and their knees are covered in blood, many of them don't get up again. They begin to doubt whether they can actually get up. They don't trust themselves or their inner strength. But life will only reward you when you prove you deserve it. When, despite your doubts, you get up and move on. Every winner, every entrepreneur, every mom, and every woman have at some point, doubted whether she was able to. Or, if she would be able to do it right. Or if she would succeed. And some do, while some don't. It worked for those who understood doubt. There are thousands of rulers in the world who have overcome doubt. Where do you find them? Usually, they're standing on the steps of the podium and are being awarded medals in sports competitions, on the stage for receiving diplomas at universities, or on the stage for moms where their children have put them...

I once spoke to an elderly lady who runs a marathon every year. She was sixty-five years old, and for the past twenty-two years, she had run a marathon every single year. "That's interesting," I thought and asked her if it was her birthday present to herself. Her response was amazing. She said: "As long as I can run a marathon for my birthday, I know I can do anything that year, and I don't have anything to doubt. After all, there aren't so many things which require such a high degree of physical and psychological fitness. If I start doubting myself about anything, I just say, 'Well, my beautiful, don't complicate things. You just ran a marathon.' And then the marathon woman in me wakes up in an instant. And keeps running."

Two Steps to Friendship With Doubt:

1. **Reframe your thoughts.**

   Most women are cloned by doubt because they notice it a little too late, usually only when it has already taken over their entire lives. And so, it's necessary to take action as soon as doubt arises, just like it is with all other challenges. The longer something grows, the bigger and harder it is to remove. It's your job to pay attention to all your cynical, sarcastic, and pessimistic thoughts, which are the perfect food for doubt. If you recognize them, you can also remove them. If you deprive a plant of what it needs to grow, it dries up.

Thoughts and words that build doubt	*Thoughts and words that build dreams*
If I ...	I'll ...
I hope that ...	I know that ...
I'll never succeed ...	I'm looking for a way to succeed ...
Well, it's not so bad ...	It could be even better ...
I'm not good enough ...	I can become anything I want...

2. **Create a result - take action.**

   Results are the chief destroyers of doubts. Doubt increases the most when you're active but aren't achieving any results. If you want to reduce the amount of doubt, create some results. Even the smallest win works. In the same way, that acetone works on nail polish - it dissolves it. Have you ever noticed that the more successful you are, the less you doubt? Set a smaller goal and make it happen. It's important that you see progress and proof so that you can successfully walk your own path.

Queen, your charismatic future is getting closer. Bit by bit, you're building it up so that you can, in it, reign proudly like a Ruler who's fearless and free of doubt. Allow yourself to experience all of its aspects on your journey, because only in this way will you be able to truly understand yourself and the world.

"A day without night simply doesn't exist."

Hanna opened her eyes and had to blink repeatedly, for the sun had already found its way to shine on her face.

"Oh, my God ... I'm late! If the sun was already shining through the window, it meant that it had to be already ... eight?" she quickly calculated, adding water to the stream of her exasperation. "Work! I can't be late! Not now!" feverish thoughts quickly awakened her.

She jumped out of bed and rushed to the bathroom. Her heart was beating wildly as she nervously brushed her teeth. She quickly smoothed down her hair, almost ran to the wardrobe, and impatiently demanded her pants to find their way onto her body all by themselves. She could feel the tingling of fear quickly spreading through her muscles.

"Oh my God," she repeated, "they're going to fire me." The message from last week's staff meeting echoed through her head, when Boris, the restaurant manager, made it clear that they could be late. Just once. And, if it happened again, there'd be no point in going back, as there'd be nothing to go back to. Their position would be taken by someone else with a more reliable alarm clock and a greater sense of responsibility. Fortunately, this was the first time for Hanna, but the feeling was still frightening. She couldn't afford to lose her job.

Half an hour later, she was already at the restaurant. She quickly changed into her uniform and walked over to Boris's office. It was empty.

"He's not in," her coworker said. "He called earlier and said he'd be a little late because some things came up that he had to take care of. Don't worry, I won't tell," she winked in a friendly kind of way. "Otherwise, you wouldn't end up being here for very long," she smiled, heading toward the kitchen.

"Jane, wait a minute! What do you mean I wouldn't be here for very long?" Hanna asked fearfully. "Do you know something I should know? Did Boris say anything about me?"

"No, silly ..." Jane reassured her. "Nobody said anything. It's just that I've got a feeling. Simply ... that you're far too smart to be stuck here. And you've got that spark in your eyes that people with dreams have." Then she went.

Hanna just stood there. "Do I really?" she asked herself and for a moment allowed herself a moment of pride. It rushed through her body and was a lot more than a momentary blessing sent by the Universe through her friend. It left a fiery trail of hope in her from which something began to awaken - a Phoenix, spreading her wings, marking her birth once again ...

A beautiful smile spread over Hanna's face. "Thank you, Jane," she quietly thanked her. "Thank you for your hope."

And the signpost of life showed her the way out from the dead-end street.

Mission no. 12:

A Directed Arrow

Hanna waited impatiently by the side of the road, her hand raised high, indicating to the taxi driver that she urgently needed a ride. She usually traveled to Manhattan by subway from Brooklyn, where she had been living for the past ten months, but today there wasn't enough time. She had completely forgotten about the emergency meeting her boss, Ms. Mallock, had set for her, as the top priority that morning. For a long time, she hadn't felt so much anxiety, taking its hold on her, that demanded her every breath, both in and out. The taxi drivers continued to ignore her as if she was an invisible ghost until one of them finally stopped and asked her in a strong Russian accent where she was headed.

"The center of Manhattan," Hanna said quickly, getting in the back seat, which looked totally worn out from all the demanding passengers that had sat in that seat before her, who were probably also time stricken. She just had to arrive on time. Mallock repeatedly made it clear that New York is the most competitive city in the world and that there are plenty of other suitable candidates if any employee doesn't do his best. So, it was clear that there was no way of saying no to her demands. Either you reached her highly set bar, or you experienced the pain of a deep fall that seemed to have no end. Her job was her lifeboat, which she relied on so she could escape the unpromising life she had in Boston. And she desperately needed it. And her fast-beating heart quickly reminded her of that.

The cab driver fought his way through the traffic, while she looked on in insecurity at the tall skyscrapers, which, like every morning, welcomed her and promised yet another intensive workday.

But then her gaze came to a halt at a restaurant by the road, one from the same chain that she had worked for in Boston. The memory took her back about a year, to a time when her life was completely different - nothing was going on, she had no money ... and the smell of fried food.

Destiny's mother was clearly gracious, as it only took one email to change the course of her entire life. The New York-based organization she sent a request to for work, only because she no longer knew who else to contact, unexpectedly answered her. They wrote that they weren't looking for any new associates themselves, but that a subsidiary, a newspaper that publishes one of the most important popular science magazines, were always on the lookout for new people. And they wanted to interview Hanna - the very next day, at midday.

Of course, she grabbed the opportunity with both hands and begged that it not try and slip away from her this time. So, the next day, after having let work know that she was ill, she bought the latest issue of the magazine at the first newspaper stand that morning, to find out what they wrote about, and then taking the first train, headed off for the Big Apple, to her unknown destiny. As she walked into the offices of the publishing house that published truly magnificent magazines, she felt that the dynamics were a little different to what she had been used to. The people there were constantly working and didn't have time to talk to each other, and it almost seemed as if they were hunting ... something ...

And not long after, she realized what it was - they were chasing the opportunity to hold onto their jobs. But although they were chasing something, something even bigger was chasing them - Ms. Mallock, an ambitious but unrelenting editor, who believed that the only thing that sounded right was her conductor's baton. Hanna had the first interview with her. She remembered every word of it, or rather, the monologue of her future boss.

"Miss Lane, we always strive for excellence in our magazine. When we received your request, our HR department checked you out. You are otherwise educated in the field of archeology, which is good, but not the

reason we called you; we called you because of the blog you write, and we're of the opinion that it's good and that you have the potential to be a writer. Above all, your unique style of presenting things could breathe some fresh air into some parts of our magazine, as well as some of the supplements.

As was also the excellent recommendation from our longtime external correspondent, Mr. Mark Howard, whose work we value greatly. We are often the first form of media to publish his archaeological research and findings. When we checked the references on his recommendation, he explained that you were a key part of the team at his expedition in Egypt and that you were a reliable person who wanted to learn and get ahead. To further enhance the quality of our magazine, we are looking for creative people who, in addition to writing, have hands-on experience that brings a unique energy to the text. We are looking for people who feel what is written, not just understand it. Mr. Howard said you were the ideal person to do this, and so, according to what you have written in your blog, we also think the same.

That is why we are offering you a position to be the author of some texts as well as being the assistant editor of our historical attachment, which we have recently introduced for a trial period of two months. For the time being, you would be looking for suitable topics, checking information, contacting research societies, drafting columns, looking after appropriate pictorial material, and doing whatever your editor-in-chief asks of you, as his assistant. Of course, later on, once you have proven that you understand the way our magazine is run, you would be able to advance in accordance with the career options we have available. And now, Miss Lane, because we have the utmost trust in Mr. Howard, we won't be using the standard recruitment process in your case. We are offering you work immediately, so if you agree, you can start tomorrow. The initial payment is fifteen dollars an hour, with additional rewards for published articles and contributions. Do you see a connection between your personal goals and the vision of our company, and can you bring to the table what it is we are looking for?"

Although Hanna had already wanted to comment, she quickly abandoned the idea of expressing her doubts, reluctant to ask her how to move from Boston to New York in half a day. She had a feeling that Ms. Mallock wouldn't want to have the same conversation with her one more time. With a lump in her throat, she simply accepted the offer. Twenty minutes later, with tears streaming down her face on the sidewalk in front of the office building, that was about to become her new work 'home', she had no idea at all how she was going to be able to find a roof over her head in one of the most expensive cities in America, all in one day. Life had given her a tremendous opportunity but also a new challenge, one that she didn't know how to deal with. She felt as if she had once again found herself in some quicksand that she couldn't escape from.

But when she calmed down a little, she remembered ... someone. Peter, who had moved to New York a long time ago and who was the only person she knew there. She decided to call him. Maybe he had some advice for her. The sound of some keys from his phone could be heard, and just seconds later, his voice sounded. Peter was extremely pleased to hear from her. When he heard about the situation she had found herself in, he offered her until she sorted things out, to stay at his place, as there was, in his two-bedroom apartment, a small study which used as a wardrobe, while he was moving in. Hanna, like so many times before, was grateful for having such a sincere friend, while at the same time amazed at how their lives had crossed paths again.

She headed back to Boston with a little more peaceful heart, packed everything essential into two suitcases, a bag, and a small backpack, while giving everything else to her co-worker, Jane. She canceled her lease and, despite the landlord not being overly happy, managed to avoid not having to pay the rent for the coming month, then set off to start her new life.

New York was an unbelievably dynamic city, and hard-working Hanna quickly got used to its rhythm. Her new job was demanding but paid enough for her to move into a small attic a month later, just two blocks away from Peter's apartment. She was finally beginning to get back on her feet and felt, for the first time in a long time, that long-forgotten inner feeling, letting her know that everything was heading in the right direction. However, her life now was totally different - she had a lot on her plate. Everything in New York was much more expensive, and again, after paying her bills, there wasn't much left over. She felt like a mouse on a running wheel, and it seemed that if she stopped, she'd lose everything. So, she ran and ran. She was genuinely grateful for the new opportunity and felt deep down inside that it represented an important step in her life, but despite this, she was scared to death, not knowing if she would succeed or not. She was aware that she was at the mercy of Mallock, who had in her whimsical and unpredictable hands ... the tremendous power of deciding the on lives of others, the consequences of which she saw every week on the sad faces of those who failed to satisfy her demands. She usually saw them for the last time in front of the elevator with boxes in her hands, leaving another job and marking up another failed attempt on their CVs.

Hanna was standing on very thin ice and knew that it could break at the slightest of hits, upon which she would fall into the icy water of doom and failure. She had never been so scared about whether she would be able to survive and whether everything would be all right. Not even the time she learned that she had become an orphan.

Hanna was so caught up in her thoughts that she didn't even notice that they had already reached the glass tower where she had spent most of her days these past few months. She quickly shook herself to clear her thoughts, almost threw the taxi driver some money, then ran into the building. The headquarters and place which would decide her fate in less than a minute were on the thirteenth floor. She could already see Mallock with a judge's hammer in her hand, convicting her of being guilty. With a lump in her throat, she stood in front of the door and could have sworn that she could hear someone pounding out some quick beat on a massive drum ... as if predicting that something was about to happen. But, there was no big drum ... just her little frightened heart.

"Is Mallock already here?" she thought, a thousand times a second. With a look of horror in her eyes, she opened the door and walked toward the conference room. Everyone was already there. Except her ... and Mallock.

"Good morning, Hanna. So, we can see that you've decided to challenge God today?" joked Nicky, who was responsible for advertising and had already seen Mallock dismiss newcomers before, just because they were minutes late. Hanna, out of breath, just looked at her and just smiled sourly, then found an empty chair and sat down.

She quickly smoothed down her hair and checked that everything was tied back, just the way it had to be. Mallock didn't like long hair. Once, a student brought her some coffee, and her hair accidentally fell into it. Mallock apparently lost it, just as the girl lost her will to live. That was the last time women wore their hair long at work. Although Mallock never said anything, Hanna was nonetheless afraid that her beautiful long ponytail would also make Mallock lose it, and so, already for a few months, she had been carefully tying it back. Hanna also smoothed down her black blouse. She no longer wore the beautiful vibrant colors that had become an everyday part of her wardrobe ever since she left Egypt; Mallock once said at a meeting that only street-people and children dress in flashy colors, not refined businesswomen doing serious work.

"Good morning," said Mallock's personal secretary as she walked in a second later. "Ms. Mallock has announced that today's meeting is canceled so you can all get back to work."

There were some sighs of relief in the room, and the atmosphere changed just like a day that sees the sun after a period of rain.

"Maybe she was picking up trash on her street today and accidentally ended up staying on the sidewalk," a co-worker joked, followed by a wave of laughter. "No, she probably found out that she didn't like herself anymore and fired herself," his colleague added, underpinned by a dose of sarcasm that was rarely expressed. The room filled with laughter, and the working day began. Hanna went to her desk and got lost in her thoughts.

Her co-workers' jokes were far from funny to her. Most of them came from the city and lived with their parents and didn't have to pay rent or buy food. It was easy for them to make fun of their jobs since reality was not breathing down their necks, reminding them that tomorrow could be darker than today. Her circumstances were completely different: She was totally alone, with no one to cover her back, and if she lost her job, she could be left homeless. Yes, it's true that Peter helped her, but she didn't want to burden him since he was also trying to get his life together. And, no, jokes at the expense of someone who enabled her to pay her bills were not funny to her. The rocky path reminded her that at every turn, huge abysses were only a stone's throw away.

She felt respect for Mallock as she was her ticket to a better life. But it was true that sometimes she felt uncomfortable alongside her. Often, she aroused intense fear within her, so she was constantly making sure that she didn't do anything to antagonize her. She didn't eat bananas in front of her, because she knew she didn't like them. She didn't talk about animals because she knew they weren't exactly on her list of favorite creatures. She didn't listen to music at work, because Mallock thought it disturbed creativity. From the day she took the job at the magazine, her life had turned into a heavily controlled fairytale that no one knew how it would unfold. But at that moment, the ending didn't matter - if the job gave her security, she'd also breathe the way Mallock wanted. For the past year, she had been trying so hard to get ahead in life, so she wanted to make sure that nothing could bring down her new house, which she still knew was not made of solid bricks, but of paper cards.

The day passed quickly; she spent it writing an article about Inca symbols. Despite having to constantly control everything she did, as well as her behavior, somewhere inside herself, she was happy - after all, she was studying history, just like she had always wanted to.

Night had already come to the city as she pressed the last key on her keyboard and decided it was enough for the day. She had worked four hours longer than her regular working day. She felt quite a lot of pain in her neck from staring at the screen the whole day, but she couldn't have expected anything less. The enormous number of hours spent at work were taking their toll, but the way she felt was now the last thing on her mind. She had come in sick at least three times in the past six months. Although her body had told her many times that it had had enough, her mind took control and forced it to continue on working. She stretched her neck, put on her coat, then left. She was catching up with Peter. Twice a month, they caught up and went out for a friendly meal. She felt relaxed in his company, and around him, she didn't have to pretend to be someone else. And so, despite her twelve-hour working day, she could hardly wait to see him.

"Hanna, how are you doing?" Peter asked cheerfully, then changed his expression the next moment, and asked, somewhat worried, "Is everything alright?"

She couldn't hide anything from him - he knew immediately that something was wrong with her when she injured her leg in Egypt, and he knew it again, today.

"I'm fine, just a little tired," Hanna replied.

"Obviously, the words 'a little' have taken on a new meaning," Peter replied sternly. "Hanna, you look exhausted. You need some rest."

He thought for a moment, then continued, "I've got an idea; let's skip going out for dinner. I'm taking you home. You can have a bit of a rest, and I'll make you some pasta with a vegetable sauce. And that's not a question."

Hanna just smiled tiredly and nodded. "He's so nice," the thought whispered through her mind, and the next moment they disappeared down the stairs leading to the subway.
A little less than an hour later, the smell of roasted onions wafted through her apartment ... Peter masterfully chopped up some peppers, while making sure that the cup of chamomile tea in Hanna's hands was never empty.

"Hanna," Peter began, "I've noticed over the past few weeks that you've changed. You don't laugh as much as you used to, you've changed the way you dress, it's been forever since I last saw your ponytail, and you've even started talking differently."

"Yeah, maybe a little; I'm trying to get in good with my boss. It's not so easy to satisfy her. Her standards are higher than the mountains of Colorado ... "

"Hanna," Peter said in a deep voice, putting the wooden spoon down. He went over to her, took her by the hand, and looked her straight into her eyes, "You're good enough just the way you are. Those who don't see that don't deserve to have you in their lives. Don't change for anyone. You're amazing."

Hanna blushed. No one had ever told her anything like that before. Her heart was trembling, and her cheeks went all pink. "Am I really?" she asked, rather timidly.

"Yes," Peter replied. "I wouldn't change a thing about you. Well, maybe the only thing I would change is getting you to eat a little now."

Hanna felt something she had never felt before. The feelings inside of her were so different, so unique ... she was kind of ... pleasantly confused.

The rest of the evening seemed to be embraced in some kind of haze. Hanna and Peter ate their pasta, after which he headed off home. At the door, as he was leaving, he turned and looked at her and said, "Hanna, I'd like to see more of you ..."

Hanna looked at him and smiled shyly, "I'd like to see more of you too." Peter just smiled mysteriously, wished her a good evening, then left.

Hanna lay back down on the couch, stared at the ceiling, and mulled over what had just happened... long into the night, the image of Peter and the stars swirled about in her mind until she ... fell asleep.

The Golden Temple glowed in the light of some crystal, which broke it up into the colors of the rainbow. Hanna entered, and at the enormous doors, shouted out, "Shanti!"

"Hello, my friend," the ruler said, greeting her warmly while remaining peacefully seated on her throne. "How are you today?"

"Shanti, can I ask you a question?" Hanna somehow didn't seem to hear Shanti's question.

"Of course," replied the ruler, "Ask me anything."

"Have you ever been ... in love?" Hanna asked shyly.

Shanti looked at her with her warm eyes and replied, "Many times, Hanna. Many times."

Hanna dreamily sat down in front of her golden friend while her thoughts seemed to drift far away.

"Hanna," Shanti began, "how do you feel now that Peter has told you how he feels?"

"Heavenly," Hanna replied. "I feel like I'm floating about with some butterflies."

"Do you know why, when you think of him, that you feel something so special?" Shanti asked mysteriously.

Hanna knew that a very important lesson was coming, so she said nothing and simply waited.

"Because he knows who you are. Because you don't have to pretend when you're with him. Because you don't have to keep everything in check when you're around him. And now, Hanna, would you like to feel that way, forever and ever? Would you like every part of your life to be surrounded by such feelings?" Shanti continued without holding back.

"Yeeeaaah," Hanna almost shouted, excitedly.

"Then let go of all control over yourself and be as genuine in all situations and with all people, just like you are when you're with Peter. That's when your life will start becoming yours, and then you'll be happy. You know, when I became Queen, I started controlling myself and tried to meet the demands that tradition dictated in our family. All of a sudden, a list of things came up that I had to consider as Queen - how to talk to people, who to socialize with, how to dress, what to eat, etc. There was a specific protocol for just about everything, and I was expected to fulfill everything all down to the last request. For a while, I worked hard, just like a humble mouse, and followed all of the demands of the court and the counselors. Then one day, because of all that, I felt like I wanted to lose touch with myself. I was no longer me. In the vortex of control, I got lost. My power began to fade and disappear. And, as Queen, I began to disappear. I was no longer able to make wise decisions, and it felt like my crown was becoming too big. So, I stopped. And I looked at where I wasn't allowing myself to be me. When I did that, I once again returned to life, and so did my kingdom.

Every woman, as a being, is absolutely extraordinary, beautiful, and unique. I have met many in my life, and each of them has their own 'register of the soul,' which makes them totally and utterly exceptional. Each has their own gifts and talents, and each has their own heart that beats to its own rhythm. When we add external beauty to all this, the woman ends up a picture of perfection. And, a creation as divine as she is, allows her to act in accordance with what she is. But what if many don't know that. But what, when many have allowed their uniqueness to be extinguished by the wave of expectations of what they think they should be. But what, if many of them think they're not good enough, so they try and change and be someone they're not. And here I'm not talking about trying to change inappropriate habits and thoughts, which everyone should work on all the time; here I'm referring to an attempt to change one's own personality and the fundamental principles that make up uniqueness in a woman. A lot of women try to be something they're not, and many speak words they don't feel, while a lot of them do things they don't agree with ... all that they would be able to achieve the things they want in life. If you act at odds with yourself, you have to create these kinds of things; in other words, you have to control them.

Many times, we've been taught that we have to control things if they are to unfold as we imagined them to. That's why so many women start controlling things in their lives; especially themselves. It seems that, these days, the attempt to adapt or to control oneself is the strongest it has ever been. Many women in this society are trying to live in accordance with the hundreds of rules that are said to best position them to achieve their goals. So that they get, in the simplest way possible, what they want. Attempts to control themselves, in some cases, have even gone so far that they have begun to harm them. People today are trying to control almost everything: Their health, their physical characteristics, their habits, their speech, their thinking, and even their hearts. And most of them are women. Most women, consciously or subconsciously, control the greater part of their lives the whole time. With control, they try to change their reality because they're otherwise afraid that they won't be accepted for who they are or won't get the things they want. And despite the fact that they completely distort reality, there's an enormous number of these ridiculous rules and actions that we try to control.

Let's run through some of the most common ways many women try to control themselves and their lives:

Makeup

Today's society, with regard to this kind of 'fashion accessory,' views it as something that beautifies a woman, right? Many ladies apply it to make themselves, simply put, more beautiful. Many justify it as a means by which they merely emphasize their own attributes. Let me reassure all the ladies who use makeup - there's nothing wrong with it. It's just a 'tool.' However, we can use tools for more than just one purpose. With a stick, we can prop something up, or we can hit someone. What matters, therefore, is what we use it for. It's the same with makeup. With it, we can emphasize the attributes we are proud of or cover up those that bother us. Most women use it to cover up their beauty and create something 'new.' They try to control their appearance with it. Why? To be all the more accepted. To be all the more loved. Have you ever wondered why men don't wear make-up (well, at least most)? Because they're far more certain of themselves than women. Men are happy with themselves as they are, so they don't need to control their appearance. And men are also the main reason why women wear make-up. Because they just want to please them.

Once, a young girl came to me for counseling and was made up 'to the nth degree.' Her face was covered with a thick layer of powder, and her eyes, eyebrows, lips, and cheeks were all ... artistically accentuated with different shades of color. She came to me because she was interested in why she hadn't been able to find the right partner. She had been on quite a few dates in recent years and had even got into relationships with a few of them, but at some point, they all walked away. She was looking for the answer to why she hadn't been able to establish a long-term relationship.

Do you know what her challenge was? She wasn't happy with herself. There were a few things she didn't like about herself. As a matter of fact, she didn't like herself, period. So, she changed her whole look into that of a 'mannequin' that she carefully covered with makeup, by putting on trendy clothes, and by hiding behind the latest fashion and cosmetic trends. She spent almost an hour each day doing her makeup, where she literally turned herself into another person. Then, she went out on a date. Why did nothing come of these dates? Because the guys on the other side didn't even know who they were dating. The image of the girl that they were looking at somehow didn't match the energetic image they felt when they got close to her. On the outside, she was different from who she was on the inside. So, everyone felt that there was something wrong with her. They didn't know what, but something about her just didn't add up, which is something that I also felt.

When I mentioned that to her, she was pretty offended. She thought she was better with makeup on, but in reality, she was only covering up her true self. Then, I asked her if she had any other obligations after our session. When she said no, I asked her to do something totally outrageous - to go to the toilet and wash the makeup off her face and show me who she really was.

That's when she burst into tears. I realized that the problem lay elsewhere. She explained to me that she started wearing makeup at the age of fifteen because her classmates gave her a hard time about her acne. They called her 'Scarface' after the character from the movie of the same name. Then, a week after she started wearing makeup, one of the boys she was in love with told her she looked beautiful, and since then, no guy had ever seen her without makeup.

Until our session. I have to admit, she was brave when she went to the restrooms and removed her makeup. And when she came back, another girl was standing in front of me. Beautiful, authentic, and free of acne. When I asked her how she felt, she said vulnerable, as if she was naked. Understandable. After almost ten years, she had thrown away her mask for the very first time. Her confidence was at rock bottom, and she needed time to rebuild it. Above all, she needed to trust herself, because, in truth, she was good enough. She needed to trust herself not to control her appearance.

Then, I advised her to do two things: First, to start being around family members and close friends without having any makeup on. Therefore, with people who loved her because of who she was, as they were the most appropriate people to help her accept herself. And secondly, to choose the part of her face that she was most proud of (eyes, lips, cheeks, etc.), and to emphasize it as she has been doing, but to apply her makeup to all the other areas in a rather minimalistic way. Honestly speaking, I didn't think she would do it. But she did. Half a year later, she came and attended one of my courses, looking almost completely natural. I didn't recognize her. And she confessed to me that in the weeks following the introduction to the new makeup regime, at least ten people had spontaneously told her how good she looked. And slowly, she began to believe them.

So, what happened to her? Was makeup really that important to her before? Yes. Because with it, she controlled how others saw her. And because of it, she wasn't able to establish sincere relationships. When she let go of that control, there was no more 'confusing energy' in her relationships, which then became all the more sincere.

Think about why you wear makeup (of course, if you wear makeup): Either because you're ashamed to show your true self, or because you want to emphasize even more what you're so proud of. Makeup is not just an accessory that seems to change you a bit but is a powerful tool that has the power to turn you into a slave, or into a ruler.

Scales

Scales are something invented by man to determine the correct quantity of goods, allowing a person to make an appropriate trade or monetary exchange. However, most people, especially women, use them for something else - to control their weight. The number that appears tells them something every morning - usually how much they are worth that day. If the number is smaller, they typically feel good, but if it's larger, then they feel worse. Today's society has created ridiculous expectations and benchmarks for what an ideal woman should look like. They have determined the ideal body mass index, the ideal skin fold thickness, and the ideal dress size according to a woman's height. A lot of people then say that only those women who meet these criteria are attractive, beautiful, and sexy. And many women have come to believe that. And so, they bought themselves a device to control their weight - a set of scales. And the weighing began. With it, they control themselves.

Many women step on the scales every morning and check with fear in their eyes whether they have gained any pounds since the previous evening. They don't want to check, but they think they have to. They have to be beautiful for their partners or husbands, for they're afraid that otherwise they'll be tossed aside, rejected, or even abandoned. So, they try to control the amount of candy they eat, and the calories they put in... and whenever you offer them something sweet, they look at it wantingly, but then decline and reject it, saying ... "Oh, I shouldn't, I'll get fat ...", even though you can see the desire in their eyes for a fresh cream slice. But, the feeling of control inside of them, which is often mixed up with a sense of guilt, is often too strong.

Once, a very slender girl came to one of my workshops. The workshop lasted eight hours, and so I made sure there was a lot of fruit, as well as sweet and savory snacks for all the participants. When it was time for a break, the whole group very quickly made their way over to the place where the food had been laid out and started replacing the calories they had burned in the workshop. That girl, however, just took a glass of water. When I asked her if she was hungry, she said that when she looked at the chocolate-filled croissants, she started drooling, but said she shouldn't, as she was watching her waist-line. I asked if she was on a diet, but she replied that she wasn't, but was careful of what she ate mainly because of her boyfriend, who likes skinnier girls. That girl was controlling her weight because she knew that her boyfriend would like her even more. If you've also found that other people's love for you correlates to the amount of fat you have on your body, let me tell you very clearly that these people don't deserve to have you in their lives. If a few extra pounds can change their affection for you, they genuinely don't love you, and as such, don't deserve your love.

'Ideal Pounds'

Ruler, now it's time that you find out the truth about weight and 'ideal pounds.' The ideal body doesn't have to be what nutritionists and doctors have defined it to be. The ideal body, for you, is one that enables you to fulfill your desires and goals or to face your challenges. Full stop. For you, the ideal number on the scales is determined by the situation you're currently in, which may be different for particular periods in your life. Your body cannot be the same all the time because your life is not the same all the time. Different situations require a different body from you, meaning that it's not always reasonable to follow some general recommendations about an ideal body, but that it's sometimes better to follow your own.

FOR EXAMPLE: What kind of patient has an easier time dealing with cancer - one that has the right weight, as determined by society, or one that's a little more on the heavier side? The one that's a little more on the heavier side, of course. A body that's fighting cancer requires a lot of energy, which gives a patient that is not too skinny more possibilities of winning the fight, than a patient having what is considered to be an 'ideal weight.' So, in this case, is her 'too-high' number on the scales inappropriate? No, quite the contrary! The 'high' number on the scales enables her a better chance of surviving. The example may be a little extreme, but it clearly shows that we really shouldn't compare ourselves to others. And any attempt at control to fulfill some general criteria is simply a waste of time. If your goal is to be an Olympic swimmer, you need a completely different body to accomplish your goal than if your goal is to be a successful, world-renowned writer. In both cases, you may have a completely different body, but if it allows you to achieve your desired goal, then it's ideal, isn't it?

Of course, it has to be healthy, but healthy in the way you see 'healthy.' Your body is yours, so form it the way you want it to be. Don't go to the gym and don't go on a diet for the sake of others, but for yourself, because only in that way will you be happy to do it. If you want to weigh yourself, weigh yourself. But again, do it just for yourself. So, you'll be happy. You're the owner of your life, so you decide what place the scales have in it.

That's what I did. After the death of her mother, my wife gained a lot of weight. Mourning, stress, and the extra pounds strongly started to affect her self-image. In a negative way. Because she had been active in dance her whole life, she was far from being used to the changed shape of her body. When the first stages of mourning passed, she decided to lose some weight. She took up some sports activities, changed the way she ate, and bought a set of scales. She diligently applied herself to her new activities, and indeed, the pounds began to disappear. She worked out every day and ... every day she weighed herself. First, once a day, then twice and then even more often. Because our body weight fluctuates, sometimes we have a pound or two more, sometimes less ... but with it, so too did her self-esteem. If the number on the scales was what she expected, she was calm that day in relation to herself, however, if it was higher, she wasn't happy with herself.

I didn't want her self-esteem to be conditional on the number, so I did something that a lot of families should do – I threw the scales into the garbage. From that time onwards, we don't have them anymore. And that kind of control is no longer carried out. Does that mean we don't care about how much we weigh? Not at all. Quite the opposite. From that time onwards, we have bodies that are more realistic given the goals we have in life. We decided that instead of an ideal number on the scales, we would rather chase our dreams and use our bodies, that we take good care of. Our bodies are incredibly intuitive, and they let us know what they need. Our job is simply to listen.

High Heels

They're the most uncomfortable kind of shoes man has ever invented. They cause deformation of the feet, toes, and ankles, causing the Achilles tendon to change, as well as our calves. They cause additional stress to the knee joints, change the dynamics of the hip joints, the spine, and our balance ... all for women to control their height.

The vast majority of women wear high heels just to make themselves look nicer, more attractive, more interesting to other people – again, particularly men. By wearing them, their legs appear longer, and women stand taller.

But, a person's height is one of their fundamental characteristics. Height, therefore, encapsulates everything that a person is. If someone isn't satisfied with their height, they're not satisfied with an entire part of themselves. High heels aren't just an innocent 'pedestal,' making someone taller, but it suggests that those who wear them aren't particularly satisfied with themselves. But the fact is that women wear them for other people and not for themselves. I know a lot of women who wear high heels in public, but not one who wears them at home, particularly when they're alone. Why? Because they're incredibly uncomfortable, and there's no one at home to see them wearing them.

High heels are like some kind of fashion trend, very heavily rooted in the mindset of modern society, so much so that a lot of women can't even imagine life without them. However, that also means that a very strongly rooted tendency to control exists. Once you remove control from your life, it becomes more straightforward, or in this case, particularly more comfortable.

Here, I've described just a few of the most common ways a lot of women try to control things in their lives, in the hope that their expectations will pan out just as they want them to. Many more attempts at control, in fact, exist, and a lot of women are caught up in them. Many people take on customs and traditions in their lives that are not theirs, and by doing so create artificial desires, and deny things that they themselves love, but that others don't, as well as accepting lifestyles that aren't natural to them. For example, by deliberately forcing stimulants into their bodies leading to some kind of unnatural functioning ... all to accommodate others. Before you start any kind of new kind of control, know that if others don't accept you when you express your true self, then they won't accept you even when you dance the way they want you to. So, it's not your job to adapt to the world around you and become a puppet just so you belong, but to create your own world in which you can be you. As a matter of fact, you don't have a choice, because, in truth, these controls can't ever help you fulfill the overall picture of your life. For whatever reasons, if you try to control yourself, you'll only limit yourself, and you'll have less of a chance of success. I understand that sometimes people have the urge to control, but it might still be a good idea to read about the illusions of control:

1. **The Illusion of Control:**
   By Controlling Things, We'll Achieve Things Faster.

   Even though many women who control their words, thoughts and even actions think that they'll get what they want faster, the opposite is true - they only further distance themselves from what they desire because instead of directing energy towards their wishes and their fulfillment, at the same time they also have to take care of being successful in their control. Control may really seem like it's a strategy for achieving goals, but it's so difficult to create this way because, within it, there is no creativity - something that is crucial in establishing it. So, if you let go of control, you'll have more time and energy to create.

2. **The Illusion of Control:**
   Control Reduces Fear.

A lot of women who control themselves and their lives find that it reduces their fear. But the opposite is true. Control comes from feelings of fear. People control because they're afraid that things won't go the way they want them to. The energy of control is actually the energy of fear. If you heighten control, you're actually reinforcing the fear that you're trying to control. Trying to control fear is the same as trying to catch your tail - eventually, you'll find that it's attached to your body.

3. **The Illusion of Control:**
   Control Increases Trust In Your Life.

A lot of women control because they think they'll get the trust in life they're after (or in people, circumstances, themselves, etc.), which isn't possible because control doesn't increase trust in life, it diminishes it. Control and trust are opposing energies - the more you control, the less you trust, and vice versa: The more you trust, the less you control. What kinds of people are imprisoned in the most tightly-controlled prisons? The ones that are the least trusted in society, right? Let go of control, and the cage around you will start to disappear.

4. The Illusion of Control: Control Is Necessary.

Many women think that they have to control if they want to achieve something. But again, as with so many things before, this is also an illusion. Control in life isn't necessary. Life, nature, the planet ... they all have their own flow. Natural flow. A flow that does so in accordance with the Laws of the Universe. Water flows without being controlled, fires rage uncontrollably, and so does the wind ... but it all makes sense, right? Look at nature in itself - in it, everything is logical, and everything in it works the way it should. The only thing in nature that doesn't work as it should is man himself and what he has created. Why? Because of the control he's trying to impose. But perhaps it's time for man to also discover that he's not able to control the natural state of things. But even before that, he has to realize that he is also a part of nature. Then he'll be able to connect and sail in its flow. Which does so ... uncontrollably. Or does it only seem that way, at first glance?

5. The Illusion of Control: A Successful Relationship Without Control is Impossible.

Many women continue to want to control their partners and their relationships. They want their relationship to be exactly as they had envisioned it.

I once met a girl who wanted to prevent her boyfriend from leaving her by getting pregnant. She had secretly stopped taking 'the pill' and, of course, fell pregnant. By having a baby, she tried to control things, so he'd stay with her. It didn't work. They broke up, even though she was going to have a baby.

Relationship control is something so toxic, that it sets the two people in it, even further apart from each other. Mutual trust is an essential component of a good relationship. If the trust isn't strong, the relationship can't be either. And control, as we have already found out, is the opposite of trust. If you don't trust a person, you control him. But we're emotional beings. If someone tries to control us, we immediately perceive it and resist it. Which, in turn, damages the relationship even more. And so, a good relationship without control is possible. Instead of controlling, focus on trust and service.

The Inner Feeling Of Entrapment

Queen, the illusion of control is sometimes very tempting and can quickly convince you that it's right for you. However, know that it won't lead you to your dreams, but into a trap, in which those who don't trust themselves, get caught up in. By controlling yourself, you won't turn you into a powerful Queen, but into an even more entrapped slave, who will find it harder and harder, every day, to deal with the chains that she is bound to. Because the main consequence of control is being captured. Your ego, which wants to control, traps you in your ideas of who you should be, and at the same time, prevents you from being all you can be. That's why when you control yourself, you also feel trapped. Because you're trying to be different.

Because you're trying not to be you.

And how can you now, in this state of control, when you're not in touch with who you are, honestly build your life? How can you be a sincere partner, co-worker, friend, etc. if you're not even honest with yourself? How can you respect the wishes of other people if you don't even respect your own?

The answers to these questions can fundamentally change the course of your fate, if only you have the courage to admit that you really can't control anything. You can't control your life, you can't control your body, you can't control whether someone loves you or not, and you can't control neither life nor death. So, save your energy and stop trying to control things, but most of all, yourself. Be who you are. In that way, you'll know which people are right for you and which are not. Let me console you by saying that you've got nothing to lose, because the people who aren't right for you, aren't, as a matter of fact, able to do anything that would be important for your life. So, stop chasing ghosts, because you can't catch them. Maybe it's time to acknowledge who you really are, and then show that to others. And this is the point of life when your 'destiny' turns in the right direction and brings partners, friends, associates, etc. into your life, who are aligned with your energy. And, as a result of all of this, something will come your way that you strongly desire - your happiness.

Ruler, maybe it's time to realize that everything is fine, that everything is as it should be, that everything comes at the right time, that everything has a purpose, that everything is meaningful, etc., that it's time to realize that you're perfect exactly the way you are. That you realize that you're a daughter of the Universe, the world of which offers you everything you want. That you've got all the talent and gifts you need. The only condition for all of this to work for you is that you are what you truly are. That's when your energy shows its true charisma, and when everything you deserve and want comes rushing your way. And then, you don't have to control anything. You simply express what you feel and follow the order of your heart, which leads you in the right direction.

"Let go of control, and the cage around you will start to disappear."

Hanna opened her eyes. Although she could clearly see how the sun was drawing bright lines through the slits of the blinds in the room, part of her heart was still floating somewhere up in the space above her. In every cell of her body, she could still feel the way Peter looked at her as he stood at the door before he left to go home the night before. She was happy. She hadn't felt that way in a very long time. Or maybe she had, but perhaps didn't want to admit it. She had already felt something for Peter in Egypt, which she wasn't able to put into words, so the whole time she pushed those magical feelings to the side because, in any case, there was no time for them. Her fears, doubts, and disappointments were obviously more important since it was those in recent years that reigned in her heart. But now, they were no longer. They were disappearing. Every day, there were fewer of them, and every day, she was happier.

She remained in bed a few minutes longer and indulged in the pleasure that was circulating throughout her body. She wasn't even aware of how much she needed him. She felt like a fragile flower, which had been watered again after a long time, and which was now getting the fluids necessary for life, that were bringing her energy and energizing all parts of her. She felt different that morning. Because of Peter. Once again, she thought of him and was flooded with warmness. Nothing, as a matter of fact, had really happened between them, but she knew he was the one. She simply knew. Nothing up until that point had been so clear or so powerful. He was the one. He had been the one for a long time. Why hadn't she seen this before?

Even before she completely formulated her question, the image of Shanti had already come over her, telling her with a smile, "Because only now are you ready to fully accept yourself. Because you can only see love around you when you first see it in yourself."

Hanna smiled. She had dreamed about Shanti so many times that she was slowly beginning to think like her. Which she liked. A lot. Although she only saw her in her dreams, she quietly wished that she could one day stand so upright and proudly as she did. She admired her. She was her friend, like some kind of guide, who helped her climb out of the abyss and find her own mission. She would be grateful to her for the rest of her life. That night in Egypt, she brought color to the grayness. A color she didn't even know existed. And, just when she thought she had seen everything, Peter came with a new palette of colors in his hands, promising her to paint new shades of happiness in her life.

Full of life, she got up and out of bed, and headed for the bathroom. It was time to make arrangements for a new game, which she would soon begin playing in Ms. Mallock's playground. She looked at herself in the mirror, combed her beautiful hair, and began to put it into a bun. Then, at some point, she stopped. Her thoughts stopped her. Once again, she was taken over by feelings of déjà vu. Once again, in the mirror, she saw someone who wanted to change for the sake of others. She looked herself in the eyes and saw something tiny that was shining. Images from her dreams began to flood her mind.

"Enough!" reverberated around in her mind. "I'm done controlling myself and yielding in the hope that I won't step on anyone's toes. It's enough."

She closed her eyes, breathed deeply, held it a little, then for a moment it seemed that she had drawn upon some energy, then exhaled. She felt as if she had exhaled from herself the last of her doubts and fears, that she had held within. It's now or never. It was time to free herself. It was time to break the last steel bars that surrounded her. She remembered Shanti asking her if she wanted to feel the way she felt about Peter all the time. Her answer was a clear YES. And then she heard again in her head, "Then be what you are, all the time."

She knew she had to make some changes. And she had to start at work. The thought of resisting Ms. Mallock somehow frightened her at first, but in the very next moment, the image of Peter came to her mind. She felt it was a gift, and that life was rewarding her for being genuine. The most wonderful gift. Deep down, however, she knew that life had a lot more in store for her. And the time had come to accept those things too.

That morning, Hanna made the decision - to always and everywhere express what she felt within. Once again, it was time for her ponytail.

Mission no. 13:

A Hunter and a Doormat

Like every day for the past two years, Hanna stopped by a nearby cafe that morning, ordered some hot chocolate, then sat down on a bench by the trail and sipped her sweet-smelling beverage. She was enjoying the sunshine that embraced the streets of New York that morning. She noticed how the sun reflected against the glass walls of Manhattan's skyscrapers and how people were rushing to get to work.

Despite the everyday hustle and bustle of the city, Hanna felt peace in her heart. Complete peace. She was happy. Her life had never been as perfect as it was that moment. A lot had happened that past year. It seemed that an invisible force had torn the last shackles away that were trying to hold her to the ground, freeing her so that she could fully spread her wings. Everything had changed so much. Hanna had never known the feeling that was now reigning in her heart, but she suspected it was the 'holy grail' that so many had been searching so furiously for their entire lives. For a sense of peace of the soul, of belonging to something and for joy for life. Finally, everything in her life was in the right place. The pieces of the puzzle had fallen into place and together embraced one another, showing the charm of their painting.

And even though she was sitting on a dirty wooden bench, she felt like a proud ruler. Shanti was right. In life, the best way to attract happiness is by being loyal to yourself. The principles she had been living in accordance with ever since the Golden Temple had given her the key to creating happiness in her life. Despite having a large lump in her throat in the beginning, she somehow forced herself that she would no longer submit to anyone, ever again. Most of all, she no longer changed herself, nor controlled herself, for anyone else. She was who she truly was. At work, this meant that she once again had her hair in a long ponytail, dressed in the clothes that she liked, and if she didn't agree with Mallock's suggestions, she made that clear. At some such events, her colleagues often turned pale, as they didn't know how their authoritative boss would react to her presumptuous behavior and, if truth be told, many times, Hanna also turned pale on the inside. But, it obviously worked. Mallock miraculously left her alone. At times it seemed that she attacked everyone else in the office, except her. She could have even sworn that she saw her secretly watching her a few times.

And Peter no longer secretly observed her. That night, when he told her he would like to see her more often, he obviously took it seriously, as he invited her out on their first date shortly after. Which was followed by another. And then another ... and a few months later, she moved in with him. That was when her life finally changed. Until then, she had somewhat forgotten what it was like to have someone genuinely care for you. The last time she felt it was the day before her parents died. The only two people who genuinely loved her disappeared from her life in an instant, then a gaping hole existed for more than twenty years that no memory of them could ever fill.

All until Peter came along. Peter reminded her again, how strong love could be. He was so gentle and so attentive. He truly loved her. And she him. And she loved herself the most when she was around him. When she was with him, she felt like she could do anything. And achieve all her dreams. And Peter strongly believed in her. His every move and every look communicated that his love for her was true. He even believed in her when she didn't believe in herself.

And she would never forget the evening when she finally realized that he was the one for her: That morning in the office when she was biting into a sandwich, then dropped everything and ran toward the restrooms. Her body was suddenly overcome with nausea, which led to a bout of vomiting, which was more than annoying.

When she got back to her desk, Nicky, her colleague, playfully laughed and said, "Babe, I think I know what's going on with you. You're pregnant." That's when Hanna turned pale, and immediately took a break, and almost ran to the nearest pharmacy to buy three pregnancy tests. Half an hour later, in the magazine's restrooms, all three showed that Nicky was right. When she got home that evening, she burst into tears at the door. Peter hugged her and asked her what was wrong. She remembered that she couldn't even convey the news to him because of the shock of it all.

"I'm pregnant," she finally said. Peter looked at her in astonishment, then cried. Out of joy. She remembered how he screamed out loud and almost yelled about how he was going to become a daddy. And then she cried even more.

When Peter asked her again what was wrong, she looked at him, all frightened and replied, "I'm scared that I'm going to be a bad mom. I don't know how to be a mom. I don't know what it's like. I've never seen anyone be one ... mine died so young and ... "

And she would never forget how Peter turned to her, hugged her, and then said, "Darling, this little being can be happy to have you as her mother. You're going to be the best mom in the world. Don't worry. We'll make it together." Then she felt something in his voice that she had only felt with someone else - with her father. At that moment, she knew everything was going to be okay.

Then, an impatient cyclist whizzed past her and shook her from her thoughts. She looked around and realized it was time to head back to the office as the clock ticking by relentlessly.

And, with a little bit of reluctance, she got up. Over the past few days, she had felt a little bit of pain in her lower back. Her gynecologist had mentioned that it might be something she would experience, which she nevertheless hoped she wouldn't. But the pain came. And there was nothing to suggest that it would go away either. "Still three more months ..." she said, quietly counting down, hoping that her twins wouldn't hear her softly spoken thoughts.

When she walked into the magazine's offices, she could already sense the tension at the door. Already, first thing in the morning, shouting could be heard from the main office, which was somewhat muffled by the heavy door that led to it. Hanna stood still and listened. Every now and then, she could understand a word and realized that her boss was yelling at someone over the phone. "Damn, I wouldn't want to be in his place right now," Hanna thought to herself after hearing the word "bastard" already for the third time.

"What's going on?" One of her friends saw him hugging a stranger this morning. And apparently, not for the first time. Now Mallock was on the phone with him. She's been yelling at him for ten minutes. It's a good thing we don't have any meetings today."

"Last week, her boyfriend was here. There's no doubt he's a good catch, but he obviously can't be tamed. Typical of those 'fashion guys.'

"Hunters" interjected Maggie, the new girl who had been in charge of public relations for the past four months and who, like the whole office, was listening in on the entire conversation.

"I know a couple of guys like that: Handsome and smart, just like the devil himself. They think they're God's gift to the world. And they choose sexy

vixens, just like Mallock. But there's a problem when they're attached to a chain that's a little bit too long. Then they start prancing around. It's Mallock's own fault. Why does she have to choose those who think they need to smell every flower they pass. Mine wouldn't even think of looking at another, let alone cheat on me."

Maggie approached Hanna and Nicky, looked around as if she was about to divulge a secret, then said in a quiet voice, "Girls, they've got to be kept on a short leash. Look, I told Bill at the beginning how things were going to be - no video games, no poker, no female friends, no hanging out with dubious friends, and at home in the evenings and on the weekends with me. And, after five years of being together, I've got no problems. That's how it is ... they've got to be trained, and sometimes you've got to tighten the screws. Then, everything's the way it should be."
Hanna felt a little bit sorry for Bill and was already imagining a frightened man in glasses, wearing a checkered shirt and holding a baby in one hand while cooking dinner with the other, and nodding to his woman giving him commands from the couch while she's watching television. She wanted to say something to Maggie, when the door of the main office opened and their boss, furious and completely red in the face, quickly stormed out. They all immediately sat down in their chairs and began working. All of a sudden, there was silence. Anger could be felt in the air, which was so apparent that they all hoped that she wouldn't unload some of her bad mood onto them, and so they kept their eyes glued to the screens of their computers. Lightning bolted from her eyes, looking for a victim to burn. Only Hanna looked at Mallock. And it seemed, for the first time, that she could feel something in her that she had never been able to. Not even in her wildest dreams did she think she would see in her - a wounded and hurt woman. She didn't know what exactly happened, but she had a feeling her boss didn't deserve it.

The day dragged on like there was no tomorrow, and Hanna could hardly wait for it to end. That day, she seemed to experience more cramping in her stomach than usual, and the events of that morning aroused in her a strong need to hug Peter as soon as possible. The clock sounded, finally announcing that the workday had come to an end. Although Hanna usually stayed longer, she finished that day as soon as she could. An hour later, she was already at home in her comfortable tracksuit, which of late had more and more embraced her growing tummy. Finally, the sound of a key in the lock of the door could be heard. It was Peter. Even before he was able to say anything, Hanna had already thrown herself around his neck and squeezed him tightly.

"Wow, that's a welcome. Wait a minute, I'll come in again," he joked, hugging his sweetheart.

"How are you, 'Mommy'?" he asked sweetly.

"Happy you're home," Hanna replied. She hugged him and felt that he was real. At work, some fear of losing him had come across her mind, but now he was here. Everything was just fine.

They quickly had something to eat, then sat down on the couch. Peter took her legs into his lap and began massaging her feet. With his every move, it seemed that she was becoming more and more relaxed. And more and more tired.

"And what was your day like?" he asked her curiously, triggering the memory of that morning's events in Hanna's head. But even before she could tell him all about Mallock, her boyfriend, Maggie, and Bill ..., she felt how the twins in her belly were becoming restless, so she slowly rocked them back and forth, until all three of them started to fall asleep.

"It was okay ..." she replied, then sank into a deep sleep.

An intense glitter shone in her eyes, and before her was revealed ... the Golden Temple. Once again, she was there. Although she had come through its door a hundred times before, she still marveled at its beauty. She entered, as if it was her home, and took a look around. She was searching for her. Shanti. And then, she found her. She was sitting at the end of the temple, on a beautiful light-blue stone that gently glowed.

"Hello, Hanna," Shanti smiled at her. "How are you today?"

"I'm well," Hanna replied. "As a matter of fact, I'm great. Once again, I saw how wonderful Peter is."

"He really is wonderful," Shanti replied. "He loves you and would do anything for you. You're his queen."

Hanna smiled shyly, and her cheeks turned red. "Yes, I am." Then she went on, "At work today, I was feeling quite a bit of anxiety, and I thought I would lose him. When I saw Mallock trying to hide her pain from someone she loved, I realized that I never wanted to be in a situation like that."

"Hanna, don't worry. You won't. Peter is different to your boss's boyfriend," Shanti replied reassuringly.

"I know he's different, Shanti. And I'm so grateful for that. And although he often cooks me lunch, I feel he's also different from Maggie's partner, Bill," Hanna added.

"Ha, ha, ha," laughed Shanti. "From a hunter to a doormat. Today you've come to know the both sides of men who've got lost in their own uniqueness.

You're lucky you didn't run into any of them."

Hanna looked at her heavenly friend, then curiously asked, "Why have I got the feeling that you've come across both of these types already before?"

"Because I have," Shanti replied.

Hanna sensed a so-called 'conversation between friends,' so she leaned in closer and said, "Tell me more."

The Ruler gazed out across the temple and then began to tell her story: "The last man I loved was a handsome prince from a neighboring country. Black hair fell over his copper-colored face, and his dark eyes could see into the heart of my soul. When he first looked at me, sparks flew. There was kindled animal lust and endless unpredictability in his eyes. I could feel how much he wanted me. He really did. When he caught me, he took me insatiably... he showed me the stars of the night and gave me things I never expected in my wildest dreams..." Shanti replied.

Hanna asked, "And what was that? It must have been so very romantic ... "

Shanti sharply broke the ice of truth: "His unpredictability put me into the sarcophagus, the one that you discovered."

And then it was Hanna's turn to be surprised to hear the truth ...

Hunters

A lot of women say they want a hunter. Already at elementary school, they've carefully learned that men are hunters and women are gatherers. Men should, therefore, hunt. But what is hunting at the end of the day? Hunting is another word for supremacy or even killing. It's an activity where a living creature, that is, a hunter, determines the fate of another; how he is to live ... if he is allowed to live at all.

And now a question for you - do you really want a hunter? Most women do. They want a man who hunts his prey. A man with fire in his eyes, who energizes a woman that doesn't have it, and then through his searches for her own, which she doesn't dare express by herself. And what is that fire of his, that hunting fire? Being full of adrenaline, having the desire for supremacy, and demand for total control. Yeah, that's really a hunt. What kind of passion does that bring for the prey? We should probably ask the deer, that's bleeding to death under the 'wonderful fire.' A lot of women would argue with me, that you can't compare hunting animals with hunting women, or with loved-based hunting. But is that true?

Let's first look at what hunting love is all about. When a guy is on the hunt for love, which representatives of the fairer sex get so caught up in, it's usually about a man who wants to show a woman with all he has and everything he's got, that she's wanted. If he does it right, he awakens in her an immeasurable sense of acceptance, sexuality, and admiration, which can make her quickly and powerfully fall in love with him. He traps them by using carefully chosen words and gestures that spark passion in her.

Putting a gentler guy alongside the hunter, who would be genuinely interested in her and her life, the woman, desiring to be hunted, would quickly overlook and mistake his words, flattering her and her beautiful dress, her smile and promising her the moon, the stars, and all the other planets.

Why do some women want to hear it so much that they're even prepared to become the prey? Because so many women have convinced themselves over the centuries that they're worthless. And most of them have accepted this belief. The hunter, with his promises, therefore, brings back to them what they've been missing for so long - their power. That's why some women do everything they can to conquer them and let them know that they're prey worthy of them. For the wonderful loud words and actions that only 'they' can do is necessary food for their soul. That's why they've learned all the tricks you usually find in gossip magazines that teach you how to get a hunter, by playing. And so, the game begins.

She's cold and inaccessible. For the hunter, this is a sign that she's running away and that he might not be able to catch her. Which is something he can't let happen. Because he's a hunter. He has to have her. Which she knows, even though she may have hidden her true nature. The hunt has begun. And she can't wait to become his prey. Usually, it happens, only a short time later that this woman, just like a lonely animal, will cry out and call her hunter ... her dream man whom she wants something more from. She won't be able to handle that he's gone off on a new hunt. And this time, he's not after her...

Once, a lonely woman, just like this, came to relationship counseling, who had been rejected by her man. She was an extremely beautiful and emotional girl, and accidentally opened her boyfriend's profile on a social network platform and learned that he's not only hunting her but others as well. And there was a list of his trophies on his profile. Lots of trophies. And they all had something in common - they were extremely attractive, just like her. When she told him what she'd discovered, he said to her that those 'bimbos' were anything but important and that there was only room in his heart for her.

She even believed him at first, since he was able to sell her anything. But then he became even bolder until one of those women called him, while he was still at home. The girl instantly knew what was going on. If she had been turning a blind eye in the past, the current circumstances right in front of her eyes were very real now. She could no longer deny she had a problem. When she asked him again about other women, he replied that these were guy's things. And that she'd never understood them. After that happened, she came to see me. She cried and cried. Although she knew he was poison, something continued to draw her to him. She described him as being so very desirable. Her boyfriend was a hunter. And she was his prey.

Passion or Habit?

It's good to have passion in relationships. It awakens emotions in people, which excite, so they can access the feelings in their lives that had subsided. But passion is usually quite fleeting. Often it happens at that time, when life takes its path, goes blurry, and what was once some wonderful passion becomes a habit. Which is the passion that a woman sees in a hunter, but in truth is not passion at all but rather a habit. His habit. And something is a habit because we keep repeating it and repeating it. That's when most women come to the realization they've gotten caught up with a hunter. When they realize they got it wrong about him, the game ends.

Hunting Rules

If a hunter has also disappointed you, or if you realize that you're getting involved with them all the time, it might be time to find out why you have to carry scars on your heart so often. Hunters don't hunt women with all possible weapons at their disposal (promises, flattery, posing, proving, bragging, making her jealous), because of her and her qualities. But because he wants to win. A lot of women want a hunter for a partner so that he'll hunt and capture every day. That every day they'll feel that passion and desire of someone wanting them. But the fact is that a hunter cannot capture the same prey twice. Once the hunter catches his prey, it's over. The next day he goes after a new one. He's not expected to capture a deer, take it home, and then lovingly take care of it for the rest of its life. He wants blood. And tomorrow he'll hunt fresh blood. Of course, this fresh blood can be one and the same woman every day. Which also means she'll have to run every day. Over time, her legs will ache, and her neck will be sore from always looking behind her. If she stops, she'll get caught, which also means the end of the game. Yes, hunting rules are a little different ...

But sometimes hunting doesn't happen according to the 'rules' ... sometimes a hunter becomes the prey, and the prey becomes a hunter, which is often the goal of women who outwardly appear frightened and weak like a young deer, but inwardly think: "A little more, and he'll be mine. Then I'll turn him into what I want him to be." But this strategy doesn't work either. Why? Because a woman with such a partner will never be happy. If she becomes the hunter, he's no longer one, because he becomes the prey. And then he starts behaving like one. His extraordinarily powerful and seductive qualities that made her fall in love with him in the first place slowly disappear into the gaze of a trapped animal who has been deprived of his freedom.

Lions at the zoo have that look about them. The lion, such mighty animal that is crowned the King of all Animals. The ruler. Strong. Fast. Capable of hunting down animals larger than itself. Capable of seeing in the dark. Capable of climbing trees. Even capable of tearing apart think skin with its sharp claws and teeth. That's a lion. A natural hunter. An animal lazing about in a zoo inundated by the gazes of hundreds of curious visitors, no longer even the shadow of what it once was ... in the wild. In the cage, there's a creature that they've changed. A hunter banned from hunting and imprisoned ... just like a prey. And little kids, on school excursions, full of expectations that the lions will roar mightily thus drive admiration through their veins, just like they wanted to see, won't happen. Because the hunter has become the prey. That's the truth of the hunted hunters. They lose their charm, which is the thing that they were admired for, right from the beginning.

So, if a woman wants to be caught by an attractive 'lion hunter,' she has only two choices: Either accept a wild, untamed lion who wants to catch new prey every day, or a trapped animal with no will to live.

Up until now, you may have believed in the game that was promoted by many as a successful way of building a partnership, but in reality was just a house of cards that slowly collapsed onto the heads of many wonderful women, who let others tell them who they were ... It's time for you to understand that, dear Queen.

As a seeker of happiness, you're not looking for a hunter. You're looking for someone who'll love you. To love does not mean to have. You're looking for someone who only wants happiness for you. Not someone, whom you bite your nails over because their deception and empty promises. For a happy life, full of love, you need harmony and communication, not games in which you'll unquestionably end up the loser. And it's also not about you winning either. It's about love that wins and embraces the two of you. You may not see your partner, who'll enable you this, as quickly as you see a hunter, who shines in his charms, because illusions are always more visible than hidden truths. Your job is to respect yourself enough to know what you're looking for. Hey, if you're looking for a hunter, no one's judging you. But, when the time comes for him to seek out a new prey, he'll do it and head off 'into the woods' for a new conquest, which is exactly what he's after. However, if you want a partner who'll be alongside you in everything that life brings you, then you'll have to turn your compass in a new direction.

How to Recognize Hunters?

Although every woman has a list of how to manage her love emotions inside herself, many still end up in the hands of hunters. Instead of tears that come from being emotionally touched or from happiness, their faces are riddled with tears of sadness and pain. Therefore, it's time to learn how to identify a hunter and their intentions, which will put you in a position where you'll be able to make the right decisions for you and for your heart. So, how can you identify a hunter if you're single, or how can you determine if a hunter can even be your partner (these characteristics are general and apply to the greater majority of 'hunters.' Of course, there's the possibility that someone has these characteristics but is not a hunter):

- ***Something about them is incredibly enticing.***
  Hunters are usually charismatic, confident, and determined men who need these qualities because they're the weapons they use to hunt. Because they know that most women want someone alongside them who will make them feel safe, they promise this, with their seeming, or even real power – and usually very quickly.

- ***They decide, instead of the woman.***
  A powerful technique to entice hunters is to take the decision-making initiative fairly quickly. This often happens on the first date, when the hunter orders a drink or some food for the woman he's with. Many women who are lost in themselves, get a strong feeling that this dream man will take care of them for the rest of their lives. Which is what hunters know.

- ***They have a lot of tricks up their sleeves.***
  Most women love beautiful things, style, charm ..., which many hunters create with a neat external appearance, with carefully selected words, with gentlemanly-like behavior, with words of flattery, with promises of giving them the stars, and with selected gifts and more. Why do they do this? Because they'd like to quickly make a good impression. Hunting is fast.

Their job is to catch their prey as soon as possible. They're not interested in building a long-lasting relationship to show a woman that she's worthy, beautiful, and admired since they don't have time for her. If they want to catch their prey, they need to do it as quickly as possible. And the things listed above are tremendous aids in making that happen.

- ***They act a little boldly and are sometimes even dangerous.***
  The purpose of hunting is to dominate. If a hunter wants to dominate his prey, he has to be bolder than she is. He's continuously using 'weapons,' as this is the only way he can catch her. That's why so many hunters emanate the energy of being 'bad guys' - untamed stallions, eternal rebels, and incurable seducers. And why does that kind of energy attract so many women? Because it so very strongly and intensely expresses the emotions that women who 'fall' for hunters need to feel. Usually, they're emotionally impoverished, hungry for love, and the sudden wave of these emotions in their hearts revives them, at least for a while. But, as we've already learned, it's just a wave and not a constant flow. Once a hunter catches, the waves quickly stop.

- ***They're very egoistical.***
  Hunting is all about them. They don't care about their prey. Would the hunter still hunt animals, if he really cared about them? No. Hunters hunt because they're egoistical. Maybe the woman who is the target of the hunter seems to think that it's not so, because her hunter, while hunting, is giving her everything she needs, but it's really only about his strategy. The moment he captures her, he stops providing and shows his true nature.

So, Queen, I'm here to show you a few of the hunters' thoughts. If you understand them, it'll help you not to find yourself on their menu. And, in that way, you won't become just another trophy, but you'll have the opportunity to remain a unique and powerful Queen who deserves someone that loves and admires her all the time.

Doormats

No woman wants a doormat. Or do they? If hunters evoke feelings of passion and excitement in women, then doormats evoke in them feelings of safety and predictability. Many who have been frustrated in the past by love (and many who have been hurt by hunters), later, when their wounds have healed, at least a little, choose a 'safer' man – a doormat to be their partner.

So, let's take a look at who or what a doormat is. A doormat is something that we wipe our shoes on before we enter our homes. It serves to remove the greater part or all of the dirt and mud on our shoes so that our homes don't get dirty. A doormat, therefore, is something really good to have. It is like some kind of servant who is available the whole time and who does things we don't want to do. So, it's great to have a doormat at home, but not as your partner. Which a lot of women have discovered, by ensuring safety and stability for themselves in their partnership when they changed their partner into a doormat.

Years ago, a middle-aged woman attended a workshop of mine for confident women. She quietly participated until we got to the part about partnerships. During the workshop, I mentioned that partnerships should respect the needs and wishes of both partners equally.

She protested. Loudly. When I asked her for her opinion, she just said she disagreed. She was adamant in her point of view, so I asked her if she could explain. She told her story: "I watched, my entire life, how my father domineered my mother and somehow kept her restrained, her whole life. So, as a teenager, I decided not to let the same thing to happen to me in my relationship. When I met the guy that would later become my boyfriend, right from the beginning, I stated how things were going to be in our relationship. I told him that I'm a woman who appreciates having a clear vision for my life and that I know exactly what I have to do to make it happen, so I expect him to accept me, as well as my decisions."

At this point, I stopped her and told her that it was otherwise okay to be that way with regard to herself, but that her husband also had his own role in deciding about their lives. She said that she disagrees, and then added that her husband can make his own decisions, as long as he decides in a way that's in-line with what she has decided. That was when all the other girls laughed out loud, and I have to admit that I was also smiling. Then, I asked her what her husband thought about that. She said he had no choice. She made it clear to him that it was going to be her way or no way at all. Of course, I wanted to know how that actually worked in practice. She continued: "It's straightforward. It's the way I want it. And then I asked her what happens when her husband disagrees with her. She said, "Then, he has to change his mind." I wondered how long they had been together. She replied, "Fifteen years."

Who's Not a Doormat?

Well, her husband is an example of a doormat. But, I've noticed that a lot of women don't even know what a doormat actually is, as a lot of the time they get it confused with something else – with a man who does everything for his partner. A man who does things for his partner and helps her with the chores is not a doormat but is just a good partner.

Once, I attended a seminar that was held by my wife. Because there were a large number of attendees, I went along to help her. A lot of the attendees had been watching me the whole day, how I had been helping her organize things, how I went to get lunch for them, how I often asked her if she needed anything, how I took care of everything that needed taking care of. At the end of the seminar, a woman came up to me and said, "She's got you under her thumb, hasn't she? You jump at her every request." Very few people approach me in such a way without really thinking. I looked at her and then took a few moments, just to observe. Then I put myself in her shoes and looked at myself through her eyes. And immediately realized what was bothering her. She was bothered by the fact that her partner behaved ignorantly towards her and not nearly as respectfully as I did to my wife. In truth, she wanted her partner to also behave in the same way to her. And because he didn't, she was angry, and she disguised that anger in such as way by projecting it on others. In truth, it was weighing her down – that she wasn't happy in her own relationship.

Helping your partner with things and doing things for her is not being a doormat, but the actions of a man who understands that a relationship is a two-way thing and that you, as a partner, help in it. If we cook at home, then I cook - simply because I'm a better cook. Many times, I get up in the morning and take our dogs for a walk because I know that my wife likes to sleep in a little longer in the morning. I go to the store and buy everything we need because I know that I'm able to carry it all. But these things are not about being a doormat but are acts of respect and love. I don't know why there's the thinking that only when a woman gets sick does a man do something for her. Isn't it right that he does things for her because he loves her? Because, at the end of the day, my wife does a thousand things for me - she prepares ad designs for my business, because she does it five times faster than I can. She translates some things for me because she studied a foreign language and is far better at it than I am. She's willing to listen to me, even in the middle of the night, if I need her opinion. She would totally take care of me if something ever happened to me. That's a partnership.

So, a Man is Not a Doormat, if:

- he gets up in the middle of the night and changes the baby while his partner is sleeping (which is the least he can do, considering she was pregnant for nine months and in the end gave birth)
- he cooks lunch or dinner (after all, he eats too)
- he mows the grass and cleans the house (since he also lives in it)
- he, in his schedule, first plans some time to spend with his partner, and then with everyone else (which just shows that she really matters to him)

There are plenty of examples where love is seen in the wrong 'light.' The term, doormat, most likely originated as a product of the male ego, which men began to call their male friends if they thought they were being too helpful to their partners. As tasks and responsibilities throughout history have been inadvertently divided into 'men's' and 'women's', the use of the term 'doormat' has become quite popular. People started using it whenever a man did something that was supposed to be a woman's job. But, dear Queen, as we discovered at the beginning of this book, tasks are neither 'female' nor 'male.' Chores are just chores. So, that's why it's smart that the one who does them best and fastest should do them. If, according to this theory, a man is a doormat just because he cooks and irons, does that then mean that women are also 'pussies' because they also do these things? Do you understand how ridiculous that is?

The Influence of Intelligent Woman

If a man is in a relationship with an intelligent woman, he can quickly be seen as a doormat, as a lot of the decision making in that kind of relationship is probably made by her. Is a man because of that a doormat? No. If he follows her lead and learns from her, he's not a doormat. He's smart because he understands that he can learn a lot from her. Of course, in this case, he has to tame his ego a little and become humble enough to allow himself to be led. In all the years I've been working with people, I've come across many intelligent women who've tried to tell their boyfriends a lot, but who didn't listen because their male egos didn't let them. They thought they were being turned into doormats. The fact is that these women just wanted to help them.

Who Is a Doormat?

A man who SUBORDINATES his thoughts, desires, habits, and dreams to the thoughts, desires, habits, and dreams of his partner IS a doormat because he has sacrificed his uniqueness to please someone else. He's preferred to give up his truth to accept the truth of someone else - his partner.

A man becomes a doormat when he introduces changes into his life that he does NOT want. For example: A guy plays football with his friends every Friday afternoon. He does this for years and years because he enjoys it. Then he meets a girl he likes. At the beginning of the relationship, everything is fine; they love each other, and the guy still goes out with his friends to play football. Then, one Thursday night, the girl tells him she'd like to spend the afternoon the following day with him. He loves her, so he's prepared to give up playing football with his friends on this occasion. Then, more and more, she starts expecting him to stop playing football until one day she demands it. That's when he has a choice: If he gives in to his girlfriend's request, then we can call him a doormat. To satisfy her whims, he gives up something important to him. He's submitted himself to her. However, if he stands up for what he wants and tells his girlfriend that Friday afternoons are reserved for him and playing football, then he shows that he stands up for his convictions - which is just the opposite of being a doormat.

As a Queen, you want to have a confident man with you who knows what he wants, not a doormat, who always lowers his head and humbly follows you around like a frightened little puppy. It's probably easier to deal with a doormat, but you'll never be able to develop into a true Queen if you have a doormat around you. So, encourage him to express his power in your relationship, don't suppress it.

However, I've noticed that a lot of women in relationships 'hunt' a little. They try to strike a balance between their own egos and their desires and the egos and the desires of their partners. Sometimes they succeed, and sometimes they don't. And the result of failure is often exactly that; it turns their men into doormats. That's right, a man is never born a doormat, but is changed into one by his partner. Who's to blame if a confident baby, at birth, is proud of himself, but then later turns into a man who is unable to stand up for himself? A lot of things, but one of the key ones is his partner's attitude towards him. Sometimes a woman, in the way she behaves towards her man doesn't give him strength, allowing him to become a king, but turns him into a doormat.

How do women turn their husbands into doormats?

- ***They forbid them.***
  Many women forbid their partners from doing certain things - either because they don't understand them or because they don't like them. But, my Queen, every man has the right to choose what he wants for himself. Even your partner. He can choose whatever he wants, even if you don't understand it. And it's not your job to make decisions for him; it's your job as his partner to respect his choices and ultimately accept him as he is. The decision to change has to be his, not yours.

- ***That they demand.***
  Very often, a woman demands a certain kind of behavior (or

assurance) from her partner. It's important that you understand that you can't demand anything because demanding is an action that communicates that the thing being demanded is more important than the thing which triggered the demand in the first place. This then communicates to your partner that your way of looking at things is more important than his. In other words, once again, some kind of control is starting to be initiated. In addition, you're responsible for your own life, so the things you want, first and foremost, are your obligation.

- ***That they use emotional blackmail.***
  A lot of women emotionally blackmail their partners as they're very good at instilling in them feelings of guilt or even fear. This leads to their partners feeling guilty, and then eventually doing whatever their women expect of them. But, let me just warn you about something here: Your partner may respond to your emotional blackmailing because he loves you. If he didn't, he probably wouldn't care about you or your emotional blackmailing. But with a person who loves you, any kind of emotional blackmailing is unnecessary, as there are many more suitable ways and approaches for building a successful relationship.

Dear Queen, life in itself is beautiful, but it's even more beautiful if it's accompanied by someone who loves you. Having the right partner is one of the most beautiful gifts that life can give you. So, be honest with yourself, because you'll also be honest in your partnership. Once you find a person who makes you feel good, loved, and happy, do everything in your power to show them.

"For a life together, you have to walk side by side, not one after the other."

Hanna opened her eyes. She had obviously fallen asleep on the couch. But now, she was covered by a warm blanket, and her head was supported by a comfortable pillow. And Peter was lying next to her. Like so many times before, they had fallen asleep in the living room. She often asked Peter to wake her so she could get up and go to bed if she had fallen asleep on the couch, but his answer was always the same: "You're so beautiful when you sleep, and I don't have the heart to wake you." It was obvious the same had happened that evening. She wanted to move, but she then felt Peter's arm around her. She looked at the love of her life and felt happiness in her heart. Although he was hugging her tightly, she never felt she was trapped, and even though he always stood by her side, there was no way she could call him a doormat, either. He was simply ... perfect.

Mission no. 14:

A Queen of a Charismatic Future

Hanna entered the premises of the magazine, as she had, already for the past few years, took off her coat, filled her bottle of water in the tearoom, then headed for her desk. There, as always, she looked at the photo of Peter holding Zoe in the large freestanding frame, and of her with Aiden in her lap. Even though she had looked at it countless numbers of times, looking at her three pearls always reminded her heart how lucky she was. "I love you," she said quietly to herself, then sat down, turned on the computer and started the new workday. But even before the home screen came into view on her computer, on which there was a photo of her and the other members of the team from the expedition in Egypt years ago, a voice brought her back to the present moment:

"Good morning, Miss Lane. Ms. Mallock wants to see you in her office," said her boss's secretary, greeting her with an edge to her voice, letting her know that something was up. Hanna kindly thanked her for letting her know. Ever since they had increased the number of pages in the magazine, Ms. Mallock had repeatedly called her into her office. "It's probably something to do with the article I submitted yesterday," she thought, making her way up to her office.

"Good morning, Miss Lane," said her boss, greeting her without taking her eyes from her computer.

"Please, sit down."

Hanna greeted her in return and sat down in the 'hot chair,' as her co-workers like to call the one opposite the main table because you never knew what it would bring.

"Time is money, so I'm going to get straight to the point," began her boss, without any politeness. Hanna felt some strange energy in the air and

began to wonder why she had been called. Numerous thoughts ran through her head. Was she getting the sack? Did she do something wrong? Or will her boss deprive her of the possibility of coming to work later, three times a week, because she has to take the twins to daycare? Or was it something else ...?

"Hanna, six months ago, I told you at one of our group meetings that our magazine had a new co-owner. At the time, they predicted changes to the business, which we're beginning to see."

"Now she's going to tell me there's no more room for me ..." Hanna thought, expecting the worst and, at the same time, trying to hide her own uncertainty in front of her boss.

"As of next month, we're opening a new department," her boss continued. "We're going to start working in collaboration with a television station and have our own show, which will portray the development of man and his life through time. The concept is very interesting because it will mix historical and contemporary aspects of the world. The newspaper market has become incredibly saturated, so it's time to move on and expand. And because of the opportunities the new owners have brought with them, that's now possible for us to do. So, we're putting together a team to co-create the show. The programming and design team has already been put together; all we need now is a field manager. The show is going to be recorded all over the world, so I need someone who'll take care of getting the required recording permits, find local people at the recording locations, communicate with the necessary institutions such as museums and archives, as well as cooperate with field teams of archaeologists, researchers, etc. Oh, by the way, we'll also be filming with Mark Howard. As a matter of fact, he'll be one of the co-creators of some of the shows. That's a rough draft of everything. In short, I want that you would lead the field team."

Hanna looked at her in surprise. She expected anything but that. She was in shock, and for a moment, the world stopped spinning. What had just happened? Did she hear right? Had Mallock just offered her a new job? And no ordinary job, but a job that was so strikingly similar to what she had always wanted to do. History, traveling, learning ... everything, all in one? And she was offering it to her? Was that really happening?

As she forcefully processed all she had heard, she looked at her boss: "Ms. Mallock, thank you very much for the opportunity. I don't know what to say. I'll be more than happy to take on the role."

"Good. Another smart decision, Lane," replied Mallock. "My secretary will fill you in on everything you need to know in the coming days."

Then Hanna got the chills. "But, what about my columns? Are they going to be cut?" she asked a little worriedly.

"No," her boss replied, "I'll partially pass them on to others. They'll still be written, and you'll still end up authorizing them, but from now on, your primary job will be the program."

Hanna smiled in relief. In recent years, she had been creating wonderful pieces, columns, and attachments that had got them many new readers. It was good to know that her work would continue. But obviously, it was time to move on. It was time for her creativity to grow some new wings. She wanted to get up when a voice in her head told her to ask Mallock why she was the one that had been chosen. At first, she tried to silence it, but the voice didn't give up.

So, she turned to her boss and asked, "Ms. Mallock, there's something I'd like to know. Given that our magazine has at least three people who have been here significantly longer than I have, and who have more experience and even more knowledge, why me?"

Mallock looked her in the eye and said, "Hanna, your coworkers should not be your concern, but mine. But since you asked, let me tell you that I think you're the only one in this department who knows what she wants. As for this job, I need someone stable and strong. Your obedient and timid coworkers aren't the right ones for it. They're well suited to the office work they do, but not much else. I need a leader for the job I offered you. How can someone, who can't even lead himself, lead others? Lane, you're one of the few who's able to think with your own head."

Hanna remained seated, surprised. She didn't know what to say. But after a few seconds, her confidence began to return, and with it, also a little bit of pride: "Ms. Mallock, thank you for the compliment. But the others are also good ..."

"Lane," Mallock interrupted, "I've been one of the most influential editors in the newspaper world for more than ten years. And do you know why? Because I know what I want, and I can read people. I didn't find my way to this position by silently laughing at my superiors and constantly agreeing with them, as most of your colleagues do, but with the character and courage to be who I am. Just as I am your superior, I also answer to certain people. And, I've never lowered my head in front of them, nor in front of others. I've also had some testing times, believe me. And I know what the company says about me; I know all my nicknames. I know everything that goes on here. And, no, I'm not a nasty or a pain-in-the-ass boss. But, if someone's not prepared to go forward, to learn, and to develop, then it's my duty to take action. And unfortunately, most of the time there's no alternative but to let people go.

Hanna replied, "Yes, a lot of them have come and gone ..."

Mallock continued: "Do you think I like doing that? No. I want every one of you to be able to succeed and to get your life in order. That's also why I offered you the opportunity to work in this organization. Everyone who works here has the chance to move up. But, I can't want success for them, any more than they want it themselves. And people are fired because that's the way they've decided, not me. I've heard stories about how I fired people just because they spoke too loudly. I've never fired anyone for that. I fired them because they did NOTHING BUT talk. I've never fired anyone for being late. But I've fired people who are ALWAYS late. Everyone holds the reins to their lives in their own hands. Just look at you; I've been watching you all year. You're diligent, dedicated, and you look for solutions. If you don't agree with something, you say so. You suggest improvements, and you take it upon yourself to do extra work, etc. And that's why I offered you the opportunity first ... and I'm pleased I can count on you, also again this time."

Hanna listened. Although she had known her for years, she found that she didn't really know who she was. The external appearance of an influential and tough editor was hidden by an extremely understanding and sensitive woman. Added to which, that remarkable woman only spoke of her, a simple girl, by using the most beautiful words. But most of all - she noticed her. At times she thought that no one saw how hard she was trying, how she always submitted her projects on time, how she dedicated her entire self to whatever it was she was undertaking, how sincerely she wanted to get ahead, etc., but she was obviously wrong. She was seen. Someone had been observing her. And that someone decided to reward her for her devotion with a new career path.

Hanna thanked her boss again and left her office. Deep in thought, she made her way back to her desk and sat down in her chair. Her thoughts went back to the day when she first came in for the interview. At the time, Mallock offered her a job, and she immediately knew that she couldn't say no. And she had exactly that same feeling today. Somewhere inside, she sensed that she had been searching for this opportunity, the whole time. She didn't completely understand what it was that her boss was actually offering her, but up until then, she had learned that sometimes you just don't need to understand life. And that you simply have to trust that it's leading you in the right direction. Trust was her virtue. The 'ups and downs' she had experienced in her life - the death of her parents, Egypt, Mark, Peter, Boston, New York, etc. - taught her how to trust. Because, in many of those situations, she didn't know if she would land on her feet or not, but at the end of the day, it always seemed to turn out right. And today, it was time for a new step! A sense of triumph began to awaken within her. Like a fiery phoenix, she became aware that she was following the path she was supposed to take. It had waited a long time for her. And now it was beginning to happen. She was excited. The world had opened its doors to her, and her book of life was turning a new page.

Hanna looked one last time through the window of the plane, leaving the Peruvian capital, Lima. She had just completed yet another of her travels. At a meeting about the show she had with Mallock five months before, she never thought that one of her greatest wishes in life - to visit the cradle of the Inca civilization - would come true so quickly. Her heart was beating to the rhythm of her fulfilled wish, and she was reminded of how her life was once again listening to her. But now it was time to return home. The two seats beside her weren't occupied, so she afforded herself the luxury and stretched out across them. She tried to fall asleep, but she couldn't. The faces of the people from the Native American tribe, about whom the last show was filmed, were still dancing about in front of her eyes. She never thought she would be the first woman from the civilized world to contact, until then, an unknown tribe that had existed in the Peruvian rainforest for thousands of years. Not only that, but they even allowed them to film them - them, their customs, their lives, etc. Those 'living wonders' from the past awakened admiration in her once again. Until then, she had been used to thinking that everything from the past had already been discovered. And dead. But it was just her, a lover of archeology, who awoke the past again, and through her work, breathed it back to life.

With that tribe, however, she had the feeling that they were thousands of years old but had never actually died. She felt exactly the same as when she saw Shanti for the first time. Someone who should have already passed away but was surprisingly 'alive' instead. She began to ask herself if people actually ever died or not. Or was it just an illusion that the world had come to believe because it didn't understand the changes that time brought? These were difficult questions for her tired mind, but the answers to them were of great interest to her. Or would her great discovery be proof that something actually never really ends? That people never really die? That old civilizations never really cease to exist? This would shake the foundations of some of the most fundamental archeological beliefs and push the world into a new way of thinking, which would somehow have to ... awaken? Just like she had? Was it possible that her mission would be one to help awaken people and really make them see?

More and more questions came to her mind until ... her eyes submitted to the weight of the fatigue from the arduous expedition and slowly closed.

The colors of the rainbow shone on her face as she, once again, gazed at the Golden Temple in front of her. Whenever she saw it, her heart was embraced with heavenly peace. But even before the mist around it had completely dissipated, a familiar voice greeted her, "Hello, my friend." It was Shanti. She stood in a beautiful golden gown on the shiny white steps that led to the golden home.

"Shanti!" Hanna called out, ran to her, and hugged her tightly.

The Ruler smiled, then asked her mysteriously, "Hanna, how are you today?"

Hanna stopped for a moment and seemed to search for the right words. She looked at her with a somewhat perplexed look on her face and replied, "Shanti, I don't know. I don't know how to describe the way I feel. I feel so ... different. "

The Ruler frowned, "Do you perhaps feel inside excitement and peace at the same time?"

"Yes," Hanna almost shouted.

"Do you have an overwhelming feeling of perfection inside, mixed up with feelings of endless possibilities?" Shanti continued.

"Yes, that too," Hanna was all the more elated.

"Do you feel a never-ending well of water inside of you that gives you strength and hope?" Shanti asked.

"Yes, Shanti! How did you know? "Hanna asked in admiration.

"Because that's how I feel," replied the Ruler. "When you realize why you were born, you're then rewarded with these feelings."

"And when you know what your mission is, that's when you feel it," Hanna proudly concluded, just like someone who had just come into contact with herself.

Shanti looked deep into her eyes, smiled at her mysteriously, and said, "Exactly. These are the feelings of a real mission. Now, please follow me."

She turned toward the temple and walked elegantly toward the mighty door, which at some point opened, all by itself. Hanna followed her without question, as they slowly entered the Golden Temple. They walked through the shimmering crystal hall, step by step until they reached the mighty golden throne.

Just before it, Shanti stopped, turned around, faced Hanna, and said, "Dear Hanna, you've seen me sit on this throne many times. From it, I guided you in the directions that were right for you, advised you wisely, and encouraged you, all from my heart. But today, I'm not going to sit on it. You will."

Hanna stood there, totally surprised. She couldn't believe what she was hearing. She looked at Shanti in confusion and said, "Shanti, this is ... I can't ... this is your throne ... how can I sit on it ... I'm just ... me."

Shanti looked at her affectionately, and in a tone that left no doubt, replied, "Hanna, your intentions are sincere, your dreams clear, your heart pure and your power mighty. Your crown and scepter have been forged. You're ready. It's time to take your seat on your throne, Queen."

Hanna remained speechless. She looked at Shanti, but then a movie of her own life came into vision - of a frightened orphan, crying all alone at the grave of her parents, a girl that no one even seemed to see, who not only felt left out but also had a look of contempt as she wandered down the school hallways, a kind but a weak student who didn't know how to stand up for herself ... and then a rebel who resisted and demanded what she needed, a warrior who realized her fears and pursued her dreams despite them, and most recently a woman who opened her heart and began to love, etc.

The movie stopped, and once again, she saw the beautiful Ruler in front of her. She was right. Shanti was right. She really was ... a Queen. It was time to occupy her throne. She climbed up and sat down. She proudly looked at Shanti, and Shanti looked back at her. Then the Ruler bowed deeply, right in front of Hanna. And, as if the Universe was dancing, fate also danced when Shanti, with her head bowed, said for the last time:

"And when you find out who you are, you also find out that maybe you didn't know, who you truly were. Maybe you were more than you thought you were the whole time. Maybe you just weren't able to see it." She said as she lifted her head. It was so beautiful. It was Hanna's face ...

Usually, the last chapter of a book announces the end. But not here. Here, the final chapter is an announcement of the beginning. Your beginning. Dear Queen, congratulations. You've made it. In your depths, you've found the power that has brought you to your throne. You've discovered the power that has forged the crown on your head and the scepter in your hand. Now it's time to take control of your life. Now you have the wisdom you need for that. Life has shown you both sides, the dark side, and the light side. So that now you can decide. That you understand. That you feel. To recognize your role in this world. Which needs Queens, who will proudly lift their heads and realize their missions. And you're one of them. That mighty inner beauty has transformed you into something so extraordinary - into yourself. Your light is shining more brightly than it ever has before. Your heart loves you more sincerely than it has ever loved before. And your mission is forged in the stars more clearly than it ever has before. You were born for this, to be extraordinary. You were born that way, and you're it, right now. Exceptional and perfect. Never let anyone tell you otherwise, not even you, yourself. The throne on which you are sitting is real. It's proof that you're true to yourself and true to your mission. It's a gift that'll always remind you of where your true place is.

Yes, the journey of life is extraordinary. Just like yours is. Your journey is unique, and so too is your experience. Now you know how. Now you know where. Now you know who. There's no question that has been left unanswered. Everything now makes sense. Your place. But the way to it has been a winding road. On this journey, you were sometimes tired, thirsty, and scared. But the fog disappeared, and then you reached the top of the mountain. And in front of you, a new horizon opened up. A horizon that reaches out into the distance, infinitely. Yes, Queen, your kingdom has no borders. Everything is here for you. It's all here to help you accomplish your mission. Take care of your mission and nurture it. Respect it in the way it respects you. Your mission is the reason you exist, after all. And the accomplishment of your mission is the seal that'll forever mark your existence. With which you'll show what a heart can do with sincere intentions. A heart that loves. So, do your best to do what you were born to do. Use all your talents, gifts, and experiences to breathe life into your mission. Let the many missions you have come across with me on this journey help you along your way. Missions on every page that reminded you and awakened you. Missions that helped you remember who you really are - A QUEEN OF A CHARISMATIC FUTURE!

"You are a Queen of a charismatic future."

"Miss, wake up," the friendly stewardess said, as she gently woke Hanna. "We're approaching New York, and we'll soon be landing. Please put your seat in the upright position and fasten your seat belt."

Hanna smiled at her, a little confused, and sat up. "New York, how can we be in New York already?" she began to ask herself. "For the love of God, how long have I been sleeping?" She looked at her watch and couldn't believe her eyes. "Six hours ???"

She knew she was tired, but she didn't realize she had been that tired. She rubbed her eyes and stared out the window. There through the clouds, she was already able to clearly see the ground and some buildings which proudly stood upon it. A little longer, and she would see the three loves of her life - Peter, Zoe, and Aiden. Oh, how she missed them! It seemed to her that she hadn't seen them for an eternity, and just like flowers that haven't been watered for a long time, she was also thirsty for their hugs and kisses.

A good hour later, she was already on her way home by taxi. When the cab pulled up in front of their apartment building, it was already nighttime. Very quietly, she unlocked the door, because she didn't know if the twins were already asleep, or not.

"Hanna!" Peter almost shouted, rushing towards her and hugging her tightly.

"Peter, I'm home!" whispered Hanna with a smile that told him she was glad to see him. They hugged, and for a moment it seemed that they were trying to make up for all the hugs they hadn't been able to give each other for the past two weeks.

When they let go, Peter overwhelmed her with questions: "How are you? How was your flight? Are you tired? Are you hungry? How was it? I saw the pictures you sent me. They're fantastic ... tell me everything!
Hanna smiled, "It was unforgettable. I'll you everything. But first, I just want to take a look at Zoe and Aiden. They're sleeping, right?"

"Yeah, we were in the park all afternoon. Aidan decided that he wants to be a football player when he grows up, so they kept running after the ball the whole time. When we got home, they were asleep within five minutes," Peter said proudly.

Hanna went to their room, gently opened the door, and snuck a look inside. Two little bodies with tousled hair were covered with warm blankets, each in their own beds, breathing peacefully. And it seemed as if they were still playing football in their dreams. Hanna went over to their beds, stroked their foreheads, gave them a kiss, and wished them beautiful dreams.

"Get some sleep, because tomorrow I won't be letting you go for anything in the world," she whispered softly, then slowly left the room.

When she returned, she noticed that Peter had already made some hot chocolate, lit a few candles, and put on some quiet music. Embracing one other, they lay down on the couch, then talked long into the night. The stars also listened to their words and co-created that perfect moment.

"Mommy, you're home!" was the sound of a tiny voice approaching from the side. It was Zoe. With sleepy eyes and a frightened look on her face, she stood by the door, clutching her little blanket in her hand.

"Zoe!" Hanna said in surprise. "I'm home, baby."

She got up, walked over to her, and hugged her tightly. When she felt her tiny arms around her neck, she wished she could have stopped time.

"Why aren't you sleeping?" she asked a little worriedly.
"I had a bad dream," Zoe replied.

"We can't let that happen, can we?" Hanna reassured her. "Come here, princess, let's see if both of us can find a better dream for you."

They quietly made their way back to the children's room. Aidan was sleeping peacefully in his bed.

Hanna put Zoe in hers, then lay down beside her.

"Zoe, everything's going to be okay now. You can go back asleep," Hanna reassured her.

"Mommy, can you please tell me a fairy tale," Zoe whispered in such a cute voice that Hanna, despite it being three in the morning, couldn't say no.

"OK," Hanna replied, getting herself comfortable and bringing Zoe closer to her chest, then began ...

"Once upon a time, the most beautiful temple in the world was hidden behind some brilliant clouds. It was called the Golden Temple. And the ruler who lived in it was the most beautiful woman that had ever lived. And her name was ... Shanti."

Mission no. 1:
"Look inside, and you'll see who you are."

Mission no. 2:
"The anvil on which you forge your strength,
is your self-esteem."

Mission no. 3:
"The scepter in the hands of a ruler
is only a consequence of her specific decisions."

Mission no. 4:
"True force is triggered by energy, not by form."

Mission no. 5:
"The hook of guilt which you get caught up on, is,
as a matter of fact, always thrown by you, yourself."

Mission no. 6:
"The time which you spend with yourself
is the best quality spent time."

Mission no. 7:
"Obviously, it is so important how we 'serve' the truth.
The difference can be a completely different life.
And a completely different woman."

Mission no. 8:

"People show their true colors when they are at the peak of their power, and not when they are fighting for their lives."

Mission no. 9:

"Your heart is the owner of your life, while your mind is its director. Your heart has a mission, while your mind has a strategy."

Mission no. 10:

"You are not born a Queen, you become one. By working on it."

Mission no. 11:

"A day without night simply doesn't exist."

Mission no. 12:

"Let go of control, and the cage around you will start to disappear."

Mission no. 13:

"For a life together, you have to walk side by side, not one after the other."

Mission no. 14:

"You're a Queen of a charismatic future."

Want to read more from Michael?You might want to give this book a try.

»This book is a must-read for the man eager to unleash the hero within, but also for the woman who wants a real-life hero by her side.«

This book will transform any man into a hero. Because let's face it, every man wants to be one – to feel like a hero on the inside and to be praised as a hero on the outside. Being the master of one's own life and living from the heart are the ultimate goals to which every man aspires.

This book will show you how to get there.

Because one thing is for sure: Heroes aren't born. Heroes are made!

Through a compelling tale and powerful lessons, this remarkable book builds up the hero inside every man by revealing:

- how to build confidence to face every challenge life throws your way
- the ways to accept the responsibilities of life
- techniques to keep the male ego in check, making it a friend, not a foe
- how to find real friends, and how to tell real friends from fake ones
- the path to emotional intelligence and heart energy
- the secrets of a good relationship
- the biggest personality pitfalls to avoid
- action steps for fostering powerful manifestation
- the tools to facilitate the transformation from average Joe to hero
- what it means to be gay and what informs the gay experience
- the spiritual truths the awakened man on Earth should live by

Title: A Queen of a charismatic future

Printed in Great Britain
by Amazon

56096574R00245